PENNSYLVANIA GENEALOGIES AND FAMILY HISTORIES

A BIBLIOGRAPHY OF BOOKS ABOUT PENNSYLVANIA FAMILIES

Compiled and Edited by

Donald O. Virdin

Arlington, Virginia

1992

Other Books By The Author:

Delaware Bible Records, Volumes 1 and 2

*Virginia Genealogies and Family Histories:
A Bibliography of Books about Virginia Families*

The Virdins of Delaware and Related Families

Published 1992 By

HERITAGE BOOKS, INC.
1540-E Pointer Ridge Place
Bowie, MD 20716
(301) 390-7709

ISBN 1-55613-590-4

A Complete Catalog Listing Hundreds of Titles on
History, Genealogy & Americana
Free on Request

INTRODUCTION

All of the books in this bibliography (about 2,800) deal with families who have some connection to Pennsylvania. Most of the books (about 2,000) can be found at the Library of Congress in Washington, D.C.; the Daughters of the American Revolution (DAR) Library in Washington, D.C.; and the National Genealogical Society (NGS) Library in Arlington, Virginia. If you should want to examine one of the family histories listed here, you should first contact one of these libraries (their addresses follow) to see if they have the book. You could also ask your own public library if they can obtain the book on inter-library loan.

In some cases, titles listed here are not available in the Washington, D.C. area; over 800 of these books are in other locations. The New York Public Library holds over 110; the Historical Society of Pennsylvania has more than 325; the Allen County Public Library in Fort Wayne, Indiana holds about 330. (Books that can be found at one of these three libraries are indicated by "N", "P", or "A" following the title.) In addition, there are more than 100 listed books that are scattered throughout the United States, at the Long Island Historical Society, the Sutro Branch of the California Library, and the Los Angeles Public Library. Of course, some of these books may be available from more than one library.

If you find a family name listed here, do not assume that the family was primarily or exclusively associated with Pennsylvania. There may be other published material on the same name or the same family in another area. Many of the books cited here include references to other states.

Keep in mind that no bibliography of this kind can ever be complete. Many family histories are privately printed and never turn up in large libraries. At the same time, there will be new family histories published after the printing of this book.

Allen County Public Library
900 Webster Street
Fort Wayne, IN 46802
(219) 424-7241

DAR Library
1776 D Street N.W.
Washington, DC 20006
(202) 879-3229

Historical Society of Pennsylvania
1300 Locust Street
Philadelphia, PA 19107
(215) 732-6200

Library of Congress
Local History and Genealogy Room
Washington, DC 20540
(202) 707-5537

NGS Library
4527 17th Street North
Arlington, VA 22207
(703) 525-0050

New York Public Library
5th Avenue and 42nd Street
New York, New York 10018
(202) 340-0849

- A -

AARON -- Shannon, Catherine and Paul B.
 Aarons of Crates, Pa., 1820-1980. Mayport, Pa.

ABBEY -- Wallace, J. A. Wallace
 The Abbey genealogy. Martin and Allardyce. Frankford, Pa.,
 1911.

ACKERMAN -- Vliet, Claire (Ackerman)
 THE ACKERMAN FAMILY ASSOCIATION, descendants of George
 Ackerman, Mennonite, Laws, Milford Township, Bucks County,
 Pa., and Stephen Ackerman, Lutheran, Haycock Township,
 Bucks County, Pa. No city, 1950.

ADAMS -- (Author unknown)
 Adams family pedigree. No City, no date.   (P)

ADAMS -- (Author unknown)
 Supplement to: The family and descendants of William ... (N)
 and Martha ... Adams of Laurel, Indiana. Pittsburgh, Pa.,
 1959.

ADAMS -- Adams, Elizabeth H.
 Adams - Va., Md., Pa., Del., etc. Ogden, 19__.

ADAMS -- Adams, Rolland L.
 Adams family history; a history of Joseph Washington Adams
 and John Leedy Snyder, both of Newport, Pennsylvania, and of
 their ancestors and descendants. No city, 1971.

ADAMS -- Adams, Enid Eleanor
 Ancestors and descendants of Jeremiah Adams, 1794-1883, of
 Salisbury, Connecticut, Sullivan County, New York, Harbor
 Creek, Pennsylvania, and Vermillion, Ohio, including known
 descendants of his brothers and sisters, most of whom went
 to Michigan: seventh in descent from Henry Adams of
 Braintree, Massachusetts. Ancestor Hunters. Victor, Idaho,
 1974.

ADAMS -- Adams, Glenn D.
 Pioneers of Chestnut Ridge: their origins and life on the
 frontier. Waverly, Pa., 1985.

ADAMS -- Adams, Glenn D.
 Pioneers of Chestnut Ridge, Bedford County, Pennsylvania: a
 family history, 1700-1977. Waverly, Pa., 1977.

ADAMS -- Darling, Flora Adams
Founding and organization of the Daughters of the American
revolution and Daughters of the revolution. Independence
Publishing Company. Philadelphia, 1901.

ADAMS -- Daughters of the American Revolution, Iowa,
         Spinning Wheel Chapter
Adams family of Chester County, Pa.   Marshalltown,   (A)
1971.

ADAMS -- Iowa D.A.R.
The Adams family of Chester County, Pennsylvania. No
City, 1972.

AEBI -- Newman, George F.
A preliminary report on the European Aebi-Eby   (P)
family. Philadelphia, 1974.

AGNEW -- Adams, J. Howe, M.D.
History of the life of D. Hayes Agnew. F. A. Davis Company.
Philadelphia, 1892.

AGNEW -- Agnew, Mary Virginia
The book of the Agnews. James Agnew of Pennsylvania,
U.S.A., his race, ancestry, and descendants. J. E. Caldwell
& Company. Philadelphia, 1926.

AIRGOOD -- Airgood, James M.
An Airgood, Airgod, Ehrgott genealogy: some of the
descendants of Michal Airgod of Indiana County, Penna.:
preliminary materials for a genealogy of the Airgood and
allied families: includes related families (among others
such as Blystone, Fisher, Harris, Hatherill, Jacoby,
Kanouff, Lewis, Parons, Shields, Stiver, Winters, etc., etc.
Pittsburgh, Pa., 1979.

ALBRIGHT -- (Author unknown)
Index to: A genealogical history of Bernard   (P)
Albright ... No city, 1958.

ALDERFER -- Alderfer, Edwin S.
Descendants of Franklin and Catharine Alderfer.   (A)
Scottdale, Pa., 1965.

ALDERFER -- Stanley, Helen Alderfer
The Alderfers of America: history and genealogy.   (A)
Schlechters. Allentown, Pa., 1972.

ALDRED -- Williamson, Eva A.
   William Aldred of Brandywine Hundred, New Castle   (P)
   County, Delaware, and some of his descendants with
   history and biographies. Departmental Supply Co.
   Philadelphia, 1970.

ALEXANDER -- Alexander, Haughwout, James Ard
   A tracing to 1949 of certain lines of descent from John
   Alexander, of Lanarkshire, Scotland, who with his wife,
   Margaret Glasson, emigrated from County Armagh, Ireland,
   to Chester County, Pennsylvania, in 1736. No city, 1949.

ALEXANDER -- Alexander, John
   Index to: A record of the descendants of John   (P)
   Alexander. Philadelphia, 1878.

ALEXANDER -- Alexander, Rev. John E.
   A record of the descendants of John Alexander, of
   Lanarkshire, Scotland, and his wife, Margaret Glasson, who
   emigrated from county Armagh, Ireland, to Chester County,
   Penna., 1736. A. Martien. Philadelphia, 1878.

ALEXANDER -- Alexander, Virginia W.
   The Alexanders. No city, 1962.

ALEXANDER -- Alexander, Hon. Walter Scott
   Sketch of Alexander Alexander, who emigrated from county
   Down, Ireland, in the year 1770 and settled in Cumberland
   County, Pennsylvania. Press of Commercial Printing Co.
   McConnellsburg, Pa., 1898.

ALEXANDER -- Alexander, William G.
   Index to: Family biographies of the families of   (P)
   Alexander ... Cripple Creek, 1892.

ALEXANDER -- Powers, Robert B.
   A record of my maternal ancestors. Edwards Bros.
   Ann Arbor, Mich., 1967.

ALLEGER -- Alleger, Daniel E.
   The genesis of the Allegers of Ulster County, New York,
   Hunterdon County, New Jersey, and northeastern Pennsylvania.
   Gainesville, Fla., 1970.

ALLEMAN -- Alleman, Henry Snyder
   A genealogy of the Allemans in the United States.
   Harrisburg, Pa., 1954.

ALLEN -- Alleman, Henry S.
   Genealogy of the Allemans in the U.S.: who are the offspring
   of John Christian Alleman and John Frederick Christian
   Alleman. J. Horace McFarland. Harrisburg, Pa., 1954.

ALLEN -- (Author unknown)
Supplement to: Jesse Allen of Wysox ... Wysox, Pa.   (N)
Sacred Art Press. Wysox, Pa., 195-.

ALLEN -- Allen, John Kermot
George Allen of Weymouth, Mass., 1635; of Lynn, Mass., 1636,
and of Sandwich, Mass., 1637-48. Together with some of his
descendants. Brooklin, Mass. (Brookline), 1924.

ALLEN -- Allen, Samuel
A record of the Allen family from the first settlement in
Pennsylvania. Philadelphia, 1899.

ALLEN -- Allen, Samuel
Index to: A record of the Allen family.   (P)
Philadelphia, 1899.

ALLEN -- Allen, William J.
Early Pennsylvania genealogical gleanings. Washington,
D.C., 1978.

ALLEN -- Hoagland, Edward Coolbaugh
Twigs from family trees. Sacred Art Press. Towanda, Pa.,
19__.

ALLEN -- Hoagland, Edward Coolbaugh
Jesse Allen of Wysox, Pa., 1784. Sacred Art Press.
Wysox, Pa., 1952.

ALLEN -- Knox, M. B.
Allen history. Waynesburg, Pa.?, 1937.   (A)

ALLEN -- Price, John
Index to: Genealogy of the Allen family. Salem, 1888.   (P)

ALLEN -- Seaver, J. Montgomery
... Allen family records. American Hisotrical-Genealogical
Society. Philadelphia, 1929.

ALLENDER -- Rinkenbach, William H.
The Allender family of Lehigh County, Pa. No City. 1958.

ALLGAIER -- Allgaier, George P.
The Allgaier family history and genealogy: Austria to Berks
County, Pennsylvania, 1751. No city. No date.

ALLYN -- Evarts, Mary
Ancestry and descendants of Nancy Allyn (Foote) Webb,   (P)
Rev. Edward Webb, Joseph Wilkins Cooch. Star Pub. Co.
Wilmington, Del., 1919.

ALMY -- (Author unknown)
Henry Augustus Almy, his descendants and lineage from the immigrant William Almy. Crafton, Pa., 1956.

ALT -- Reeser, Nellie Wallace
Valentin Alt. York, Pa., 1949.

ALTHOUSE -- Reed, Herbert P.
Althouse family; (as related to the Reed family). (P)
Wernersville, Pa., 1974.

AMBLER -- Ambler, Frank Rhoades
The Ambler family of Pennsylvania, 1688-1968. Old York Road Pub. Co. Jenkintown, Pa., 1968.

AMBLER -- Ambler, Mary Grace
The Ambler family of Pennsylvania, 1968-1977. No city. No date.

AMBLER -- Baldwin, Aubrey H.
Index to: The Ambler family of Pennsylvania. (P)

No City. No date.

AMEY -- Eckel, Marie Monroe II.
Leases, releases, bonds, deeds, and indentures of Peter Amey and associated families of Pennsylvania and New Jersey, 1768-1888. No City. 1952.

AMSTUTZ -- Amstutz, Evelyn J.
Benjamin Amstutz family record, 1853-1966. Scottdale, (A) Pa., 1966.

ANDERSON -- (Author unknown)
Notes of family history: the Anderson, Schofield, Pennypacker, Yocum, Crawford, Sutton, Lane, Richardson, Bevan, Aubrey, Bartholomew, De Haven, Jermain and Walker families. Stephenson-Bros. Philadelphia, 1948.

ANDERSON -- Anderson, Alvin L.
The Anderson family; a genealogy of the two immigrant brothers, John and Frederick Anderson, who emigrated from Oetisheim, to northern Pennsylvania, in 1838 and 1859. Medellin, Colombia, 1965.

ANDERSON -- Battey, George Magruder, III
... The Andriessen (Andriezon, Anderson) family of East Tennessee, Pennslyvania, Delaware and elsewhere. Washington, D.C., 1940.

ANDERSON -- Battey, George Magruder
<u>The outlaws of North Carolina and Tennessee, the Hamiltons</u>
<u>and Campbells of Virginia and Tennessee, as related to their</u>
<u>inlaws, the Andersons of Pennsylvania and Tennessee</u>.
Washington, D.C., 1940.

ANDERSON -- Wolff, Elizabeth B.
<u>Early history and genealogy of the Anderson-McCullough-</u>
<u>McCune families and related lines of Franklin County, Pa</u>.
No city. No date.

ANDREWS -- Arthaud, John Bradley
<u>Notes on Andrews, Carlisle, Foley, and Hagarty families of</u>
<u>Washington County, Pennsylvania, 1790-1870</u>. Denver, CO.,
1982.

ANGELL -- Gruber, Walter Wilbert
<u>Genealogy of Charles Angel, Sr., pioneer of Frederick</u>
<u>County, Maryland</u>. Dover, Pa., 1948.

ANNIN -- (Author unknown)
<u>Centennial celebration by the Annin family at the old Stone</u>
<u>house in Somerset County, N.J., August 15, 1866</u>. Printed
for F. J. Dreer. Philadelphia, 1866.

ANSHUTZ -- Anshutz, Philip J.
<u>Sketch of the Anshutz family, Pennsylvania</u>.   (A)
Cincinnati, Ohio, 1895.

ANSLEY -- Davidson, Harold Ansley
<u>"Our Ansley family"</u>. Jenkintown, Pa., 1933.

ANSPACH -- Anspach, Donald Ray
<u>The genealogy of the Anspach family</u>. Sayre, Pa., 1954.

ANTES -- McMinn, Rev. Edwin
<u>A German hero of the colonial times of Pennsylvania; or,</u>
<u>The life and times of Henry Antes</u>. W. J. Lovell.
Moorestown, N.J., 1886.

ANTES -- MacMinn, Edwin
<u>On the frontier with Colonel Antes; or, The struggle for</u>
<u>supremacy of the red and white races in Pennsylvania</u>.
S. Chew & Sons. Camden. N.J., 1900.

ARMBRUSTER -- Armbruster, Mary Agnes
<u>Armbruster-the cross bowman</u>. Pittsburgh, Pa. No date.

ARMITAGE -- Orbison, Mary H.
 A short sketch of the Armitage family. Philadelphia,   (P)
 1905.

ARMOR -- Armor, C. Wesley
 Ancestral records from the seventeenth to the twentieth
 centuries. Philadelphia, 1971.

ARMSTRONG -- Armstrong, Thomas Elmer
 History of the Armstrong family from 980 to 1939 A.D.
 Pittsburgh, Pa., 1939.

ARNDT -- Arndt, John Stover
 The story of the Arndts; the life, antecedents and
 descendants of Bernhard Arndt who emigrated to Pennsylvania
 in the year 1731. Christopher Sower Co. Philadelphia,
 1922.

ARNOLD -- Arnold, James
 Descendants and relatives of Johannas Arnoldt, 1715-   (A)
 1803, and Anna Elizabeth Garman, 1726-1814, Lebanon,
 Pa. Claremont, Calif., 1976.
ARNOLD -- Taylor, Walter Kingsley
 The lives, families, and descendants of Arnold, Philip,
 and Benjamin Taylor: from Pennsylvania and New Jersey to
 Kentucky. Winter Park, Fla., 1984.

ASH -- Kysor, Mrs. Willis E.
 The Ash family, Washington County, Maryland, Somerset
 County, Pennsylvania. No city. 1980.

ASHMEAD -- Du Bin, Alexander
 The Ashmead family; one of the series of sketches   (P)
 written by Frank Willing Leach for the Philadelphia
 North American, 1907-1913, and brought down to date.
 Historical Publication Society. Philadelphia, 1933.

ASHMEAD -- (Author unknown)
 The voyages of Capt. John Ashmead of Philadelphia, Pa.   (P)
 between the years 1758 and 1780. Philadelphia. No date.

ATCHISON -- Acheson, A. W.
 A history of the Acheson family on the paternal side.
 S. A. Clarke & Co. Pittsburgh, Pa., 1878.

ATCHISON -- Acheson, James C.
 A history of the Acheson family on the maternal side.
 No city. 1879.

ATKINS -- Gordon, Colin
A richer dust: echoes from an Edwardian album.
B. Lippincott. Philadelphia, 1978.

ATKINSON -- (Author unknown)
Wilmer Atkinson, An autobiography. Founder of the Farm
Journal. Wilmer Atkinson Co. Philadelphia, 1920.

ATKINSON -- Ellis, Emily Quinby Atkinson
Thomas Atkinson, a Quaker patriot. Philadelphia, 1935.

ATKINSON -- Hough, Oliver
Atkinson families of Bucks County, Pennsylvania.
J. B. Lippincott Company. Philadelphia, 1908.

ATLEE -- Barber, Edwin Atlee
Genealogical record of the Atlee family. The descendants
of Judge William Augustus Atlee and Colonel John Atlee of
Lancaster County, Pa. W. F. Bell & Co. Philadelphia, 1884.

ATLEE -- Pennypacker, Samuel W.
Samuel John Atlee. Philadelphia, 1878.

ATLEE -- (Author unknown)
Original draft of the genealogy of the Atlee family.   (P)
No City. No date.

AUCHEY -- Achey, Fred A.
History of the Auchey family. Lancaster, Pa., 1917.

AULD -- Auld, David Walton
David Auld of Antrim: the Auld family of Middle Ten Mile
Creek with proven and apparent relatives: a synopsis of
facts and legends of Auld family members who arrived in
Cumberland Co., Pennsylvania, or that general area,
between 1775 and 1825 from Ulster Province, N. Ireland,
and their descendants. Saratoga, Calif., 1980.

AULL -- Aull, William F.
The Aull and Martin genealogy. Ware Bros. Co.   (P)
Philadelphia, 1920.

AURAND -- Aurand, Rev. Frederick
History of the American branch of the Aurand family.
A. M. Aurand. Beaver Springs, Pa., 1900.

AURAND -- Aurand, Frederick
History of the American branch of the Aurand family.
Mifflinbyrg, Pa., 1900.

AURAND -- Harbaugh, Miriam Aurandt
    The Aurandt panorama, 1550-1982. Altoona, Pa., 1983.

AVERY -- Sellers, Edwin Jaquett
    Captain John Avery; president judge at the Whorekill in
    Delaware bay, and his descendants. J. B. Lippincott Co.
    Philadelphia, 1898.

AYRES -- (Author unknown)
    The Eyre family of Philadelphia. University Microfilms
    International. Ann Arbor, Mich., 1979.

- B -

BACHERT -- (Author unknown)
Report on the ancestry of the Backerts of Schuylkill   (N)
county, Pennsylvania. Frank Allaben Genealogical Society.
New York, 191_.

BACHMAN -- Mann, Pauline Bachman
Our heritage, a history of the Bachmans of Lititz,
Pennsylvania: ancestors and descendants [sic] of
Aaron Eugene and Fannie Ritter Bachman, Monroe Eugene
and Clara Weidman Bachman. P. B. Mann. Des Moines,
Iowa, 1981.

BAER -- Bare, Daniel M. and Robert Bruce Bare
Genealogy of Johannes Baer, 1749-1910. Central Printing
and Publishing Co. Harrisburg, Pa., 1910.

BAER -- Baer, Willis N.
The genealogy of Henry Baer of Leacock, Pennsylvania   (N)
(Baer-Bear-Bare. Schlechter. Allentown, Pa., 1955.

BAILEY -- Bailey Casson Family Reunion
Genealogy and history of Stephen Bailey, descendant of
Isaac Bailey, free man, and Betsy Bailey, his wife,
slave, 1720-1982. The Reunion Book Committee.
Philadelphia, 1937.

BAILEY -- Bailey, Joseph Trowbridge
Ancestry of Joseph Trowbridge Bailey of Philadelphia and
Cathering Goddard Weaver of Newport, Rhode Island.
The De Vinne Press. Philadelphia, 1892.

BAILEY -- Cope, Gilbert
Genealogy of the Baily family of Bromham, England, and more
particularly of the descendants of Joel Baily, who came from
Bromham about 1682 and settled in Chester County, Pa.
Wickersham. Lancaster, Pa., 1912.

BAIRD -- Dall, William Healey
Spencer Fullerton Baird; a biography, including selections
from his correspondence with Audubon, Agassiz, Dana, and
others. J. B. Lippincott. Philadelphia, 1915.

BAIRD --Baird, John A., Jr.
Profile of a hero: the story of Absalom Baird, his family,
and the American military tradition. Dorrance.
Philadelphia, 1977.

BAKER -- Baker, Frank S.
The family of David Baker (1808-1882) of East Hempfield   (A)
Township, Lancaster County, Pa. Baker. Hanover, Ind.,
1975.

BAKER -- Baker, Thoreau Butler
Family records of the John Baker branch of the Conrad
(Becker) Baker family of York County, Pennsylvania
(covering all available records from August, 1739 to
March 1, 1939). No city, 1939.

BAKER -- Pennsylvania D.A.R., G.R.C.
Early New England families. No city, 1959-1960.

BAKER -- McCullough, Norma Baker
The Bakers of Sissinghurst and other relatives.
Washington, Pa., 1981.

BAKER -- Seaver, J. Montgomery
... Baker family records. American Historical-Genealogical
Society. Philadelphia, 1929.

BAKEWELL -- Bakewell, B. G.
The family book of Bakewell-Page-Campbell, being   (A)
descendants of John Bakewell (and others).
Pittsburgh, Pa., 1896.

BALCH -- Balch, Edwin S.
Elise Willing Balch in Memoriam. Philadelphia, 1917.

BALCH -- Balch, T. W.
Balch genealogica. Allen Lane and Scott. Philadelphia,
1907.

BALDWIN -- (Author unknown)
Baldwins of Chester, Pa. No city. No date.   (A)

BALDWIN -- Baldwin, James
Genealogy and reminiscences of our Baldwin family. Erie,
Pa., 1916.

BALL -- Ball Estate Association Executive Committee
A Pennsylvania pioneer. Mansfield, Ohio, 1900.

BALL -- (Author unknown)
Pedigree of the family of Ball of "Richmond," com,
Philadelphia, Pa., U.S.A. No city, 189_.

BALL -- Ball, George C.
Ball family memorial: ancestry of Nellie Castor Ball   (A)
Oldham of Wissinoming, Phila., Pa. No city. No date.

BALL -- Dodson, Richard B.
Pedigree of the family of Ball of "Richmond" com,   (P)
Philadelphia, Pa., U.S.A. No City. No date.

BALL -- Gans, Emmett William
A Pennsylvania pioneer: biographical sketch, with report of
the executive committee of the Ball estate association.
R. J. Kuhl. Mansfield, Ohio, 1900.

BALL -- Kinsey, Margaret Biser
Ball cousins: descendants of John and Sarah Ball and of
William and Elizabeth Richards of Colonial Philadelphia
Co., Penna. Gateway Press. Baltimore, Md., 1981.

BALL -- Kirk, Henry I.
Descendants of William Ball of Millenbeck, Lancaster   (A)
Co., Pa. No city. No date.

BALLIET -- Laux, James B.
Colonel Stephen Balliet. Lehigh County Historical   (A)
Society. Allentown, Pa., 1918.

BANGHART -- Mullin, Frederick L.
History and genealogy of the Jacob Banghart family.   (P)
Easton Pa., 1964.

BARBER -- Barber, Edwin AtLee
Genealogy of the Barber family: the descendants of
Robert Barber, of Lancaster County, Pennsylvania.
W. F. Bell & Co. Philadelphia, 1890.

BARCKLEY -- Armstrong, Wm. C.
Hugh Barckley and Elizabeth Kirkpatrick, Finleyville,   (N)
Pennslyvania. Shawver. Morrison, Ill., 1931.

BARCLAY -- Armstrong, William C.
Hugh Barckley and Elizabeth Kirkpatrick, Finleyville,
Pennsylvania, a supplement to Capt. John Kirkpatrick.
Shawver. Morrison, Ill., 1931.

BARCROFT -- Runk, Emma Ten Broech
Barcroft family records; an account of the family in England
and the descendants of Ambrose Barcroft, the emigrant, of
Solebury, Pennsylvania. J. B. Lippincott. Philadelphia,
1910.

BARD -- Seilhamer, G. O.
The Bard family. Chambersburg, Pa., 1908.

BAREKMAN -- Barekman, June Beverly
The colonial Barker families of the United States.
John Barrickman and his children of Shelby County, Illinois,
son of Jacob Barrickman, Revolutionary soldier of Maryland,
Pennsylvania, Kentucky, Indiana. Grandson of George Peter
Bergmann ... Chicago, Ill., 1972.

BAREKMAN -- Barekman, June B.
Barrickman-Barrackman of Crawford County, Pennsylvania.
Genealogical Services & Publishers. Chicago, 1974.

BAREKMAN -- Barrickman, June B. and Hank JOnes
The genealogy of the Jacob Barrickman family from
Pennsylvania, Kentucky to Franklin, Ripley and Marion
Counties, Indiana. Chicago, Ill., 1967.

BARKER -- Barker, Jesse H.
The colonial Barker families of the United States.
Philadelphia, 1899.

BARNES -- Conquer, Belle Barnes
Barnes and allied families of Pennsylvania and Ohio.
Sheffield, Pa., 1979.

BARNES -- McClelland, Beatrice Barnes
A history of the Barnes families in Jackson Township,
Mercer County, Pennsylvania. McClelland. Franklin,
Pa., 1977.

BARNETT -- Caughey, A. H.
The occasional writing of Isaac Moorhead; with a sketch of
his life by A.H.C. ... Erie, Pa., 1881.

BARNHART -- Wetzel, M. T.
Barnhart family of Central and Eastern Pennsylvania.   (A)
Goshen, Ind., 1965.

BARNHURST -- Laub, Leathra and Milton Rubincam
A brief genealogy of the Barnhurst family of Philadelphia,
Pa. No city, 194-.

BARR -- Miller, Dwight P.
Historical notes. Camp Hill, Pa., 1973.

BARRICKMAN -- Lent, Robertalee and June B. Barekman
Genealogy of the Michael Barrickman family group of   (P)
Frederick County, Maryland; and his sons and grandsons of
Pennsylvania, Ohio, Indiana ... Chicago, Ill., 1968.

BARRICKMAN -- Barekman, June B.
Barrickman-Barrackman of Crawford County,   (A)
Pennsylvania; records of the Barekman-Barrackman-Barrickman
Barackman family ...who moved to Ohio, Kansas and
Nebraska. Geneal. Services. Chicago, 1974.

BARTGES -- Black, Arthur G.
Descendants of Christopher Bartges (d. 1782) of Penn's
Township, Nurthumbarland County, Penna. and some
descendants of Michael Bartges (d. 1791) of Lancaster,
Pa. and his son Matthias Bartges of Frederick, Md.
No city, 194-.

BARTON -- French, Ellen Cochran
Barton & Hummel family histories' early pioneers to
Pennsylvania, to Tuscarawas Co., Ohio, to Henry Co.,
Iowa. Tribune Print Co. Fairfield, Iowa, 1967.

BARTRAM -- (Author unknown)
Bartram genealogy. Genealogical chart of the ancestors (P)
of Henry Llewellyn Jones. Philadelphia, 1928.

BARTRIM   -- Bartrim, Helen R.
Memories are more than dreams. McElvany. Pittsburgh,   (A)
Pa., 1970.

BASHAM -- Hatcher, Charles Silas
Historical genealogy of the Basham, Ellison, Hatcher,
Lilly, Meadows, Pack, Walker, and other families.
Lynchburg, Va., 1980.

BASKIN -- Bell, Raymond Martin
The Baskin family. Carlisle, Pa., 1934.

BASKIN -- Bell, Raymond M.
The Baskins-Baskin family, Pennsylvania, Virginia,   (P)
South Carolina. Washington, Pa., 1957-8.

BASKIN -- Bell, Raymond Martin
The Baskin-Baskins family: South Carolina, Pennsylvania.
Washington, Pa., 1963.

BASKIN -- Bell, Raymond M.
The Baskin(s) family, South Carolina - Pennsylvania,   (N)
with Stephens and Martin notes. Washington, Pa., 1975.

BASSETT -- Anderson, Barbara M.
   Joseph Bassett, Englishman and American.   Anderson.
   State College, Pa., 1979.

BATCHELOR -- Batchelor, Charles W.
   Incidents in my life, with a family genealogy.   (A)
   J. Eichbaum. Pittsburgh, Pa., 1887.

BAUMBERGER -- Morse, Emily Swope
   The Baumberger family book of rememberance: history
   of the first Baumberger, Bomberger families in early
   Tulpehocken Township, Berks County, Pennsylvania and
   some of their descendants.   W. M. McLachlan.
   Bloomfield, N.J., 1982.

BAUSCH -- Campolongo, Donald Ralph
   The descendants of Heinrich Bausch.   Wescosville, Pa., 1980.

BAUSSER -- (Author unknown)
   Bausser-Bowser family of Basil, Switzerland, Pennsylvania,
   Perry County, Ohio.   No city, 1973.
BAUX -- Lawrence, Schuyler
   The princely house of de Baux.   Towanda, Pa., 1937.

BAVER -- Baver, Russell S.
   Genealogical list of the descendants of Christopher   (A)
   Bewer (Baver).   Easton, Pa., 1955.

BAWEL -- Peachey, John B.
   Record of the descendants of Philip and Grace Bawel.   (A)
   Belleville, Pa., 1950.

BEAL -- Hitchens, Mary (Beale)
   The Beales of Chester County, Pa.   Abell Press. Brooklyn,
   1957.

BEAL -- Lowe, Blanche (Beal)
   William Bael, Bucks County, Pa.; an incomplete chronicle
   of one family line descending from William Beal, yeoman,
   presumably from Ross, Herefordshire, England.   Seeman
   Printery. Durham, N.C., 1961.

BEALE -- Chance, Maria Scott Beale
   A chronicle of the family of Edward F. Beale of   (P)
   Philadelphia.   Haverford, 1943.

BEALE -- Hitchens, Mary Beale
   The Beales of Chester County, Pa.   No city, 1957.

BEAR -- Baer, Willis Nissley
  The genealogy of Henry Baer of Leacock, Pennsylvania (Baer-Bear-Bare). Schlechter. Allentown, Pa., 1955.

BEAR -- Bear, Walter Scott
  A genealogy of the Bear family and biographical record of the descendants of Jacob Bear, 1747-1906. Central Printing. Harrisburg, Pa., 1906.

BEAR -- Bare, Daniel M. and Robert Bruce Bare
  Genealogy of Johannes Baer, 1749-1910. Central Printing. Harrisburg, Pa., 1910.

BEAR -- Brownfield, Robert L., Jr. and Rex Newlon Brownfield
  Baer family of Leacock Township, Lancaster County, Pennsylvania. No city, 1951.

BEAVERS -- Beaver, Rev. I. M.
  History and genealogy of the Bieber, Beaver, Biever, Beeber family ... I. M. Beaver. Reading, Pa., 1939.

BECK -- Beck, Berton E.
  The life and times of Jacob Beck, 1794-1875, a   (N)
  pioneer of the Liberty Valley in Tioga and Lycoming Counties, Pennsylvania. Bronx, N.Y., 1973.

BECKER -- Becker, Leah B.
  A biographical history of the Becker family and their early settlement in America and other unpublished information belonging thereto. Express Printing. Lititz, Pa., 1901.

BECKHAM -- Beckham, James Madison
  Genealogy of the Beckham family in Virginia and the branches thereof in Kentucky, Tennessee, Pennsylvania and West Virginia with family sketches ... O. E. Flanhart. Richmond, Va., 1910.

BECHTEL -- Gilbert, Franklin Bechtel
  Genealogical(!) family tree of John George Bechtel ... by his great grandson Franklin Bechtel Gilbert. P. S. Duval & Son. Philadelphia, 1865.

BECHTEL -- Jordan, John W.
  John Bechtel: his contributions to literature, and his descendants. Philadelphia, 1895.

BEDFORD -- Wight, Florence B.
  Some (early) Pennsylvania Bedfords. West Springfield,   (A)
  Mass., 1965.

BEDFORD -- Wight, Florence B.
   <u>Bedfords from Virginia to Maryland and Delaware</u>   (A)
   <u>(some) Pennsylvania</u>. W. Springfield, Mass., 1966.

BEEGLE -- Royer, Frederick Demont
   <u>Charles (Karl) Beegle, the original settler and his</u>
   <u>descendants, based on records of his only two sons Frederick</u>
   <u>and Daniel Beegle: genealogical records of the Beegle family</u>
   <u>in Friend's Cove, Bedford County, Pennsylvaniay</u>. Bedford
   Gazette. Bedford, Pa., 1973.

BEERY -- Wenger, Joseph H.
   <u>History of the descendants of Nicholas Beery, born in 1707.</u>
   <u>Emigrated from Switzerland to Pennsylvania in 1727; and a</u>
   <u>complete genealogical family register with biographies of</u>
   <u>many of his descendants, from the earliest available records</u>
   <u>to the present time. Dates in three centuries</u>. South
   English, Iowa, 1911.

BEERY -- Wenger, Joseph H.
   <u>History of the descendants of Abraham Beery, born in 1718,</u>
   <u>emigrated from Switzerland to Pennsylvania in 1736, and a</u>
   <u>complete genealogical family register with biographies of</u>
   <u>many of his descendants, from the earliest available records</u>
   <u>to the present time, giving dates in three centuries</u>.
   South English, Iowa, 1905.

BEGHTOL -- Maes, Virginia Ingles
   <u>The descendants of Peter Beghtol of Pennsylvania,</u>   (N)
   <u>Kentucky and Illinois, by his first wife, Polly Bruner ...</u>
   <u>With miscellaneous data on various lines of the Beghtol-</u>
   <u>Bechtol family and the Evans family in America</u>. Rushville,
   Ill., 1945.

BEHRMAN -- Alperin, Richard J.
   <u>Rimmonim bells, ten generations of the Behrman, Drucker,</u>
   <u>Hahn, Stockler, and Sztynberg families plus ten related</u>
   <u>lines</u>. Alperin. Philadelphia, 1980.

BEIDLER -- Fretz, Rev. A. J.
   <u>A genealogical record of the descendants of Jacob Beidler of</u>
   <u>Lower Milford township, Bucks County, Pa., together with</u>
   <u>historical and biographical sketches illustrated with</u>
   <u>portraits and other illustrations</u>. Milton, N.J., 1903.

BEIGHLEY -- Rodenbaugh, William B.
   <u>Beighley, 1737-1934 ...</u> The Electric Storage Battery
   Company Printing Department. Philadelphia, 1934.

BELDEN -- Belden, Jessie Perry Van Zile
Concerning some of the ancestors and descendants of Royal
Denison Belden and Olive Cadwell Belden. J. B. Lippincott.
Philadelphia, 1898.

BELDEN -- (Author unknown)
Concerning some of the ancestors and descendants of Royal
Denison Belden and Olive Bates Cadwell Belden.
J. B. Lippincott. Philadelphia, 1958.

BELL -- Bell, Frank Frederick
Bell-Sharpe; a collection of genealogical and biographical
notes on Beuttelspach(er)-Bidelspacher-Bell, Laugenstein,
Edwards, Attmore, Stull, Stroop, George, Lassatt, Sharpe,
Reese, Polk, Green(e), Tumlin, and attendant families of
Pennsylvania, North Carolina, and Georgia. No city, 1951.

BELL -- Bell, Raymond M.
Founders of the Bell family; a record of pioneer settlers
in Mifflin County, Pennsylvania. Carlisle, Pa., 1929.

BELL -- Bell, Raymond Martin
John Bell of Barree township, Huntingdon County, Pa., a
record of his ancestors and descendants. Carlisle, Pa.,
1937.

BELL -- Bell, Raymond Martin
The Bell family of Mifflin County, Pennsylvania; the
ancestors and descendants of John Henderson Bell of
Decator township. Edwards Brothers, Inc. Washington,
Pa., 1941.

BELL -- Bell, Raymond Martin
The Bells of East Pennsborough, Cumberland County,
Pennsylvania. Washington, Pa., 1958.

BELL -- Bell, Raymond Martin
The descendants of John Henderson Bell, 1791-1838, of
Mifflin County, Pennsylvania. Washington, Pa., 1966.

BELL -- Bell, Raymond Martin
The Bells of Stony Creek, Middle Paxton Twp., Dauphin Co.,
Pennsylvania. Washington, Pa., 1966.

BELL -- Bell, Raymond Martin
The Bells of Stony Creek, Middle Paxton Township, Dauphin
County, Pennsylvania. Washington, Pa., 1976.

BELL -- Bell, Susan A.
The Bell family, "The James and Isaiah Bell chart."
Westtown, Pa., 1945?

BELL -- Seaver, J. Montgomery
... Bell family records. American Historical-Genealogical
Society. Philadelphia, 1929.

BELOTE -- Macdonald, Donald B.
Belote family, Connecitcut and New York. Kingston, Pa.,
1935.

BEMIS -- Bemis, Ted H.
The history of the Bemis, Perkinson, Fay, and Lawrence
families: these being the four ancestral lines of the
compiler. T. H. Bemis. Stroudsburg, Pa., 1980.

BENDER -- Bender, C. W.
Descendants of Daniel Bender. Berlin Pub. Co. Berlin,
Pa., 1948.

BENDER -- Lenhart, John Mary
The Bender family; German pioneers of western Pennsylvania,
1798-1945. No City, 194-?

BENNER -- (Author unknown)
Detective work among the Benners; or, an analytical   (P)
study of two pioneer Montgomery County families.
Norristown, Pa., 1949-1951.

BENNETT -- Bennett, Stephen Beers
The Bennett, Bently and Beers families. Pittston, Pa.,
1890.

BENNETT -- Bennett, S. B.
The Bennett, Bently and Beers families. Pittston, Pa.,
1899.

BERG -- Berg, James
Descendants of Andrew Berg, Lancaster County,
Pennsylvania, pioneer. Bothell, Wash., 1965.

BERGE -- Wanger, George F. P.
Three generations of the descendants of Abraham Berge of
Limerick township, Montg. County, Pa. Pottstown, Pa.,
1910.

BERKEY -- Berkey, Lennie (M.)
Christian Berkey family of Somerset Co., Pa., Clark,   (A)
Washington & Jackson Counties, Indiana. Salem, Ind., 1953.

BERKHEIMER -- Berkheimer, Charles F.
     The American ancestors of the Berkheimer family:
     Birckheimer, Barkhamer, Burkheimer, Bergheimer, Barkhammer,
     Birkhimer, Berkhimer, Burkhamer, (and) Birkimer.
     Williamsport, Pa., 1966.

BERLIN -- Jones, Wayne V.
     Berlin family. Allentown, Pa., 1911.   (A)

BERSTLER -- Jones, Mrs. Urban J.
     Berstler family, Berks, Lancaster, Chester and
     Philadelphia Counties. No city, 1967.

BERTRAND -- Bartram, Violet W. and D. Kent Bartram, Jr.
     Bartram branches: genealogy of the families of West
     Virginia, Connecticut, and Pennsylvania. Gateway Press.
     Baltimore, 1984.

BERWYN -- Berwind, Elizabeth B.
     Gateways to the past. Berwind. Philadelphia, 1978.

BEWER -- Baver, Russell S.
     Genealogical list of the descendants of Christopher   (P)
     Bewer(Baver). Easton, Pa., 1955.

BIBIGHAUS -- (Author unknown)
     Descendants of John Bibighaus, of Bedminster, Bucks County,
     Pennsylvania. No city, 1951.

BICE -- Bice, Lucille (B.)
     Family tree; with branches, dates, names and data about   (A)
     the Aurandt, Bice, Bonebreak, Lykens, Miller, Oellig,
     Rhodes, Rodkey families. B. M. Bice. Martinsburg, Pa.,
     1967.

BICKNELL -- Carroll, Phyllis Bicknell
     The Bicknell genealogy, 1981: supplement to the 1913
     Bicknell genealogy. Gateway Press. Doylestown, Pa.,
     1981.

BIDDLE --
     Autobiography of Charles Biddle, vice-president of the
     Supreme executive council of Pennsylvania. 1745-1821.
     E. Claxton and Company. Philadephia, 1883.

BIDDLE -- (Author unknown)
     An eminent family honors a founder; descendants of   (P)
     William Biddle plan gathering on 250th anniversary of
     house's establishment in America. Philadelphia, 1931.

BIDDLE -- Biddle, Henry D.
Notes on the genealogy of the Biddle family, together with
abstracts of some early deeds. W. S. Fortescue & Co.
Philadelphia, 1895.

BIDDLE --Biddle, Henry D.
A sketch of Owen Biddle, to which is added a short   (P)
account of the Parke family, together with a list
of his descendants. Philadelphia, 1927.

BIDDLE -- Biddle, Nicholas
Biddle anniversary celebrating the 250th anniversary of the
arrival in America of William and Sarah Kempe Biddle, held
at the Pennsylvania Historical Society, Philadelphia,
November 12, 1931. The Engle Press. Philadelphia, 1932.

BIDDLE -- Du Bin, Alexander
The Biddle family ... Historical Pub. Soc.   (N)
Philadelphia, 1950.

BIDDLE -- Gay, Paul
A genealogical chart of the descendants of William   (P)
and John Biddle of Philadelphia, Pa., grandsons of
William Biddle, who came to New Jersey in 1681.
No city, 1933.

BIDDLE -- Leach, Frank W.
Biddle family. One of the series of sketches written   (P)
by Frank W. Leach for the Philadelphia North American,
1907-1913 ... The Historical Pub. Soc. Philadelphia,
1932.

BIDDLE -- Leach, Josiah G.
An account of the descendants of John Biddle, who   (P)
settled in Cecil County, Maryland in the years 1687.
The Historical Soc. of Pa. pHILADELPHIA, pA., 1906.

BIDDLE -- Biddle, Walter L. C.
Col. Clement Biddle, with a genealogy of the   (P)
Biddle family. Philadelphia, 1883.

BIEBER -- Beaver, Irwin M.
History and genealogy of the Bieber, Beaver, Biever,
Beeber family. Reading, Pa., 1939.

BIERBAUER -- Bierbower, James Culver
House of Bierbauer. New Wilmington, Pa., 1942.

BIERLY -- Shoemaker, Henry W.
    The Bierly family in Europe and America; an address by
    Henry W. Shoemaker ... at the annual Bierly reunion,
    McElhattan, Pa., August 16, 1922. Tribune Press.
    Alttona, Pa., 1922.

BILES -- White, Miles
    William Biles. Philadelphia, 1912.   (A)

BILLOP -- Davis, William T.
    The Conference of Billopp House, Staten Island, New York,
    by William T. Davis, Chairman, Committee on History,
    Conference House Association ... The Science Press.
    Lancaster, Pa., 1926.

BINGHAM --Bingham, Theodore A.
    Genealogy of the Bingham family in the United States,
    especially of the state of Connecticut; including notes
    on the Binghams of Philadelphia and of Irish descent, with
    partial genealogies of allied families. Harrisburg Pub. Co.
    Harrisburg, Pa., 1898.

BINGHAM -- Bingham, Theodore A.
    Bingham & other genealogies; the Bingham family in the
    United States, especially of the state of Connecticut;
    including notes on the Binghams of Philadelphia & of
    Irish descent; mediaeval records; armorial bearings; etc.
    Also partial genealogies of the following intermarried
    families: Rutherfurd, Tison, De la Beaume, Grew, Johnson,
    Deming, Foote, Clark, Whiting. No city, 1920.

BINGHAM -- Hogan, Helen Elizabeth Bingman
    Bingman-Wilson families of Pennsylvania. No city, 1946.

BIRCHARD -- (Author unknown)
    The Birchard-Burchard genealogy, with history and records
    of the kindred in North America, descendants (!) of
    Thomas Birchard (1635) Norwich, Connecticut. Mrs. Elizabeth
    Birchard, Publisher. Philadelphia, 1927.

BIRD -- Bird, Nancy Niles
    Historical sketch of the family of Michael Presbury Bird
    of Roxbury, Massachuestts, a pioneer of East Smithfield,
    Pennsylvania, in 1801, to which is added a brief history
    of the Sumner family, who were also pioneers of East
    Smithfield, Pa. Press of Fierstine Printing House.
    Utica, N.Y., 1905.

BISBEE -- Bisbee, Margaret J. (D.)
"Two brothers in the Pennsylvania triangle"; a   (A)
biographical encyclopedia of the descendants of
Reuben Bisbee (born 1776) Mass. Erie, Pa., 1974.

BISHOP -- Mervine, William M.
The Bishop genealogy. Philadelphia, 1913.

BISHOP -- (Author unknown)
Family record of descendants of Joseph Bishop and   (P)
Susanna Moyer of Bucks County, Pa. No city, no date.

BISSELL -- Jessop, Edith Newbold
General Daniel Bissell, his ancestors and descendants, and
the Hoyt, Strong, and other families with which they inter-
married. Wm. F. Fell Co. New York, N.Y., 1927.

BITSCHE -- Peachey, Samuel M.
A memorial history of Peter Bitsche, and his lineal   (N)
descendants ... J. Baer's Sons. Lancaster, Pa., 1892.

BIXLER -- Lick, David E.
Bicksler-Bixler family, 1728-1968, in the U.S.A.   (A)
Church Center Printers. Myerstown, Pa., 1968.

BLACKFAN -- Smith, M. G.
Genealogy of the Blackfan family. J. Rakestraw.   (A)
Philadelphia, 1857.

BLACKLEDGE -- Leckey, Howard L.
Genealogical records of Blackledge, Burson, Carter families.
Waynesburg, Pa., 1936.

BLACKMAN -- Plumb, Henry Blackman
The Blackmans, Darrows, Booses, Joneses, Collingses,
Stearnses, Straws, Plumbs, Hydes. Wilkesbarre, Pa.,
1894.

BLACKMAN -- Young, Henry James
The Blackmans of Night's Creek: Ancestors and Descendants
of George and Maria (Smith) Blackman. Carlisle, Pa., 1980.

BLAIR -- Blair, Charles R., Sr.
An index of the Blair magazine, official bulletin of   (N)
the Blair society for genealogical research, pub.
Erie, Pa., in 13 issues between Nov. 1925 and Nov. 1931.
C. R. Blair. Silver Spring, Md., 1964.

BLAIR -- Horner, Frederick
<u>The history of the Blair, Banister, and Braxton families</u>
<u>before and after the revolution. With a brief sketch of</u>
<u>their descendants</u>. J. B. Lippincott. Philadelphia, 1898.

BLAIR -- Kinter, W. L.
<u>The Blairs of Blair's Mills and Blair's Gap, Pennsylvania</u>.
No City, 1966.

BLAIR -- Miller, Mervin A.
<u>Meet the Blair family</u>. Blair County Historical   (P)
Society. Hollidaysburg, Pa., 1916.

BLAIR -- Miller, M. A.
<u>Meet the Blair family</u>. Blair County Historical Society.
Hollidaysburg, Pa., 1946.

BLANKENBURG -- Blankenburg, Lucretia L.
<u>(The) Blankenburgs of Philadelphia, by one of them,</u>
<u>Lucretia L. Blankenburg ...</u> The John C. Winston Co.
Philadelphia, 1928.

BLAUCH -- Blauch, D. D.
<u>History of the Blauch family</u>. Johnstown, Pa., 1909.   (A)

BLAUCH -- Weaver, Daniel D. and D. D. Blauch
<u>History of the Rev. Bishop Samuel Blauch of Conemaugh</u>   (A)
<u>Township, Somerset County, Pa., and his descendants</u>.
D. D. Blauch. Johnstown, Pa., 1921.

BLEW -- Engle, Charles Henry
<u>A genealogical study of John Blew, (Revolutionary war</u>
<u>veteran) of New Jersey and Pennsylvania</u>. Mahanoy City,
Pa., 1954.

BLINN -- Walker, George G.
<u>John Adam Blinn (1864-1892) and Caroline Anna Stuber</u>
<u>(1863-1949) of Beaver County, Pennsylvania: their</u>
<u>ancestors and descendants</u>. G. G. Walker. Manchester,
Conn., 1983.

BLISS -- Detty, Victor C.
<u>P. P. Bliss, July 9, 1838-December 29, 1876; a centennial</u>
<u>sketch of his life and work, 1838-1938, with selected</u>
<u>gospel hymns</u>. Wysox, Pa., 1938.

BLOSSOM -- Blossom, Walter L.
<u>The Blossom family</u>. Erie, Pa., 1942.

BOLICH -- Bolich, Mary Margaret
   The Bolich family in America. Allentown, Pa., 1939.

BOMBERGER -- Bomberger, Henry H.
   Bomberger chronicles. Jeanette Publishing Co.
   Jeanette, Pa., 1935.

BOONE -- Du Bin, Alexander
   Boone family and collateral lines of Paxton, Taylor,   (N)
   Dumbauld. The Historical Pub. Co. Philadelphia, 1950-54.

BOONE -- Hoagland, Edward C.
   Some brief notes on the Boone family. Sacred Art   (P)
   Press. Wysox, Pa., 1955.

BOONE -- Hoagland, Edward C.
   More twigs from family trees, no. ccxxxiii; or, Some   (N)
   brief notes on the Boone family. Sacred Art Press.
   Wysox, Pa., 1955.

BORDEN -- Du Bin, Alexander
   Borden, Powers, Harvey, Wood, Peck. The Historical
   Publication Society. Philadelphia, 1950.

BORNEMAN -- Borneman, J. H.
   The history of the Borneman family in America since the
   first settlers, 1721 to 1878. Boyertown, Pa., 1881, 1879.

BORTNER --Glatfelter, Charles Henry
   George Bortner of Codorus Township, York County,
   Pennsylvania, and his descendants. Glen Rock, Pa., 1949
   (i.e. 1950).

BOSBYSHELL -- Bosbyshell, Oliver Christian
   Descendants of Christian and Elizabeth (Oliver) Bosbyshell.
   Philadelphia, 1910?

BOUCHER -- Burkhardt, Franklin A.
   The Boucher family (Bowsher, Bauscher, Bausher, Bousher)
   comprising a genealogy of branches of Strawn, Harpster,
   Tedrow, Cryder, Reichelderfer, Critchfield, Stahl, Straw,
   Brant and other families. Descendants of Daniel Boucher
   of Albany Township, Berks County, Pa. Notes of other
   Boucher families. Henry Boucher descendants (Indiana,
   Pa.) A brief history of the Ohio reunions of kindred
   families. F. E. Burkhardt Press. New York, N.Y., 1917.

BOWEN -- Seaver, Jesse Montgomery
   The Bowen genealogy. Philadelphia, Pa., 1962.

BOWER -- McNeil, Mary (Bower)
    Genealogy of the Bower family. West Grove, Pa., 1892.   (P)

BOWER -- Bower, Luther M.
    Christopher Bower story. Blain, Pa., 1971.   (A)

BOWERSOX -- Bowersox, George E.
    Historical notes and genealogic i.e., genealogical record
    of the Bowersox family with full record of the Jeremiah
    Daniel Bowersox (1851-1870 i.e. 1890) descendants.
    Leechburg, Pa., 1950.

BOWLES -- Farquhar, Thomas M.
    The history of the Bowles family; containing an accurate
    historical lineage of the Bowles family from the Norman
    conquest to the twentieth century, with historical and
    genealogical notes and some pedigrees of Bowles families
    in various sections of the United States and Britain.
    Farquhar Pub. Philadelphia, 1907.

BOWMAN -- Bowman, Shadrach L.
    The Bowman family. Harrisburg, Pa., 1886.

BOWMAN -- Dougherty, Charles B.
    The story of Bowman's Hill, Wilkes-Barre, Pa. (with   (A)
    Bowman genealogy). Wilkes Barre, Pa. No date.

BOWMAN -- Heinhold, Laura K.
    Genealogy of John Bowman of the Seventh Day German Baptists
    of Ephrata, Pa. and his descendants Laura K. Heinhold.
    Philadelphia, Pa., 1968.

BOWMAN -- Penrose, Maryly Barton
    Bauman/Bowman family of the Mohawk, Susquehanna & Niagra
    Rivers. Liberty Bell Associates. Franklin Park, N.J.
    1977.

BOWMAN -- Seas, Helen Chadderton
    A genealogy of Esther Bowman, August 22, 1778, Patrick
    Rice, June 24, 1774, married about 1798. Sharon, Pa.,
    1960.

BOWMAN -- Thomas, Augusta Dillman
    The Bowmans. Allentown, Pa., 1934.

BOWMAN -- (Author unknown)
    The Bowman family; a historical and memorial volume, from
    the earliest traditions to the present time, 1886.
    Publishing Dept. M. E. Book Rooms. Harrisburg, Pa., 1886.

BOWSER -- Bowser, Addison Bartholomew
    The Bowser family history. Kittanning, Pa., 1922.

BOWSER -- Bracken, Evelyn Claypoole
    The Bowsers and Claypool(e)s. Indiana, Pa., 1981.

BOWYER -- Cohen, Evelina Gleaves
    Family facts and fairy tales. Philadelphia, 1953.

BOYD -- Boyd, M. Hillis
    ... Family record. Descendants of John and Mary-Fulton
    Boyd ... L. S. Hart. Harrisburg, Pa., 1882.

BOYD -- Boyd, William P.
    History of the Boyd family and descendants, with historical
    sketches of the ancient family of Boyd's in Scotland from
    the year 1200, and those of Ireland from the year 1680, with
    records of their descendants in Kent, New Windsor, Albany,
    Middletown and Salem, N.Y., Boston, Mass., Northumberland
    County, Pa., and sketches of those from the southern and
    western states from 1740 to 1912. John P. Smith Printing.
    Rochester, N.Y., 1912.

BOYD -- Gottschalk, Katherine Cox
    Boyd family of Pennsylvania, military records. No city,
    1936.

BOYD -- Laborde, Phyllis Boyd
    From Lancaster to Lafayette, Thomas Boyd 1692-1768.
    Lafayette, Calif., 1976.

BOYER -- Boyer, Carl
    Ancestral lines: 190 families in England, Wales, Germany,
    New England, New York, New Jersey, and Pennsylvania.
    C. Boyer. Newhall, Calif., 1981.

BOYER -- Boyer, Charles C.
    American Boyers. Allentown, Pa., 1940.

BOYER -- Boyer, Charles C.
    American Boyers. Kutztown Pub. Co. Kutztown, Pa., 1915.

BRACE --Brace, Sherman
    Brace lineage. G. E. Elwell & Son. Bloomsburg, Pa., 1914.

BRACE -- Brace, John Sherman
    Brace lineage. G. E. Elwell & Son. Bloomsburg, Pa., 1927.

BRADFORD -- Darrach, Henry
    Bradford family. 1660-1906 ... Philadelphia, Pa., 1906.

BRADFORD -- (Author unknown)
Descendants of William Bradford, Dorrance branch.   (P)
Dando Print & Pub. Philadelphia, 1904.

BRADY -- Brady, Cyrus T.
The Bradys of Western Pennsylvania; a photographic   (N)
collection. New York, N.Y., 1959.

BRADY -- Brady, Edward
Birth, marriage, etc. of Edward Brady, counsellor-at-law...
Philadelphia, Pa., 1895.

BRADY -- Brady, William Young
Chart of the descendants of Hugh Brady ... W. Y. Brady.
Pittsburg, Pa., 1920?

BRADY -- Murdock, William G.
Brady family reunion and fragments of Brady history and
biography. Milton, Pa., 1909.

BRANT -- Cober, Alvin Alonzo Brant
The Brant genealogy of Somerset County, Pennsylvania.
Berlin, Pa., 1932.

BRAYNE -- Wynne, Elizabeth Maxwell Alsop
Genealogies (!) and traditions, Brayne, Benger, Barton,
French. Printing House of Park. Indiana, Pa., 1931.

BRECHBILL -- Brechbill, Earl D.
Ancestry of John and Henrietta Davidson Brechbill; a   (A)
historical narrative. Greencastle, Pa., 1973.

BREED -- Breed, John H.
A record of the descendants of Allen Bread, who came   (P)
to America from England in 1630. Hathaway Bros.
Philadelphia, 1892.

BREIDINGER -- Leavesley, Ronald J.
The Breidinger family in America. Levittown, Pa., 1961.

BRENDLINGER -- Hoyt, Theodore Charles, Jr. and Zola M. Hoyt
Some genealogies of the Brendlingers, Walbecks,
Baumgardners, Lichtenfels, Henderson, and Riddles, of
Westmoreland and Indiana Counties, Pennsylvania.
Indiana, Pa., 1941.

BRENNEMAN -- Gerberich, Albert H.
The Brenneman history. Mennonite Publishing House.
Scottdale, Pa., 1938.

BRENNEMAN -- Breneman, Charles D.
A history of the descendants of Abraham Breneman, born in
Lancaster County, Pennsylvania, December 3, 1744, and
settled near Edom, Rockingham County, Virginia, in 1770,
or soon after, and a complete genealogical register with
biographies of many of his descendants from the earliest
available records to the present time, giving dates in three
centuries. Elida, Ohio, 1939.

BRENNER -- Barley, Clara
Brenner baptisms, marriages and deaths copied from the   (N)
records of Trinity Lutheran Church, Lancaster, Pa.
Lancaster, Pa., 1919.

BRENNER -- Brenner, Scott Francis
The Brenner family history of the ancestors and descendants
of Jacob Brenner and Elizabeth Goehring. Reading, Pa.,
1946.

BRENNER -- Myers, Forrest D.
Briner family history: a genealogy of George Michael Breiner
and Anna Catharina Loy, married 1756/7 in Pennsylvania.
A. E. Myers. Harrisburg, Pa., 1984.

BRETZ -- Parthemore, E. W. S.
Genealogy of the Ludwig Bretz family, 1750-1890. Harrisburg
Publishing Co. Harrisburg, Pa., 1890.

BREVARD -- (Author unknown)
A notice of the Brevard family. Philadelphia, 1851.

BRIGHT -- Green, Albert Gallatin
Historical sketch of the Bright family. Prepared at the
request of the Historical Society of Berks County, and
read before that body Tuesday, November 13, 1900 ...
Times Book Print. Reading, Pa., 1900.

BRINGHURST -- Leach, Josiah Granville
History of the Bringhurst family; with notes on the
Clarkson, De Peyster, and Boude families. J. B. Lippincott.
Philadelphia, 1901.

BRINKMAN -- De Long, Dr. Irwin Hoch
Descendants of Otto Henrich Wilhelm Brinkman. Lancaster,
Pa., 1925.

BRINLEY --Brinley, Robert M.
The Brinleys of Pennsylvania (a detailed compendium of
eighty-eight interrelated descendants of one of the earliest
families to emigrate to America). Paramus?, N.J., 1967.

BRINTON -- Schoonover, Janetta Wright
    The Brinton genealogy; a history of William Brinton who came
    from England to Chester County, Pennsylvania, in 1684 and of
    his descendants, with some records of the English Brintons.
    (Data collected by Gilbert Cope). MacCrellish & Quigley.
    Trenton, N.J., 1925.

BRITTON -- Cronbaugh, Lois E. W.
    Pennsylvania: Brittain-Britton data. No city.   (A)
    No date.

BROBST -- Rinkenbach, William H.
    Early history of the Brobst-Probst family of Berks and
    Lehigh Counties, Pa. No city, 1939.

BROCK -- Baker, Juliette Boyer
    Early Brock data from New Jersey, Pennsylvania and West
    Virginia. No city, 1933.

BROCKMAN -- Clark, Henry W.
    Genealogy of the Brockman and Dean families.   (A)
    Harrisburg Pub. Harrisburg, Pa., 1905.

BROOKHART -- Hartshorn, Edwin Simpson
    Michael Brookhart, sometimes Michael Brugart (-1775)
    of Hellem Township, York County, Pa., and some of his
    descendants. No city, 1956.

BROOKS -- Adair, Caroline Brooks
    Our heritage. York, Pa., 1954-55.

BROOKS -- Balch, Thomas W.
    (The Brooke family of Whitchurch, Hampshire, England;   (A)
    tog. with an account of Acting governor Robert Brooke
    of Maryland and Col. Ninian Beall of Maryland and some
    of their descendants. Allen, Lane & Scott. Philadelphia,
    1899.

BROOKS -- Seaver, J. Montgomery
    Brooks family history. Philadelphia, 192-.

BROMWELL -- Bromwell, Henrietta E.
    The Bromwell genealogy, including descendants of William
    Bromwell and Beulah Hall, with data relating to others of
    the Bromwell name in America also genealogical records of
    branches of the allied families of Holmes... Payne...
    Rice and Leffler... With some descendants of Major Conrad
    Leffler of Pennsylvania, and of the Rev. Peter Fullenwider,
    Rev. Jasper Simler, and Jonathan Boone of Kentucky (Eighty
    illustrations from various sources). Denver, Colo., 1910.

BRONK -- Bronk, Mitchell
Genealogical notes: the Palatine Bronk family.   (N)
Descendants of Mattheus Brunck, settled at West Camp,
in 1710, and the related Rettelff (Radley) family.
Philadelphia, 1943.

BRONSON -- Tracy, Eliza H.
Bronson-Brownson-Brunson: some descendants of John   (N)
Bronson of Hartford (1636) who migrated to Vermont,
New Hampshire, New Jersey (and) Pennsylvania ... with
some brief accounts of their relationship to Canfield,
Chittenden, French, Howlett, Morris, and Tracy families.
La Jolla, Calif., 1973.

BROSSMAN -- Brossman, Schuyler
The Heimbach-Brossman family of Montgomery County,
Pennsylvania. Rehrersburg, Pa., 1960.

BROSSMAN -- Brossman, Schuyler C.
Notes on the family of Daniel David Brossman, Sept. 1862-5
Jan. 1927, and wife, Alice, 19 Dec. 1868-21 Mar. 1932, of
Pennsylvania and Colorado. Rehrersburg, Pa., 1969.

BROSSMAN -- Brossman, Schuyler C.
Notes on Jacob Bressman-Brussman-Brossman, 26 March 1830 -
11 January 1896; his ancestors and descendants and his life
journey from Lebanon County, Pa. to Fremont County, Iowa,
to Nevada. No city, 1971.

BROSSMAN -- Brossman, Schuyler C.
Notes on Charles Edwin Brossman, 1879-1950, and his wife,
Sarah Minerva Deck, 1884-1948, and their descendants of
Rehrersburg, Berks County, Pa. Rehrersburg, Pa., 1974.

BROWN -- (Author unknown)
... A reunion of the children and grand children of   (P)
John Adams Smith Brown upon the seventieth anniversary
of his birthday ... 1928, at the Wellington ...
Philadelphia ... Philadelphia, 1928.

BROWN -- Brown, George Williams
Historical genealogy relating to a branch of the Brown
family, including brief history of other families.
J. P. Murphy. Philadelphia, 1885.

BROWN -- Brown, Isaac Brownell
Genealogy of Rasselas Wilcox and Mary Potter Brown, their
descendants and ancestral line. Evangelical Pub. Co.
Harrisburg, Pa., 1922.

BROWN -- Brown, John Jordan
    <u>The descendants of James Brown, 1716-1922</u>. Sun Printing.
    Williamsport, Pa., 1922.

BROWN -- Du Bin, Alexander
    <u>Old Philadelphia families</u>. The Historical Pub. Society.
    Philaldephia, 1939.

BROWN -- Du Bin, Alexander
    <u>Browne-Brown family ...</u> Historical Pub. society.   (N)
    Philadelphia, 1948.

BROWN --Hoagland, Edward Coolbaugh
    <u>Twigs from family tress, CCLXXIV-CCLXXXIII</u>. Wysox,
    Pa., 1957.

BROWN -- Smith, Mary W.
    <u>The Browns of Nottingham. Pa., and related families</u>.   (P)
    Canton, Ohio?, 1969.

BROWNFIELD -- Vosburgh, Genevieve R.
    <u>Brownfield family</u>. Pittsburgh, Pa., 1932.   (A)

BROWNLEE -- John Templeton Brownlee Reunion in
              Washington, Pennsylvania, July 18 & 19, 1967
    <u>A genealogical record of the descendants of Joseph Brownlee,
    1791-1867</u>. Evans City?, Pa., 1966.

BROWNLEE -- Reed, Alexander P.
    <u>Brownlee descendants of Samuel R. Brownlee (1827-1845)</u>   (P)
    <u>Washington County, Pennsylvania, and Lee County, Iowa</u>.
    Pittsburgh, Pa., 1963.

BRUBACHER --Brubacher, Aden H.
    <u>Record of the ancestors and descendants of Jacob Sherk</u>   (A)
    <u>Brubaker, and his brother, Daniel Sherk Brubaker ...</u>
    <u>deacons in the Mennonite Church ... in Juniata County,</u>
    <u>Pa. ... in Stark and Wayne Counties, Ohio</u>. Elmira,
    Ont., 1974.

BRUBACHER -- Brubaker, Frederick L.
    <u>History-genealogy of the Jacob Sherk Brubaker family</u>.   (A)
    Middleburg Post. Middleburg, Pa., 1961.

BRUBACHER -- Gibble, Phares Brubaker
    <u>History and genealogy of the Brubaker-Brubacher-Brewbaker</u>
    <u>family in America</u>. Eastern Pennsylvania Brubaker Assoc.
    Ephrata?, Pa., 1951.

BRUBAKER -- Brubaker, Landis H.
     Family of Abraham Kurtz Brubaker, born Jan. 20, 1855,   (A)
     died May 8, 1933; married ... Lydia Graybill ...
     Lancaster, Pa., 1972.

BRUBAKER -- Zook, Lois Ann
     Who begot thee? Descendants of Jacob Brubaker of   (P)
     Snyder County, Pa. Zook. Lancaster, Pa., 1976.

BRUMFIELD -- Brumfield, Blackman O.
     Descendants of Thomas Brumfield of Berks County,
     Pennsylvania; genealogy and family history, 1720 to 1960.
     John Woolman Press. Indianapolis, Ind., 1962.

BRUSH -- Brush, Anna F.
     Concerning the ancestors of Abner Brush; and of his   (P)
     wife Laura Hubbard Brush. Philadelphia, 1908?

BRYANT -- Luke, Miriam L.
     Some descendants of Thomas Bryant of Chester County, Pa.
     No city, 1977.

BRYNER -- Belton, Cardie Snyder
     Descendants of John Bryner and his wife, Eliza Beth Hench
     of Juniata County, Pennsylvania. Co city, 1933.

BUCHANAN -- (Author unknown)
     Buchanan lineage (descendants of David Buchanan,   (A)
     1754-1818, emigrant from Ireland to Westmoreland
     Co., Pa. Colton, Calif., 1924?

BUCHANAN -- Bell, Raymond Martin
     The Buchanan family of Lewistown, Pennsylvania.
     Washington, Pa., 1972.

BUCHANAN -- Bell, Raymond Martin
     The descendants of Dorcas Armstrong Holt Buchanan:
     pioneer woman of Lewistown, Pennsylvania: with a
     note on Andrew Lycans. R. M. Bell. Washington, Pa., 1984.

BUCHANAN -- Blakemore, John Augustus
     Buchanan, the family history of James Buchanan, son of
     Alexander Buchanan of Pennsylvania, 1702-1976.
     Blakemore. Emory, Va., 1977.

BUCHANAN -- Rex, Clara Elliott Buchanan
     The Buchanan and allied families, with quotations from
     authoritative sources ... Norristown, Pa., 1931.

BUCHER -- (Author unknown)
Eighth Bucher reunion: souvenir magazine and program   (P)
No. 3, commemorating the 206th anniversary of the
Bucher family settlement in Pennsylvania. Bucher
Family Assoc. No city, 1928.

BUCK -- Buck, William J.
Account of the Buck family of Bucks County, Pennsylvania;
and of the Bucksville Centennial celebration held June 11,
1892. Jenkintown, Pa., 1893.

BUCK -- Fisher, Edith Buck
Johannes Buck, 1747-1790, Christian and Cathrine Buck
and their descendants, 1754-1958. Harrisburg, Pa., 1958.

BUCK -- Richards, Mrs. Elizabeth S.
Genealogy of the Buck family which settled in Cambridge,
afterwards Woburn, Mass., in the year 1635. Eagle Book
and Job Press. Reading, Pa., 1913.

BUDD -- (Author unknown)
Budd family. Historical Publication Society. Philadelphia,
Pa., 1940.

BUHL -- Ziegler, Gertrude Mohlin
The Christian Buhl family story. Zelienople Historical
Society. Zelienople, Pa., 1980.

BULL -- Bull, James Henry
John Bull of Perkiomen, early Philadelphia County, now
Montgomery County, Pennsylvania and his descendants,
1674-1930. San Francisco, Calif., 1930.

BULL -- Bull, James H.
The Bulls of Parkeomink, Montgomery County, Pennsylvania,
and their descendants. Prepared for Historical Society,
Norristown, Pa., for meeting at St. James Church, New
Providence, June 1, 1907, by James H. Bull ...
Norristown Historical Society. Norristown, Pa., 1907.

BULLOCK --Bullock, Paul D.
A Bullock family history: from Rehoboth to Holcomb,
1643-1957. P. D. Bullock. Monroeville, Pa., 1983.

BUNTING -- Bunting, Morgan
Genealogical chart of the Bunting family, drawn by
Morgan Bunting. Philadelphia, 1895.

BUNTING -- (Author unknown)
Bunting family, Bucks County, Pennsylvania. Lewis   (P)
Publishing Co. New York, N.Y., 1905.

BURBACH -- Calder, Treva E. G.
The Burbach-Poorbaugh-Purbaugh family in America,   (P)
1771-1974. The Poorbaugh-Purbaugh Assoc. Somerset Co.,
Pa., 1976.

BURCHINAL -- Gans, John L.
Burchinal genealogy, Jeremiah Burchinal of Mt. Harmon,   (A)
Kent County, Maryland and his descendants.
Connellsville, Pa., 1942?

BURD -- Burdge, Howard G.
Burdge and allied families. Melbourne?, Fla., 1950.   (P)

BURD -- Gillingham, Harrold E.
Notes on the Burds of Ormiston, Scotland, and   (P)
Philadelphia. Philadelphia?, 1939.

BURGER -- Bastian, Reba Mae (Beers)
Genealogy; family of Sarah Burger and Aron Beer;
descendants of Conrad Haag and Elizabeth Barger,
also Hawk family. Williamsport, Pa., 1982.

BURIAK -- Neidermyer, Paulette Buriak
The Buriak family history: "our roots." R & P Neidermyer.
Lebanon, Pa., 1982.

BURKE -- Kelly, John A.
Burk(e) family of southwest Virginia and the valley.
Haverford, Pa., 1944.

BURKET -- Patton, T. B.
history of the descendants of Peter Burket. Huntingdon,
Pa., 1897.

BURKHOLDR -- Burkholder, Henry L. and Albert N.
The Swiss origin of the Burkholder family of America.   (P)
Burkholder Family Assoc. Harrisburg, Pa., 1939.

BURKHOLDER -- Hoover, Mrs. Amos B.
Daniel S. and Anna W. Burkholder family, 1833-1957;   (A)
genealogy. Ensinger Print. Adamstown, Pa., 1957.

BURKHOLDER -- Burkholder, Elmer J.
Burkholder history. Ephrata, Pa., 1965.   (A)

BURLINGAME -- Burlingame, Evelyn E.
Ancestors and genealogical records of Evelyn Olsen
Burlingame, 1066-1960. Families from Massachusetts,
Maine, Pennsylvania, Wisconsin, Minnesota, England,
Norway, Canada. Minneapolis, Minn., 1960.

BURNER -- Barner, Harry William
More than 4,000 direct descendants of Adam & Fanny (Bunn)
Barner, their spouses & families. Barner Reunion History
Committee. Liverpool, Pa., 1976.

BURNHAM -- Burnham, Walter J.
1971 Annual since 1966: Burnham family lineage charts.
Pittsburgh, Pa., 1971.

BURNHAM -- Burnham, Walter Jefferson
Burnham family lineage charts, arranged and printed by
Walter J. Burnham for the Burnham Family Association.
Pittsburgh, Pa., 1966.

BURNS -- Seaver, J. Montgomery
... Burns family records. American Historical-Genealogical
Society. Philadelphia, 1929.

BURR -- Tyrrell, Henry G.
Burr family of New Jersey and Pennsylvania.. including   (A)
the families of Terry, Graham, Patton, Tyrrell, etc.
Washington, 1923.

BURRITT -- Burritt, Alice
The family of Blackleach, Burritt, Jr., pioneer, and one
of the first settlers of Uniondale, Susquehanna County,
Pennsylvania. Washington, D.C., 1911.

BUSHMAN -- Butt, Newbern I.
The Bushman family, originally of Pennsylvania and the   (A)
Rocky Mountains states. Provo, Utah, 1956.

BUTLER -- Butler, John B.
The Butler family of the Pennsylvania line.   (P)
Philadelphia, 1883

BUTLER --Butters, George
The genealogical registry of the Butters family ...
including the descendants of William Butter, of Woburn,
Mass., 1665 and the families of New York, Pennsylvania,
West Virginia, Ohio, Iowa and others bearing the name, who
settled in America. D. Oliphant. Chicago, Ill., 1896.

BUTLER --Garnett, Martha Roscoe
    Samuel Butler and his family relations. Folcroft Library
    Editions. Folcroft, Pa., 1976.

BUTLER -- Ravenscroft, Ruth (Thayer)
    John Newton Butler, 1878 pioneer to Spokane County,   (P)
    Washington. Spokane, Wash., 1961?

BUTLER -- Ravenscroft, Ruth Thayer
    Proof of descent of Saranne Butler Geer from Rev. Samuel
    Stone through the Butler family of Connecticut, Ohio and
    Pennsylvania. No city, 1956.

BYERS -- Sausaman, William Amel
    Jacob Byers (c. 1750-1801) of Pennsylvania and his   (A)
    descendants. Springfield, Ill., 1974.

BYRD -- Glenn, Thomas Allen
    Some colonial mansions and those who lived in them, with
    genealogies of the various families mentioned. H. T.
    Coates & Company. Philadelphia, 1898.

BYROM -- Keller, Velma Byrum
    The sons of Isaac; (a genealogy of the Byrums of North
    Carolina and Indiana). National Advertising Mfg. Co.
    Allentown, Pa., 1969.

- C -

CADBURY -- (Author unknown)
Joel Cadbury of Philadelphia (1799-1870) the families   (P)
descended from the brothers and sisters of Joel Cadbury
who was born in Birmingham, England, in 1799 and
settled in Pennsylvania, in 1815, send this message
of greeting ... No city, 1965.

CADBURY -- Cadbury, Henry J.
Cadbury pedgree. American section 1965. With sesqui-   (P)
centennial memento. Haverford, Pa., 1965.

CADBURY --Cadbury, Sarah
A reminiscent record of Joel & Caroline Warder Cadbury
of Philadelphia, and their nine children, 1840-1871.
No city, 1912.

CADDEN -- Hamlin, R. N.
Chronicle of the Cadden, McCarthy, and McManus families.
Hamlin. Philadelphia, 1980.

CADDIES --Wrathall, Claude and Jean
Caddies family of Pennsylvania. Seattle, Wash., 1966.

CALDWELL -- Weede, Fred Lewis
The James Caldwell family of Erie, Pennsylvania and
Chillicothe, Illinois; genealogical (sic) tabulation
of their descendants; including data of forebears of
Caldwell, Booth, Hay, Armstrong, and other allied
families in France, England, Scotland, Ireland, and
America. Ashville, N.C., 1959.

CAMAC -- Camac, Wm. Masters
Memoirs of the Camacs of Co. Down with some account of   (P)
their predecessors ... Philadelphia, 1913.

CAMPBELL -- (Author unknown)
The Campbell families of York County, Pennsylvania.
No city, 1951.

CAMPBELL -- (Author unknown)
Descendants of Joseph and Mary Dodge Campbell in America.
Chester, Pa., 1907.

CAMPBELL -- (Author unknown)
Genealogical account of the ancestors in America of
Joseph Andrew Kelly Campbell and Eliza Edith Deal (his
wife). Philadelphia, 1921.

CAMPBELL -- Burns, M. F.
History of the descendants of John Campbell and Ann   (A)
Christy who migrated to western Pennsylvania from
Argylshire, Scotland. Butler, Pa., 1923.

CAMPBELL -- Dunlap, Lewis Campbell
The Campbell clan. Coopersville Observer. Coopersville,
Mich., 1938.

CAMPBELL -- Seaver, J. Montgomery
... Campbell family records. American Historical-
Genealogical Society. Philadelphia, 1929.

CAMPBELL -- Sherrard, Hallock Campbell
The Campbells of Kishacoquillas. Chambersburg, Pa., 1894.

CAMPBELL -- Temple, Sarah E.
Our Campbell ancestors, 1742-1937. Traditions and history
of the family of five Campbell brothers and sisters; John,
James, Douglas, Hester, Mary and Samuel: including what is
known of them in New Jersey; York County, Pennsylvania;
Union County, South Carolina and in Ohio. A genealogy of
the known descendants of John Campbell through his son
James, and Samuel Campbell through his son Ralph, also brief
ancestral notes on families connected by marriage with the
foregoing; viz; Parnell, Clark, Spray, Wilson, Haskett,
Mendenhall and Underhill. I. Deach, Jr. Burbank, Calif.,
1939.

CAMPOLONGO -- Campolongo, Donald Ralph
Campilongo--Campolongo family history. Wescosville, Pa.,
1982.

CANBY -- (Author unknown)
William Canby, Brandywine, Delaware ... His descendants,
fourth to seventh generation in America. Friends' Book
Assoc. Philadelphia, 1883.

CANBY -- Du Bin, Alexander
Canby, Shipley, Roberts, Price, Bradford, Du Pont,   (N)
Boden, Newkirk. The Historical Publications Society.
Philadelphia, 1951.

CANTRELL -- Christie, Susan Cantrill
The Cantrill-Cantrell genealogy; a record of the descendants
of Richard Cantrill, who was a resident of Philadelphia
prior to 1689, and of earlier Cantrills in England and
America. The Grafton Press. New York, N.Y., 1908.

CAREY -- Carey, Alfred B.
Some of the Carey lines of Sussex County, Delaware who
descended from Thomas Cary, the immigrant and the
English pedigree. Home Print Co. Bryn Mawr, Pa., 1964.

CAREY -- Seltzer, Helen Estes
The Cary-Estes-Moore genealogy. Barn Hill. Huntingdon,
Pa., 1981.

CAREY -- Toennies, Dorothy Carey
Branches of the John Carey family of Buck's County,
Pennsylvania to Virginia, Ohio, and on West. No City,
1969.

CARMICHAEL --Bell, Raymond Martin
The Carmichael brothers of Mifflin County, Pennsylvania:
John, James, Daniel. R. M. Bell. Washington, Pa., 1984.

CARNAHAN -- McCreary, Dorothy G.
The Carnahan's. Salina, Pa., 1959.

CARPENTER -- Casanova, A. Y.
A Carpenter family of Lancaster. Philipsburg, Pa., 1910.

CARPENTER -- Carpenter, Edward and his son General
                    Louis Henry Carpenter
Samuel Carpenter and his decendants. J. B. Lippincott.
Philadelphia, 1912.

CARPENTIER -- Sellers, Edwin Jaquett
Genealogy of the De Carpentier family of Holland. Allen,
Lane & Scott. Philadelphia, 1909.

CARPENTIER -- Sellers, Edwin Jaquett
De Carpentier allied ancestry; ancestry of Maria De
Carpentier, wife of Jean Paul Jaquet, vice-director and
chief magistrate on the South River of New Netherland,
1655-1657. Allen, Lane & Scott. Philadelphia, 1928.

CARR -- (Author unknown)
The American Carr families. Martin & Allardyce.
Philadelphia, Pa., 1912.

CARRELL -- Carrell, Ezra Patterson
The descendants of James Carrell and Sarah Dungan, his wife.
International Printing Co. Hatboro, Pa., 1928.

CARRIEL -- Carriel, Charles Arthur
Henry Frost Carriel, M.D., his ancestors and descendants.
Pittsburgh, Pa., 1960.

CARSKADDON -- McLain, David E.
Descendants of James and Lettice Carskaddon of
Chillisquaque Township, Northumberland County,
Pennsylvania. McLain. Moorhead, Minn., 1970?

CARTER -- Carter, Floyd Raymond Nicholas
Genealogy of William R. Carter of the State of Pennsylvania,
Loudoun Co. Virginia, of Preble Co. Ohio, and Clinton Co.
Indiana. South Bend, Ind., 197-?

CARTER -- Potts, Thomas-Maxwell
Bi-centenary memorial of Jeremiah Carter, who came to the
province of Pennsylvania in 1682, containing a historic-
genealogy of his descendants down to the present time.
Canonsburg, Pa., 1883.

CARTER -- Seaver, J. Montgomery
... Carter family records. American Historical-Genealogical
Society. Philadelphia, 1929.

CARTER -- Thompson, Nora Belle
In search of grandmother. (Notes on Sarah Bradley Carter
of Derbyshire, England and Phoenixville, Pennsylvania.
Lancaster?, Pa., 1958.

CARTER -- Waterman, Thomas Tileston
English antecedents of Virginia architecture. Lancaster
Press, Inc. Lancaster, Pa., 1939.

CARVER -- Carver, Elias
Genealogy of William Carver from Hertfordshire, England,
in 1682. Loughead & Co. Philadelphia, 1903.

CASE -- Case, Lynn Marshall
The descendants of Captain Stephen Case of Marlboro, N.Y.
Ravertown, Pa., 1971.

CASHMAN -- Weaner, Arthur
History and genealogy of the German emigrant Cashman, with
reference to other Cashman surnames in America of German,
Irish, Jewish, other and unknown origins. Gettysburg, Pa.,
1957.

CASKEY -- (Author unknown)
Caskey cousins. Harrisburg, Pa. No date.   (N)

CASS --Cass, Earle Millard
Ada Bell Cass, descendant of John Cass, 1620-1675.
New Castle, Pa., 1945.

CASSEL -- Cassel, Daniel Kolb
    <u>A genealogical history of the Cassel family in America,
    being the descendants of Julius Kassel or Yelles Cassel,
    of Kriesham, Baden, Germany</u>. Morristown, Pa., 1896.

CASSEL -- Parthemore, E. W. S.
    <u>A Dauphin county centenarian in 1895 ...</u> Harrisburg   (N)
    Publishing Co., Harrisburg, Pa., 1895.

CASTOR -- Castor, Henry A. Jean
    <u>The Castors of Castorland, the descendants of John
    de Castorer, an ensign in the revolutionary army, who
    settled in Redfield, New York, after the war</u>. Martin &
    Allardyce. Philadelphia, Pa., 1910.

CATHERMAN -- Catherman-Katherman Reunion Assoc.
    <u>Report of the historian</u>. Millmont?, Pa., 1955.   (P)

CATLIN -- Weyburn, S. Fletcher
    <u>The biography and ancestry of Hon. George Henry Catlin,
    Scranton, Pennsylvania, with notes on genealogy</u>.
    Scranton, Pa., 1930.

CAUGHEY -- Rosenberg, Karl
    <u>Descendants of John Caughey, 1747-1826, a revolutionary
    War soldier of the Pennsylvania Lines</u>. Rosenberg.
    No city, 1974.

CESSNA -- Cessna, Howard
    <u>The house of Cessna, second series</u>. Berling, Pa., 1935.

CHAMBERS -- Brooks, James E.
    <u>Alexander Chambers of Philadelphia</u>. Glen Ridge?   (P)
    N.J., 1949.

CHANCE -- Chance, Hilda
    <u>Chance family, England to America, 1600-1965, Maryland,
    Delaware, Pensylvania, Missouri, Illinois</u>. Chester?
    Pa., 1965.

CHANCE -- Chance, Hilda Nancy Ersula Snowberger
    <u>The Chance family: England to America 1668 and to all
    states of America, Canada and Alaska</u>. H. Chance.
    Aston, Pa., 1981.

CHANDLEE -- Chandlee, Edward E.
    <u>Six Quaker clockmakers</u>. The Historical Society of
    Pennsylvania. Philadelphia, 1943.

CHANDLER -- (Author unknown)
Chandler. (The ancestry of Maria Louise (Chandler)   (P)
Williams and Percy Milton Chandler). Philadelphia,
19__.

CHANDLER -- Chandler Family Reunion Committee
A record of the descendants of George and Jane Chandler
(who emigrated to Pennsylvania from Wiltshire, England,
in 1687) with a pedigree of the Chandlers of Oare,
Wiltshire. Published to commemorate the 250th anniversary
of the landing in Pennsylvania, 1687-1937. No city, 1937.

CHAPMAN -- Chapman, George E.
Chapman family historical workbook. Allison Park, Pa.,   (A)
1966.

CHAPMAN -- Seaver, Jesse
Chapman family history. American Historical   (A)
Genealogical Society. Philadelphia, 1929. (American
Genealogical Research Institute. Washington, D.C., 1972).

CHASE -- Dow, Euphemia C.
The Pennsylvania branch of the William Chase family of
Roxbury, Mass. No city, 1956.

CHASE -- Seaver J. Montgomery
... Chase family records. American Historical Genealogical
Society. Philadelphia, 1929.

CHASTAIN -- Chastain, Lowell B.
Virginia Chastain (all spellings). Chastain.
Elizabethtown, Pa., 1983.

CHEW -- Konkle, Burton Alva
Benjamin Chew, 1722-1810, head of the Pennsylvania judiciary
system under colony and commonwealth. University of
Pennsylvania Press. Philadelphia, 1932.

CHEW -- Osburn, Frank Chew
Chew family, from the records of Frank Chew Osburn.   (P)
Printed by his estate. Pittsburgh, Pa., 1945.

CHEW -- Read, Elizabeth
Chews of Pennsylvania. New York, N.Y., 1880.   (A)

CHRISTY -- Christy, Bayard Henderson
James Christy of Westmoreland County, Pennsylvania.
No city, 1939.

CLAMER -- (Author unknown)
Waves of generations; or the prosperity and adversity   (P)
of a family. Being the story of the elder branch of
the descendants of Guilliam Clamer, senator of Hamburg
(1750-1774) to the year 1900. Collegeville, Pa., 1907.

CLARK -- Baer, Mabel Van Dyke
Robert Clark of Beaver County, Pennsylvania, and some
descendants particularly through Reverend Thomas Baker
Clark (1799-1853) and Clark family of Maryland,
including Harford County. No city, 1967.

CLARK -- Clark, Eunice Newbold
Clarks from Pennsylvania and allied families: from
early 1700s to 1984. E. N. Clark. Dallas, Tx., 1984.

CLARK -- Cooper, William A.
Notes on the ancestry of Ann Clarke who married John
Cooper, 1st mo. 18, 1712-13. Conshochen, Pa., 1910.

CLARK -- Clark, Phillip P.
Le Clericus: a 183 year history of the descendants of
William Clark and his wife Ann McDonald, 1801-1984.
P. P. Clark. Elizabethtown, Pa., 1984.

CLARK -- Justice, Alfred Rudulph
Ancestry of Jeremy Clarke of Rhode Island and Dungan
genealogy. Franklin Printing Co. Philadelphia, 1922.

CLARKSON -- Hall, John and Samuel Clarkson
Memoirs of Matthew Clarkson of Philadelphia, 1735-1800, by
his great-grandson, John Hall, and of his brother, Gerardus
Clarkson, 1737-1790, by his great-grandson, Samuel Clarkson.
Thomson Printing Co. Philadelphia, 1890.

CLARKSON -- Leach, Frank Willing
The Philadelphia branch of the Clarkson family.
Philadelphia?, 1912?

CLARKSON -- Leach, Frank W.
Clarkson family. One of the series of sketches written   (P)
by Frank W. Leach for the Philadelphia North American,
1907-13... The Historical Publ. Society. Philadelphia,
1932.

CLAUSER -- Blair, Beulah Hix
Some early lineages of Berks County, Pennsylvania,
Clauser (Klauser)-Hicks (Hix) and associated lines.
Boulder, Colo., 1959.

CLAY -- (Author unknown)
The family of Clay, of New Castle, Delaware, and
Philadelphia, Pennsylvania. Gibson Brothers.
Washington, D.C., 1895.

CLAY -- Shaw, Don C.
A genealogy and history of some of the descendants of   (N)
Johan Nicholas Klee of Bern Township, Berks County,
Pennsylvania; Clays of Pennsylvania Dutch ancestry.
Chicago, Ill., 1968.

CLAYPOOLE -- Graff, Rebecca Irwin
Genealogy of the Claypoole family of Philadelphia, 1588-
1893. J. B. Lippincott. Philadelphia, 1893.

CLAYPOOLE -- Graff, Rebecca I. V.
Appendix 2 to Genealogy of the Claypoole family of
Philadelphia, 1893. Philadelphia, 1894.

CLAYTON -- Clayton, Thomas J.
Rambles and reflections. Europe from Biscay to the Black
Sea and from Aetna to the North Cape with glimpses of
Asia, Africa, America and the islands of the sea. Press
of the Delaware County Republic. Chester, Pa., 1893.

CLEMENS -- Clemens, Lewis W.
Clemens family. Philadelphia, 1930.   (A)

CLEMENS -- Keyser, Alan G.
The Account book of the Clemens family of Lower Salford
Township, Montgomery County, Pennsylvania, 1749-1857,
translated by Raymond E. Hollenbach. Pennsylvania German
Society. _____, Pa., 1975.

CLEMENTS -- Bell, Raymond Martin
The ancestry of Samuel Clemens, grandfather of Mark
Twain. Bell. Washington, Pa., 1980.

CLEMENTS -- Bell, Raymond Martin
The ancestry of Samuel Clemens, grandfather of Mark
Twain. Revised. R. M. Bell. Washington, Pa., 1984.

CLEMSON -- Ball, Raymond Martin, Frank R. Baird and
         Margaret S. Ward
The Clemson family of Pennsylvania. Washington and
Jefferson College. Washington, Pa., 1971.

CLEWELL -- Clewell, Lewis B. and Lewis P. Clewell
History of the Clewell family in the United States of
America, 1737-1907. Keystone Print Co. Bethlehem, 1907.

CLOPPER -- (Author unknown)
An American family; its ups and downs through eight generations in New Amsterdam, New York, Pennsylvania, Maryland, Ohio and Texas, from 1650 to 1880. Cincinnati, Ohio, 1950.

CLOUD -- Pond, Rachel Adams
William Cloud, Pennsylvania proprietor, 1682. New York, N.Y., 1961.

CLOUD -- Pond, Rachel Adams Cloud and Clifton Ray Pond
William Cloud, Pennsylvania proprietor, 1682. 2d. ed., rev. and enl. of the "Cloud family" 1961. New York, N.Y., 1965.

CLULEY -- Cluley, David Dance
Cluley: a family from Philadelphia, 1801-1971.   (P)
Pennsauken?, N.J., 1971.

CLYMER -- (Authorn unknown)
Three generations of the Clymer family. Philadelphia, 1885.

CLYMER -- Macfarlane, James R.
George Clymer, signer of the Declaration of Independence, framer of the Constitution of the United States and of the state of Pennsylvania, his family and descendants. Sewickley Printing. Sewickley, Pa., 1927.

COAT -- (Author unknown)
Coat family of New Jersey and Pennsylvania, 1676-1823. Being a genealogical table of most of the descendants residing in Pennsylvania & New Jersey & other places in United States of America of Marmaduke & Ann Coat ... collected ... 1823... Philadelphia, 1823.

COATES -- (Author unknown)
The family in the Philadelphia city directories, 1785-   (P)
1901. No city, 1901.

COATES -- (Author unknown)
The history and genealogy of families who settled in   (P)
the provinces of Penn., N.Y., N.J., and Delaware. A compilation of original documents and records pertaining to related families: Coates, Webb, Clemson, Ash, Ross, Read, Bird, Van Gezel, Raniers, Taylor, Fleming, Clymer, Parke and others. Lancaster, Pa., 1935.

COATES -- Coates, Henry T.
Thomas Coates, who removed from England to the province of Pennsylvania, 1683. Philadelphia, 1897.

COATES -- Coates, Mary
Family memorials and recollections; or, Aunt Mary's patchwork. Philadelphia, 1885.

COBER -- Cober, Rev. Alvin Alonzo
The Cober genealogy of Pennsylvania, Iowa and Canada. The Berlin Press. Berlin, Pa., 1933.

CODER -- Huffman, Richard Glenn
The Conrad Coder's-Koder's, 1751-1985. R. G. Huffman. Whitney, Pa., 1985.

CODY -- Cody, Edward P.
Genealogy of the Cody family of Philadelphia. No City, 1953?

COLCORD -- Colcord, Doane B.
Colcord genealogy. Coudersport, Pa., 1908.

COLLINS -- Clement, John
Genealogy of the three daughters of Samuel and   (P)
Rosanna Collins, late of Waterford Township in Gloucester County and state of N.J. Leisenring. Philadelphia, Pa., 1871.

COLLINS -- Collins, John
Reminiscences of Isaac and Rachel (Budd) Collins, with an account of some of their descendants, together with a genealogy of the Collins family, and also a history of a reunion held at Philadelphia, May 9, 1892. J. B. Lippincott. Philadelphia, 1893.

COLLINS -- Collins, Margaret Hill
The Collins family. Collins. Ardmore, Pa., 1980.

COLTON -- Colton, George Woolworth
... A genealogical record of the descendants of Quarter-master George Colton; collected and arranged from all available public and private sources. Wickersham Printing. Lancaster, Pa., 1912.

CONKLIN -- Hoagland, Edward C.
Some brief notes on the Conklin and Conkling families.   (P)
Sacred Art Press. Wysox, Pa., 1955.

CONKLING -- Hoagland, Edward C.
More twigs from family trees, nos. ccxxxiv-ccxxxviii;   (N)
or, Some brief notes on the Conklin and Conkling families. Sacred Art Press. Wysox, Pa., 1955.

CONNELLY -- Waite, Frances Wise
Conley--Connelly, descendants of Thomas Connelly of northern Lancaster and York counties, Pennsylvania.
F. W. Waite. Doylestown, Pa., 1980.

CONNOR -- Hand, Robert
The American descendants of Henry Connor of County Antrim, Ireleand. Chadds Ford?, Pa., 1971.

CONNER -- Myers, Albert Edwin
The ancestry and genealogy of William Conner, Jr. who   (A)
married Emeline Snowman... 1829 at Penobscot, Maine.
Myers. Harrisburg, Pa., 1976.

CONOVER -- Conover, Charles Hopkins
The Conover family. Frankford, Pa., 1912.

CONSER -- Horan, John P.
The Conser family. Punxsutawney? Pa., 1966?

CONSTANT --Roebling, Emily Warren
The journal of the Reverend Silas Constant, pastor of the Presbyterian church at Yorktown, New York; with some of the records of the church and a list of his marriages, 1784-1825, together with notes on the Nelson, Van Cortlandt, Warren, and some other families in the journal.
J. B. Lippincott. Philadelphia, 1903.

CONYNGHAM   -- (Author unknown)
The reminiscences of David Hayfield Conyngham,   (P)
1750-1834, of the revolutionary house of Conyngham and Nesbitt, Philadelphia, Pa. No city. No date.

CCOK -- Cook, Joseph B.
Life history of Oliver and Elizabeth Cook. J. B. Cook.
York, Pa., 1979.

COOK -- Glenn, Thomas Allen
Welsh founders of Pennsylvania. Vol. 1 page 106.
Co city. No date.

COOK -- Seaver, J. Montgomery
... Cook family records. American Historical-Genealogical Society. Philadelphia, 1929.

COOLBAUGH -- Hoagland, Edward Coolbaugh
The Coolbaugh family in America, from the earliest appearance at New Amsterdam, 1686-1938, including a genealogical register of the descendants of William Coolbaugh, revolutionary patriot. 1st Edition.
Weldy's Print Shop. Towanda, Pa., 1938.

COOLBAUGH -- Hoagland, Edward Coolbaugh
<u>Twigs from family trees; or, 162 early American and foreign</u>
<u>lineages of first settles in this country and their descen-</u>
<u>dants who were pioneers in northern Pennsylvania and central</u>
<u>New York; together with royal lineages, revolutionary</u>
<u>journals, incidents and anecdotes of the old timers, and a</u>
<u>register of the marriages and deaths of the pioneers.</u>
<u>Carefully compiled from authentic sources</u>. Wysox, Pa.,
1940.

COOLBAUGH -- Hoagland, Edward C.
<u>Christopher Cowell of Macedonia, Pa., and some of his</u> (P)
<u>descendants</u>. Sacred Art Press. Wysox, Pa., 1957.

COOLBAUGH --
<u>Consolidated index to Twigs from family trees, sections</u> (P)
<u>I, II and III, numbers 1 to 400. Including Coolbaugh</u>
<u>family in America ...</u> Sacred Art Press. Towanda. Pa.,
1965.

COOLEY -- Cooley, George E.
<u>A record of the descendants of Jacob Cooley ... and</u> (N)
<u>Abigail Bartlett ...</u> Washington, Pa.? 1944.

COON -- McTeer, Frances Davis
<u>Coon-Gohn descendants from Chanceford Township, York</u>
<u>County, Pennsylvania</u>. Holiday, Fla., 1979.

COOPER -- Cresson, Joshua
<u>Genealogical table of the Cooper family, formerly of</u> (P)
<u>New Jersey beginning with William and Margaret Cooper</u>
<u>who came from Amersham (England) in the year 1678 and</u>
<u>settled ... opposite Philadelphia ...</u> No city, 1853.

COOPER -- Clemens, William M.
<u>Cooper marriages in Pennsylvania</u>. W. M. Clemens. (A)
Hackensack, N.J., 1917.

COOPER -- Cooper, George
<u>Descent of Coopers from 1771</u>. Unger. Philadelphia, (P)
1953.

COOVER -- Coover, Melanchthon
<u>A limited genealogy of the Kober-Cover-Coover family and</u>
<u>cognate families</u>. Times News and Publishing. Gettysburg,
Pa., 1942.

COPE -- The Gilbert Cope Foundation of
        Genealogical and Historical Research
<u>Cope notes</u>. West Chester, Pa., no date.

COPE -- (Author unknown)
Major John Andre's residence in Lancaster. Lancaster, Pa., 1904.

COPE -- Cope, Gilbert
A record of the Cope family. As established in America, by Oliver Cope, who came from England to Pennsylvania, about ... 1682, with the residences, dates of births, deaths and marriages of his descendants as far as ascertained. King & Baird. Philadelphia, 1861.

COPE -- Cope, Gilbert
Ancestral chart. West Chester, Pa., 1879.

COPE -- Cope, Gilbert
Ancestral chart. West Chester?, Pa., 1934.

COPE -- Hensel, W. U.
Major John Adre as a prisoner of war at Lancaster, Pa., 1775-6, with some account of a historic house and family; read before Donegal chapter, Daughters of the American Revolution. Lancaster, Pa., April 13, 1904?

CORBETT -- Corbett, E. Clark
Genealogy of the Corbett family. Clarion, Pa., 1917.

CORDELL -- Cordell, Glenn R.
Shaking the Cordell family tree: The history of a family in Franklin County, Pennsylvania since 1779: with a genealogy of the descendants of Henry Cordel, Jr., 1767-1842. Craft Press. Chambersburg, Pa., 1977.

CORMAN -- Mohr, James C.
The Cormany diaries: a Northern family in the Civil War. University of Pittsburgh Press. Pittsburgh, Pa., 1982.

CORNBOWER -- Diehl, Harry A.
Ancestors and descendants of Francis Wesley and Lucinda Elmira (Shearer) Cornbower (originally Kornbau) and allied families of Shearer, Sterner, Gerberick, Kroll-Croll of York County, Pa. and Baltimore and Carroll County, Md. Wilmington, Del., 1982.

CORNMAN -- Cornman, Charles A.
Genealogical record of descendants of Ludwig Kornman, Sr. in America. Carlisle, Pa., 1916.

CORSON -- Corson, Hiram
The Corson family. Philadelphia, 1896.

CORSON -- Corson, Hiram, M.D.
The Corson family; a history of the descendants of Benjamin Corson, son of Cornelius Corssen of Staten Island, New York. H. L. Everett. Philadelphia, 1906.

CORSON -- (Author unknown)
First reunion of the Corson family association, Valley Park, Pa., June 3, 1916. No city, 1916.

CORYELL -- Coryell, Ingham
Emanuel Coryell of Lambertsville, New Jersey, and his descendants; being a brief history of the origin of Emanuel Coryell and the Coryell family, with an outline of his descendants to the fourth generation. Philadelphia, 1943.

COTTER -- Dromey, John H.
Cotter kin: a brief history of James Cotter (1799-1877) from County Kerry, Ireland, through Pennsylvania and Ohio to the state of Iowa, his wife Mary (Conley) Cotter (1810-1850), and some of their descendants. J. H. Dromey. Baring, Mo., 1984.

COVERT -- Jones, Edson Salisbury
Covert ancestry. T. A. Wright. New York, N.Y., 1906.

COWAN -- Royes, Elizabeth Huron
Cowan family and other descendants of William McKinney of Pennsylvania, Revolutionary War soldier, also the family of Hugh Brown of Mercer County, Pennsylvania. Imbler, Oregon, 1978.

COWDEN -- Welch, James Marcus
Ancestry and kin of the Cowden and Welch families. Indiana, Pa., 1904.

COX -- (Author unknown)
Cox and Nelson families of Pennsylvania and New Jersey. Co city. No date.   (A)

COX -- Cox, H. P.
History of Joshua and Elizabeth (Spanogle) Cox family, pioneer residents of Warriors Mark Valley and their descendants in Pennsylvania and elsewhere, 1789-1954. Spring Mount, Pa., 1954.   (A)

COXE -- Du Bin, Alexander
Coxe family; based on the sketch by Frank Willing Leach, July 26, 1908. The Historical Pub. Society. Philadelphia, 1936.   (N)

CRAIG -- Craig, Jane Maria
Samuel Craig, senior, pioneer to western Pennsylvania,
and his descendants. Greensburg, Pa., 1915.

CRAIG -- Craig, Washington
Graphic sketch of the life of William Craig, Sr.   (A)
(1761-1854). Greenville, Pa., 1854.

CRAIG -- Clemens, William Montgomery
The Craig family of Pennsylvania, 1708 to 1895. W. M.
Clemens. Pompton Lakes, N.J., 1921.

CRAIG --Sutton, Esther Craig and Lois Craig
The Craig-Meyer Families of Pennsylvania, Michigan,
and Iowa, 1742-1977. JiFi Print. Fort Dodge, Iowa, 1977.

CRAIG -- Wainwright, Nicholas B.
Andalusia, Countryseat of the Craig family and of
Nicholas Biddle and his descendants. Historical Society
of Pennsylvania. Philadelphia, 1976.

CRAIGHEAD -- Craighead, Rev. James Geddes, D.D.
The Craighead family: a genealogical memoir of the
descendants of Rev. Thomas and Margaret Craighead, 1658-
1876. Sherman & Co. Philadelphia, 1876.

CRAMER -- Cramer, Alma H.
Miscellaneous notes on Cramer families of Lancaster
County, Pennsylvania. No city, 1960.

CRANMER -- Trousdale, J. B.
The Cranmer, Maynard, and Taylor genealogies: the
descendants of Noadiah Cranmer of Monroeton, Bradford
County, Pa., and the descendants of Nathan Maynard and
Benjamin Taylor of Rome, Bradford County, Pa. Ithaca,
N.Y., 1965.

CRARY -- Frost, Josephine C. (Mrs. Samuel Knapp Frost)
Ancestors of Jerry Crary and his wife Laura Antoinette
Dunham, of Warren, Pennsylvania. F. H. Hitchcock.
Brooklyn, N.Y., 1924.

CRATER -- Crater, Lewis
History of Greter, Grater or Crater family. Reading,
Pa., 1894.

CRAWFORD -- Chenoweth, Alexander C.
Col. William Crawford of Greene Co., Pennsylvania.
Genealogical chart of his descendants. New York, N.Y.,
1917.

CRAWFORD -- Stark, Helen D.
The Crawford Sample family tree. No City. No date. (N)

CREE -- Inman, Mrs. Gerald O.
The Cree family of Pennsylvania and Iowa and related lines,
Morse, McCormick. No city, 1975.

CREE -- Inman, Gwendolyn L. (P.)
Cree family of Pennsylvania and Iowa and related lines. (A)
Cedar Rapids, Iowa. No date.

CROLL -- (Author unknown)
First reunion of the John Croll family, July 4, 1900.
Trexlertown, Pa., 1900.

CROMLEY -- Hewlett, Hoseph M.
The Cromley family (Gramlich) of Philadelphia. (P)
The descendants of Heinrich and Elizabeth Gramlich.
Wyncote, Pa., 1959.

CRONBAUGH -- Cronbaugh, Lois E. Wilson
Cronbaugh of York County, Pennsylvania, 1807-1977 and
many cousins, Jacob Cronbagh...John Cronbaugh...
Nicholas Cronbaugh. Cedar Rapids, Iowa, 1977.

CROSSEN -- Taylor, Mrs. Donald W.
Crossen; descendants of Henry Crossen (Crossan) of
Pennsylvania, 1750-1971. Alexandria, Va., 1975.

CROSSMAN -- History Comm.
Partial history of the Crossman-Kressman-Cressman- (A)
Crissman-Crisman family. Mechanicsburg, Pa., 1972.

CROUSE -- Crouse, John H.
History of the Crouse family of Pennsylvania and (A)
Ohio. A. C. Printers. Chicago, Ill., 1932.

CROW -- Crow, James Homer
The history of the Jacob Crow family in Greene County,
Pennsylvania and in Marshall County, West Virginia.
Cameron, W. Va., 1977.

CROWNOVER -- Crownover, Helen
Crownover families in USA. A. G. Halldin Pub. Co.
Indiana, Pa., 1984.

CROZER -- (Author unknown)
A record of the Crozer family, of Bucks County, (P)
Pennsylvania. Murphy and Bechtel. Trenton, N.J., 1866.

CRYER --Galbraith, William Howard
Brief genealogy, family of William Cryer of Bucks
County, Pennsylvania. Washington, ?, 1955.

CULVER -- Colver, William H., Jr.
Various information and history of Edward Colver-Culver,
1600-1686, descendants from London, England to Mystic,
Conn., to all parts of the United States, etc.: encluded
[sic] a cemetery map of the church of Christ Lutherans
at Shoenersville, Pa., showing the locations of five (5)
generations of Colver-Culvers there interned [sic].
W. H. Colver, Jr. Highspire, Pa., 1978.

CUMMINGS -- Neale, Anne Rebstock Cummings
A peak (i.e. peek) at the past, my family history: a
family history of our Pennsylvania and New York first
immigrant American ancestors with some surnames, traced
in England and Switzerland to 1000 A.D. Anundsen Pub. Co.
Decorah, Iowa, 1982.

CUNNINGHAM -- Cunningham, John, Francis, Robert & Fern Bain
History of the Cunningham family, descendants of John
Cunningham and his wife, Elizabeth, who emigrated to
Americam from the Scotch settlement in the North of
Ireland about the year 1748. Cunningham & Co.
Williamsport, Pa., 1930.

CUNNINGHAM -- Historical Publication Society
Conyngham family. Philadelphia, 1940.

CUNNINGHAM -- Cunningham, James L.
Our family history, subsequent to 1870. Herald Press.
Pittsburgh, Pa., 1943.

CURWEN -- Davis, Patricia Talbot
A family tapestry; five generations of the Curwens of
Walnut Hill and their various relatives. Livingston Pub.
Co. Wynnewood, Pa., 1972.

CUSHMAN -- Burt, Alvah Walford
Cushman genealogy and general history, including the
dscendants of the Fayette County, Pennsylvania, and
Monongalia County, Virginia, families. A. W. Burt.
Cincinnati, Ohio, 1942.

- D -

DALLAM -- Dallam, David E.
   The Dallam family, an effort to assemble and preserve the
   history of an Anglo-American family from 1690 to 1929, and
   a brief story of the English family from 1066 to 1690.
   G. H. Buchanan Co. Philadelphia, 1929.

DALLAS -- (Author unknown)
   Dallas, of Cantray and Saint Martin's, Scotland. Dallas-
   Yorke, Walmsgate, county Lincoln, England, representing
   Dallas, of that ilk, and Cantray and Saint Martin's.
   Dallas, of Philadelphia, state of Pennsylvania, United
   States of North America, representing the American family,
   founded by Alexander James, son of Robert. No city, 1877.

DALLETT -- Dallett, Francis James
   The genealogy of the Dallett family. Innes. Philadelphia,
   1946.

DAM -- Sheppard, Walter L.
   Ancestry of Loring Dam, 1896. Havertown, Pa., 1961.   (P)

DAMON -- Wharton, Anne Hollingsworth
   Genealogy of the Philadelphia branch of the Damon family
   of Massachusetts. Philadelphia, 1896.

DARBY -- Alderks, Marjorie Carmichael
   The descendants of John and Fanny (Edwards) Derby.
   Alderks. Tunkhannock, Pa., 1977.

DARBY -- Darby, Milton M. and Clarence A. Miller, LL.M.
   ... The lineage of the Darby family and allied families of
   Fayette County, Pennsylvania. No city, 1930?

DARLINGTON -- (Author unknown)
   Sesqui-centennial gathering of the clan Darlington: at the
   residence of Brinton Darlington, in East Bradford, Chester
   county, Pennsylvania, on the 20th of August, 1853...
   E. C. Darlington. Lancaster, Pa., 1853.

DARLINGTON -- Cope, Gilbert
   Genealogy of the Darlington family. A record of the
   descendants of Abraham Darlington of Birmingham, Chester
   Co., Pennsylvania, and some other families of the name.
   Press of the Manufacturers' and Publishers Print Co.
   West Chester, Pa., 1900.

DARLINGTON -- Herbert, Anne Hemphill
   Personal memories of the Darlington family at Guyasuta.
   University of Pittsburgh Press. Pittsburgh, Pa., 1949.

DART -- Bolton, Thaddeus Lincoln
Genealogy of the Dart family in America. Philadelphia, 1927.

DAVENPORT -- Grant, Eleanor Brewster
The ancestry and descendants of John and Jane Ann (Lounsbery) of Ulster County, New York and Meadville, Pennsylvania. River Forest, Ill., 1960.

DAVIS --Davis, Eleanor M.
Davis: a Quaker family: Charles Davies, the immigrant to Pennsylvania about 1725, from there to North Carolina, his wife, Hannah Matson, and their descendants. Gateway Press. Baltimore, Md., 1985.

DAVIS -- Davis, Harry Alexander
The Davis family (Davies and David) in Wales and America; genealogy of Morgan David of Pennsylvania. H. A. Davis. Washington, D.C., 1927.

DAVIS -- Davis, Helen E.
Kindred: Davis Stansbury lines. Dorrance. Philadelphia, 1977.

DAVIS -- Davis, T. Carroll
A brief genealogical history of the Davis family and allied lines. Downington, Pa., 1934.

DAVIS -- Seaver, J. Montgomery
Davis family history. Philadelphia, Pa., 1929.

DAWSON -- Ditchfield, P. H.
The history of the Dawson family of Farlington and North Ferriby, York, of Ackworth Park and Osgodby hall, in the County of York, of Greystock, Cumberland, of Arborfield house, Berkshire, and of Philadelphia, United States of America. G. Allen & Company. London, 191-?

DAY -- Day, James Edward
Descendants of Christopher Day of Bucks County, Pa. Los Angeles?, Calif., 1959.

DAY -- Day, James Edward
Descendants of Christopher Day of Bucks County, Pa. --And with a supplement to Volume I, the ancient families of Dee and Day of Wales, England, and Ireland. L. F. Day. Pontiac, Mich., 1976.

DEAN -- (Author unknown)
Deans of Dorchester. Second series. v. 1; 1950.   (N)
Jersey Shore, Pa., 1968.

DEAN -- Dean, Cynthia A.
"My Dean family of Fayette County, Pennsylvania" currently
back to 1837: ancestors of Christina Renee Dean-Schnaible.
C. A. Dean. Santa Clara, Calif., 1982.

DEAN -- Dean, Arthur D.
Genealogy of the Dean family. Scranton, Pa., 1903.

DEARDORFF -- Deardorff, Richard F.
Our Dierdorff ancestors in early America: a personal search.
R. F. Deardorff. Pennsylvania? 1984.

DeBOLT -- Blank, Joseph P.

19 steps up the mountain: the story of the DeBolt family.
Lippincott. Philadelphia, 1976.

de CARPENTER -- Sellers, Edwin Jaquett
De Carpenter allied ancestry. Philadelphia, 1928.

DECK -- Brossman, Schuyler C.
Notes on Frederick Deck (also known as Johan Frederick
Deck), b. 2 Feb. 1741--d. 9 June 1820, and his wife
Maria Veronica Seirer, August 1743--28 March 1828, of
Tulpehochen Twonship, Berks County, Pennsylvania, and
some of their descendants. Rehrersburg, Pa., 1973.

DECKARD -- Deckard, Percy Edward
Genealogy of the Deckard family. Richfield, Pa., 1932.

DEERY -- Weldy, George W.
The early Deerys of Chester County in Pennsylvania.
G. W. Weldy. Springfield, Pa., 1983.

de HAAS -- Smith, Dorothy M.
Brigadier General John Philip de Haas and some of his
descendants. Mechanicsburg, Pa., 1975.

DE HAVEN -- Ross, Howard De Haven
History of the De Haven family. Press of Smith & Salmon.
Philadelphia, 1894.

DE HAVEN -- Ross, Howard De Haven
History of the De Haven family ... 4th ed. deluxe; rev.
and re-illustrated. The Pandick Press. New York,
N.Y., 1929.

DE HAVEN -- Wright, Helen Marth, M. A.
The de Haven family (alias Im Hoffe or ten Heuven) of early
Philadelphia county, Pennsylvania, through Ann (De haven)
Wright. Jersey City, N.J., 1935.

DE HAVEN -- Cody, Edward Perrine
Genealogy of the De Haven family of Philadelphia, Penna.
Wethersfield? Conn., 1950.

DEHOFF -- McCurley, James B.
Dehoff (Dahuff, Dehoof(f), or Dehuff, later Da(y)hoff,
Dayhuff, Deahofe, or De Hoff) of Penndylvania (1757):
preliminary outline of the family (only partly verified).
J. B. McCurley. Louisville, Ky., 1980.

DELONG -- Delong, Irwin H.
Early occurrences of the family name Delong in Europe   (P)
and in America. Delong. Philadelphia, 1924.

DE LONG -- De Long, Dr. Irwin Hoch
The lineage of Malcolm Metzger Parker from Johannes De Lang.
Lancaster, Pa., 1926.

DE LONG -- De Long, Dr, Irwin Hoch
Pioneer Palatine pilgrims. Art Printing Co. Lancaster,
Pa., 1928.

DE LONG -- De Long, Dr. Irwin Hoch
My ancestors. Art Printing Co. Lancaster, Pa., 1930.

DELP -- Delp, Priscilla L.
A genealogical history of the Delp and Delp Cassel families;
descendants of John George and Barbara Moyer Delp and Hupert
and Sydge Op Den Graeff Cassel, with complete records of
descendants of Abraham Freed & Ann Cassel Delp. Souderton,
Pa., 1962?

DELP -- Delp, Leonard A.
Delps galore, a gathering of genealogical information   (P)
concerning several Delp families lines. Monticello,
Fla., 1971.

DE PEYSTER -- Law, James D.
Here and there in two hemispheres... 1st series. Home Pub.
Co. Lancaster, Pa., 1903.

DEPPEN -- Deppen, E. E. and M. L.
Counting kindred of Christian Deppen and history of
Christian Ruchty and other collateral families, also the
complete genealogical register of Christian and Veronica
(Ruchty) Deppen's family, including the Carpenter, Yeakley
and Kechendorn lines, surnames of Barbara, Anna and
Veronica, daughters of Christian Deppen, with biographies
of all their descendants from the earliest records
available. Church Center Press. Sinking Spring, Pa., 1940.

DEPPEN -- John W. Deppen Family History Committee
Genealogy of John W. Deppen, with a brief history of   (A)
his ancestors. Mechnicsburg, Pa., 1974.

DERR -- Derr, Charles A.
Derr-Dorr family of Pennsylvania, descendants of   (P)
Johann Heirich Dorr, who came to Pensylvania in 1742.
No city, 1937.

DETURK -- DeTurk, Eugene P.
History and genealogy of the DeTurk, DeTurch family;
descendants of Isaac De Turk and Maria De Harcourt.
DeTurk Family Assoc. Kutztown, Pa., 1934.

DETWEILER -- Hostetler, Lizzieann J.
Descendants of Gideon Detweiler and Lydia Kanagy
(Detweiler).   L. J. Hostetler. Volant, Pa., 1940.

DEWEES -- La Munyan, Mrs. Philip E.
The Dewees family; genealogical data, biographical facts
and historical information. W. H. Roberts. Norristown,
Pa., 1905.

DEWEY -- (Author unknown)
Our birthright of kinship with distinguished descendants
of the immigrant Thomas Dewey who settled at Windsor,
Connecticut, in 1633, and many notable non-Dewey ancestors.
Containing an abstract of ancestry for the founder of this
legacy. The whole vitalized by instantaneous keys to all
relationships ... W. E. Dewey. Philadelphia, 1913.

DEWOODY -- Russell, Virginia Gordon
The Dewoody family of Venango County, Pennsylvania.
Speciality Printers. Cochranton, Pa., 1981.

DIEFENBACH -- Diffenbaugh, Milton Hess
Dieffenbach-Diffenbaugh ... Lancaster, Pa., 1930.

DIEHL -- (Author unknown)
An account of the family reunion of the descendants   (P)
of Samuel Diehl of Friend's Cover, Pa., 1890, with a
genealogical table. Bedford, Pa., 1891.

DIFFENDERFFER -- Diffenderffer, Frank Ried
Some of the descendants of John Michael Dubendorf,
1695-1778. More especially those directly descended
through his grandson David Diffenderffer, 1752-1846.
New Era Printing Co. Lancaster, Pa., 1910.

DIFFENDERFFER -- Owen, William Henry, III
Some of the descendants of John Michael Dubendorf, 1695-1778; more especially those directly descended through his grandson David Diffenderffer 1752-1846, by his great-great-grandson Frank Ried Diffenderffer, 1833-1921; as revised and continued through David Rittenhouse Diffenderffer, 1822-1900, by his grandson William Henry Owen, III ... with addendum Dunham and Owen families, Lebanon, Mo. Printing by Prouty. Lebanon, Mo., 1940.

DILL -- Dill, Rosalie Jones
Mathew Dill genealogy; a study of the Dill family of Dillsburg, York County, Pennsylvania, 1698-19. Spokane, Wash., 1934.

DILLER --Ringwalt, J. F.
The Diller family (published in November, 1877) . New Holland, Pa., 1942.

DILLMAN -- Baer, Mabel Van Dyke
Dillman family research, Pennsylvania, Ohio & Indiana, including Revolutionary War pension of Andrew Dillman with Dillman deeds of Clermont County, Ohio, 1800's. No city, 1964-65.

DILWORTH -- Cook, Lewis D.
The Joseph Dilworth family of Bucks County, Pennsylvania. No city. No date.   (P)

DISE -- Dise, Ronald W.
Henry M. Dise of Springfield Township, York Co., Penna. and his descendants. Glen Rock, Pa., 1975.   (A)

DOANE -- MacReynolds, George
The new Doane book. Doylestown, Pa., 1952.

DOBBIN -- Barekman, June B.
Some Dobbin(s)-Skiles lines from Pennsylvania to North Carolina. Also with additional lines: Coker-Cowan-Dailey-Graham-Hess-Palmer-Barekman. Chicago, Ill., 1966.

DOBBIN -- Foster, William J.
John Dobbin of Connagher, descendants. The Science Press. Schenectady, N. Y., 1936.

DODSON -- Ege, Thompson P.
Dodson genealogy, 1600-1907. Philadelphia, 1908.

DONALDSON -- Donaldson, Alexander
A history of the Donaldson family and its connections. J. M. McMillin. Sun City, Ariz., 1972.   (P)

DONALDSON -- Donaldson, Wayne
    The Donaldson line: from Donaldson, Nicodemus, Lefever,
    Simpson, Ashbaugh, Jones, 1730-1981: Maryland, Pennsylvania,
    Ohio, Wisconsin. W. Donaldson. Ann Arbor, Mich., 198-?

DONALDSON -- McKitrick, May Donaldson
    A genealogical record of one of the Donaldson family in
    America, descendants of Moses Donaldson, who lived in
    Huntingdon County, Penn., in 1770. F. J. Heer. Columbus,
    Ohio., 1916.

DORRANCE -- Welch, Emma Finney
    Dorrance inscriptions. Germantown, Pa., 1909.

DOTEY -- Doty, Ethan Allen
    Edward Doty, a Mayflower passenger and Plymouth settler,
    also Doten family. Philadelphia, 1954.

DOTTERER -- Duttera, William B.
    Descendants of George Philip Duddra or Dodderer ...   (A)
    of Pa. and Md. Dushore, Pa., 1929.

DOTTERER -- Dotterer, Henry S.
    The Dotterer family. Philadelphia, 1903.

DOWNING -- Snow, Helen F.
    The Downings, Pennsylvania Quakers. Madison, Conn.,   (P)
    no date.

DOWNS -- Downs, Arthur Channing
    The Downs family of Long Island. Primros, Pa., 1959.

DRAKE -- Avery, Lillian Drake
    Drake genealogy in the line of Samuel Drake of Lower
    Smithfield Township, Northampton (now Monroe) County,
    Pennsylvania. Ann Arbor, Mich., 1926.

DRAYTON -- Taylor, Emily Heyward
    The Draytons of South Carolina and Philadelphia.   (P)
    Wickersham. Lancaster, Pa., 1921.

DREIBELBIS -- (Author unknown)
    Dreibelbis bicentenary anniversary, 1732-1932 ...   (N)
    Kutztown, 1932.

DREIBELBIS -- Dreibelbis, Charles B.
    Excerpts from the Dreibelbis genealogies and   (A)
    biographies of the John Jacob Dreibelbis cousins in
    America, 1966. Dreibelbis Historical Committee.
    Philadelphia, 1966.

DREISBACH -- Helman, Laura M.
<u>History and genealogy of the Dreisbach family</u>. Berkemeyer, Keck & Co. Allentown, Pa., 1924.

DREISBACH -- Smith, Charles A.
<u>Dreisbach families of Pennsylvania and Ohio. Martin Dreisbach - descendants Pennsylvania to Fairfield-Pickaway Counties, Ohio, 1717-1925</u>. Findlay, Ohio, 1933.

DREXEL -- M. Dolores, Sister?
<u>The Francis A. Drexel family</u>. Cornwell Heights, Pa., 1939.

DRINKER -- Biddle, Henry D.
<u>The Drinker family in America, to and including the eighth generation</u>. J. B. Lippincott. Philadelphia, 1893.

DRINKER -- Drinker, Henry S.
<u>History of the Drinker family</u>. Merion? Pa., 1961.

DRUM -- Helman, Laura M.
<u>History and genealogy of the Drum family</u>. Allentown, Pa., 1927.

DUBOIS -- (Author unknown)
<u>Bi-centenary reunion of the descendants of Louis and Jacques De Bois (emigrants to America, 1660 and 1675), at New Paltz, New York, 1875 ...</u> Rue & Jones. Philadelphia, 1876.

DUCACHET --
<u>Last will and testament of Ann D. Ducachet</u>. Philadelphia, 1871.

DU COMB -- Kahlert, Fern D.
<u>Vincent DuComb of Philadelphia</u>. No city. No date.

DUDDRA -- Duttera, Wm. B.
<u>Descendants of George Philip Duddra or Dodderer,</u>   (P)
<u>spelling their names Duttera, Dutterer or Dodrer, Dudderar, Dotterer, Dutrow, etc. natives of Pennsylvania and Maryland</u>. Dushore, Pa., 1929.

DUFF -- Duff, William Boyd
<u>The forefathers and families of certain settlers in</u>   (A)
<u>Western Pennsylvania</u>. Duff. Pittsburgh, Pa., 1976.

DUKE -- Morris, Jane
<u>The Duke-Symes family</u>. Philadelphia, 1940.

DUKE -- Smyth, Samuel Gordon
A genealogy of the Duke-Shepherd-Van Metre family.
Lancaster, Pa., 1909.

DUNDAS -- Dundas, Francis de Sales
Dundas. Hesselius. The Historical Pub. Society.
Philadelphia, 1938.

DUNDAS -- White, William
In re Dundas family; pedigree of Jane Dundas White, born
May 27, 1919, as far as the same has to do with the
Dundas family and its earlier female lines. Philadelphia,
1922.

DUNDORE -- Dundore, Nathan
A genealogical record of the Dundore family in America.
Philadelphia, 1881.

DUNGAN -- Folker, Howard O.
Dungan ancestry; chronicles of family. First   (P)
settler preceded Penn in America. Doylestown, Pa.,
1906-(07?)

DUNGAN -- Folker, Howard O.
The Dungan family of Eastern Pennsylvania; Levi   (P)
Dungan, the Westmoreland pioneer. Daily Intelligencer.
Doylestown, Pa., 1910.

DU PUY -- Du Puis, Nicholas
The two hundredth anniversary of the settlement of Shawnee,
Pennsylvania ... under the auspices of the Monroe County
Historical Society, Wednesday, July 15, 1925. 1725-1925.
Stroudsburg?, Pa., 1925.

DUPUY -- Dupuy, Charles Meredith
A genealogical history of the Dupuy family. Philadelphia,
Pa., 1910.

DUTTON -- Cope, Gilbert
Genealogy of the Dutton family of Pennsylvania, preceded
by a history of the family in England from the time of
William the Conqueror to the year 1669; with an appendix
containing a short account of the Duttons of Conn.
F. S. Hickman. West Chester, Pa., 1871.

DYMOND -- Dymond, Robert Herschel
Genealogy of the Dymond, Williams, and related families.
Gateway Press. Baltimore, Md., 1981.

- E -

EAGLE -- Town, Charles M.
Descendants of Henry Eagle who settled in Connewago,   (P)
Pa., 1682. Philadelphia, 1953.

EAKER -- Baker, Lorena S.
The shoe cobbler's kin: genealogy of the Peter (Ecker)
Eaker, Sr. family, 1701-1976. Gateway Press. Baltimore,
Md., 1976.

EARHART -- Ansen, Cornelia E.
Some lateral branches of the Peter Earhart family of   (A)
Penn., Ohio and Indiana. Muncie, Ind., 1975.

EARNEST -- Replogle, Mrs. Emma A. M.
Indian Eve and her descendants. An Indian story of Bedford
County, Pennsylvania. J. L. Rupert. Huntingdon, Pa., 1911.

EASTBURN -- (Author unknown)
The Eastburn family. Ancestors first settled in Bucks
County in the year 1684 (paper) read by Eastburn Reeder,
at Doylestown... 1902. No city, 1902.

EASTBURN -- Walton, Hettie A.
The Eastburn family, being a genealogical and historical
record of the descendants of John Eastburn, who came to
America in 1684 from the parish of Bingley, Yorkshire,
England, and of Robert Eastburn, who married Sarah Preston
in 1693, in Yorkshire, England, and who came to American
in 1713... The Intelligence Co. Doylestown, Pa., 1903.

EASTWOOD -- Eastwood, Eric K.
The Eastwood family; ... descendants of Abel Eastwood,   (N)
who settled in Washington County, N.Y., around 1780.
Pittsburgh, Pa., 1950.

EBERLY -- Martin, Levi E.
Biographic memorial of John Eberly and genealogical family
register of the Eberly family. United Evangelical Pub.
House. Harrisburg, Pa., 1896.

EBERLY -- Eberly Family Assoc.
A history of the Heinrich Eberly family and their   (P)
descendants. Allentown, Pa., 1927.

EBERLY -- Eberly, David G.
History and genealogy of the Alsacian branch of the   (A)
Eberly family in Europe and America; together with a
Survey of the Cloister at Ephrata, Lancaster, Pa.,
1935-40. No city. No date.

EBERLY -- Bennetch, Paul C.
Eberly family history, 1700-1974. Saul Print. (A)
Denver, Pa., 1974.

EBY -- (Author unknown)
The Eby report. Philadelphia, or Glenolden, Pa., (P)
1975.

ECKEL -- Rubincam, Milton
The Eckel family of Maryland, Pennsylvania, Tennessee,
North Carolina, and Delaware. Hyattsville, Md., 1955.

ECKERT -- Rinkenbach, William H.
Eckert families of Northampton County, Pennsylvania.
No city, 1962.

ECKMAN -- Barr, Ruth Eckman (Mrs. James L.)
Descendants of Hans Jacob Eckman of Pennsylvania and
Maryland, and miscellaneous Echmans. Austin, Tex., 1969.

EDDY --Horton, Byron Barnes, A. M.
The ancestors and descendants of Zachariah Eddy of Warren,
Pa. The Tuttle Company. Rutland, Vt., 1930.

EDEBURN -- Caylor, Thelma Lee
The Edeburn family of Pennsylvania. No city, 1955.

EDMUNDS -- Edmunds, Franklin D.
Bible records. Philadelphia, 1933.

EELLS -- Pennsylvania DAR
Eells genealogy. No city, 1973.

EGE -- Ege, Rev. Thompson P.
History and genealogy of the Ege family in the United
States, 1738-1911. Star Printing. Harrisburg, Pa., 1911.

EICHHOLTZ -- Rodriguez, Janic Eichholtz
Johan Jacob Eichholtz, 1712-1760, a pioneer settler of
Lancaster County, Pennsylvania, and his descendants.
Baltimore, Md., 1978.

EISENHARD -- Eisenhard, Irvin George
Ancestry of the Charles Henrich Eisenhard family.
Boyerstown, Pa., 1961.

EISENHART -- Eisenhart, Willis Wolf
Ancestry of the John Franklin Eisenhart family.
Abbottstown, Pa., 1951.

ELDERKIN -- Elderkin, Dyer White
Genealogy of the Elderkin family with intermarriages.
Pittsburgh, Pa., 1888.

ELFRETH -- (Author unknown)
The Elfreth necrology. Philadelphia, 1902.   (P)

ELFRETH -- Hodge, Susan Winslow
The Elfreth book of letters. University of Pennsylvania
Press. Philadelphia, 1985.

ELLARD -- Burnham, Walter J.
The American descendants of Richard (Thomas) Ellard with
other Ellard lines. Pittsburgh, Pa., 1968.

ELMORE -- Glass, Willie Elmore
Miss Willie: happenings of a happy family, 1816-1926.
Huntingdon Press. Essington, Pa., 1976.

ELY -- Bell, Raymond Martin
The Ely-Ealy families of Washington County, Pennsylvania
and their German neighbors, Dennis, Horn, Stricker, Wolf.
R. M. Bell. Washington, Pa., 1984.

EMBREE -- Price, E. K.
Biographical sketches of James Embree, Philip Price   (A)
(By E.K. Price); and Eli K. Price .... D. H. Everts.
Philadelphia, 1881.

EMERICK -- Emrich, Oran S.
Descendants of Johannes Emerick of Philadelphia,
Pennsylvania, 171-1781. Kansas City, Mo., 1986.

EMLEN -- Leach, Frank W.
Emlen family; ...for the Philadelphia North American,   (P)
1907-13 and brought down to date, 1931. The Historical
Pub. Society. Philadelphia, 1932.

EMRICH -- Emrich, Oran S.
Descendants of John Emrich, Pennsylvania and Ohio,
1769-1864. Emrich. Oxon Hill?, Md., 1980.

EMRICH -- Emrich, Oran S.
Descendants of John George Emmerich, 1730-1800, of Chester
County, Pennsylvania. Emrich. Washington, D.C., 1979?

EMRICH -- Emrich, Oran S.
Descendants of John Nicholas Emmerich, 1702-1769, of Berks
County, Pennsylvania. Emrich. Washington, D.C., 1979.

EMRICH -- Emrich, Oran S.
   Descendants of Andreas Emmerich of Lancaster County,
   Pennsylvania. O. S. Emrich. Oxon Hill, Md., 1982.

ENDICOTT -- Endicott, Charles Moses
   The Endicott family. Frankford, Pa., 1911.

ENGLAND -- England, Charles Walter
   Joseph England and his descendants: an historical genealogy
   of the England family as descending from Joseph England,
   1680-1748; a Quaker family of Cecil County, Maryland
   (prior to 1767, Chester County, Pa.) since 1723. Silver
   Spring, Md., 1975-78.

ENGLE -- Engle, Morris M.
   The Engle history and family records of Dauphin and
   Lancaster counties. The numerous lineal descendants of
   Ulrich Engel. Short sketches of Engle families not
   related. A sketch of the arrival and record of the origin
   of the brethren in Christ Church of which a large number
   of these descendants are members. The Bulletin Press.
   Mt. Joy, Pa., 1927.

ENGLISH -- English, James M.
   Early settlers in the Pine Creek Valley in   (N)
   Pennsylvania. Jersey Shore, Pa? No date.

ENGLISH -- Russell, Helen M.
   English and allied families. Jersey Shore, Pa., 1968-1979.

ENLOW -- Enlow, Eugene E.
   Enlow - Enloe - Inlow and ... Enslow family of the   (A)
   United States. E. E. Enlow. Sebastopol, Calif., 1948.

ENNIS -- Ennis, Harold E.
   History of the family of Thomas Ennis who settled in   (P)
   Philadelphia in 1793. Philadelphia, 1922.

ENNIS -- Hoagland, Edward C.
   Cornelius Ennis of Standing Stone, Pa., 1816, patriot of
   the American Revolution, and some of his descendants, with
   a few notes on others of the name. Sacred Art Press.
   Wysox, Pa., 1956.

ENOS -- Enos, Joseph G.
   A history of the Enos family of Delaware, 1463-1958.   (P)
   Philadelphia, 1958.

ENSMINGER -- Bell, Raymond Martin
The Ensminger family: Diemeringen, Alsace; Cocalico,
Pennsylvania; Williamsport, Maryland; Cowpasture, Virginia.
Washington, Pa., 1958.

ENSMINGER -- (Author unknown)
The Ensminger family: Pennsylvania, Maryland, Virginia
(and) South Carolina. Rev. Washington, Pa., 1965.

ENSMINGER -- Bell, Raymond Martin
The Ensminger family of Pennsylvania. Washington, Pa.,
1971.

ENSMINGER --Bell, Raymond Martin
The Ensminger family of Pennsylvania. Rev. Bell.
Washington, Pa., 1976.

ENSMINGER -- Bell, Raymond Martin
Supplement to The Ensmingers of Alsace and Pennsylvania: the
first seven generations in America. R. M. Bell.
Washington, Pa., 1980.

ENSMINGER -- Bell, Raymond Martin
The Ensmingers of Alsace and Pennsylvania. Rev. R. M.
Bell. Washington, Pa., 1981.

EPPLEY -- Fryburg, Mrs. L. Gertrude and family members
History and genealogy of the descendants of Jacob (Eppli,
Aeply, Ebli) Eppley, the pioneer Eppley of America and some
short accounts of other Eppley families. Hartzell Brothers.
Carlisle, Pa., 1936.

ERSKINE -- Scott, Ebenezer Erskine
The Erskine Halcro genealogy: a genealogical study of the
ancestors, kindred, and descendants of the Rev. Henry
Erskine, of Chirnside, Berwickshire, 1624-1696, and his
wife, Margaret Halcro of Orkney, 1647-1725, and their
children, the Rev. Ebenezer Erskine of Stirling, 1680-1754,
and the Rev. Ralph Erskine of Dumfermline, 1685-1752, and
their descendants. Contained in five tables, with explana-
tory notes to each. G. Bell & Son. London, 1890.

ERTEL --Calasibetta, Charlotte Mankey
Seventy-fifth reunion of the descendants of Feldbeck Daniel
Ertel, Williamsport, Pennsylvania, Sunday, August 12, 1962.
Newark?, N.J., 196-.

ERVIN -- Hoagland, Edward C.
Notes on the Ervin, Erwin, Irvine, Irving and Irwin   (P)
families, including a register of the Irvine family of
Liberty Corners, Pa. Sacred Art Press. Wysox, Pa., 1955.

ESLING -- (Author unknown)
Descendants of John Esling. Philadelphia, 1882. (P)

ESPENSCHIED -- Espenschied, Lloyd
Arrival in Pennsylvania in 1787 of three immigrant brothers,
Valentine, Peter, Daniel, Espenschied-Espenshade-Esbenshade.
Kew Gardens, N.Y., 1953.

ETNIER -- Etnier, Oliver L.
Genealogy of the families Etnier, Etnire, Intneyer, Itnyer,
Itnyr. No city, 1977.

EVANS --(Author unknown)
Evans, Whitting, Davis. Philadelphia, 1922.

EVANS -- Beam, Rose Evans
The John H. Evans (Vandling, Pa.) family, a genealogy.
No city, 1964.

EVANS -- Evans, Samuel
The Evans family. Harrisburg Pub. Co. Harrisburg, (P)
Pa., 1895.

EVANS -- Mitchell, H. C.
Genealogy of the William Evans (fl. 1831) family of (A)
Neath, Pa. No city. No date.

EVANS -- Nivin, Hon. Septimus E.
Genealogy of Evans, Nivin and allied families.
International Print. Co. Philadelphia, 1930.

EVANS -- Sica, Margaret Eleanor Evans
Evans genealogy: descendants of William and Parthenia (Hill)
Evans. M. E. Sica. New Castle, Pa., 1983.

EWING -- Ewing, Lucy E. Lee
Dr. John Ewing and some of his noted connections. John C.
Winston. Philadelphia, 1930.

EYERMAN -- Eyerman, John
The ancestors of Marguerite Eyerman, a study in genealogy.
Free Press Book and Job Print. Easton, Pa., 1898.

EYERMAN --Eyerman, John
Genealogical studies; the ancestry of Marguerite and John
Eyerman. Eschenbach. Easton Pa., 1902.

EYRE -- Darlington, George E.
History of the Eyre and Ashmead famlies who settled in (P)
Chester and Philadelphia, Pennsylvaia. Record Print.
Media, Pa., 1909.

EZEKIEL -- Ezekiel, Henry C.
   Genealogical record, 1892, of the Ezekiel family of
   Philadelphia, Pennsylvania; Richmond, Virginia; and
   Cincinnati, Ohio. No city. No date.

- F -

FAGALY --Williams, Mildred Corson
The Fagaly family in America (Vogelen-Fagaly-Fagely).
Allentown, Pa., 1982.

FAHNESTOCK -- Fahnestock, A. K.
Family memorial of the Fahnestocks in the United States.
Harrisburg, Pa., 1879.

FAIRCHILD -- Spear, Eunice Fairchild
Genealogy of the family of Fairchild. Wilkes-Barre,
Pa., 1966.

FARRINGTON -- Rochelle, Herschel B.
Farrington and Kirk family: Ancestors and Descendants
of Abraham Farrington (1765-1845) of New Jersey and
Ohio and wife Deborah Kirk (1781-1829) of Chester Co.,
Pennsylvania. Hillsborough, N.C., 1983.

FAULKNER -- Sachse, Julius Friedrich
Justus Falckner, mystic and scholar, devout Pietist in
German, hermit on the Wissahickon, missionary on the
Hudson; a bi-centennial memorial of the first regular
ordination of an orthodox pastor in America, done
November 24, 1703, at Gloria Dei, the Swedish Lutheran
church at Wicaco, Philadelphia; comp. from original
documents, letters and records at home and abroad.
Philadelphia, 1903.

FAULKNER --
A contribution to Pennsylvania history; missives to Rev.
August Herman Francke from Daniel Falckner, Germantown,
April 16, 1702 and Justus Falckner, New York, 1704,
supplemented with a (!) genealogical chart of Daniel
Falckner. Lancaster, Pa., 1909.

FAULKNER -- Helffenstein, Abraham Ernest
Pierre Fauconnier and his descendants; with some account
of the allied Valleuax. S. H. Burbank & Co. Philadelphia,
1911.

FAUST -- Faust, Harry E.
First Fausts in Pennsylvania. University Print Shop.
Lewisburg, Pa., 1930.

FEE -- McGroarty, Wm. B.
Fee family in Maryland, Pennsylvania, Kentucky &   (A)
Ohio, 1703-1944. Alexandria, Va., 1944.

FEEMAN -- (Author unkown)
Feeman family, Lebanon County, Pa. Schaefferstown,   (A)
Pa., 1974.

FELL -- Craig, Blanche
Pennsylvania heritage. West Newton, Pa., 1959.

FELPEL -- Long, Anna Mary Nolt
Little foxes: the Volpell/Felpel family in America.
Mennoite Family History. Elverson, Pa., 1982.

FELTY -- Berge, Edgar
Felty family notes: a collection of newspaper   (A)
clippings on the Felty family of Schuylkill and
Lebanon Counties in Pennsylvania, with ... nearby
areas. Philadelphia, 1959-76.

FENNELL -- Ralston, Ruby Fennell
My Fennell chronicles. Slippery Rock, Pa., 1981.

FENWICK -- Sellers, Edwin Jaquette
Fenwick allied ancestry; ancestry of Thomas Fenwick of
Sussex County, Delaware. Allen, Lane & Scott.
Philadelphia, 1916.

FERREE -- Landis, Charles Israel
Madame Mary Ferree and the Huguenots of Lancaster County.
No City. No date.

FEW -- Fruth, Florence Knight
Some descendants of Richard Few of Chester County,
Pennsylvania, and allied lines, 1682-1976. Fruth.
Beaver Falls, Pa., 1977.

FINK -- Moore, Vivian Lyon
Descendants of Jacob Fink of Pennsylvania and some allied
lines. No city, 1949.

FINNEY -- Finney, Thomas
222 years of the Finney family, 1732-1954; descendants   (A)
of Thomas Finney ... of Dauphin County, Pa. No city,
1954.

FISH -- Fish, Margaret R.
Thomas Fish of Pennsylvania-Ohio-Illinois; family   (A)
outline. Vincennes, Ind., 1970.

FISHEL -- Keller, Roberta Kennedy
History of the Fishel McKinstry family and other related
lines. Reading, Pa., 1975.

FISHER -- Black, Ruth Anne Heisey
<u>Descendants of Jacob and Barbara Redlingshafer Fisher,</u>
<u>Washington County, Pa., 1804-1975</u>. Black. Mountain
View, Calif., 1975?

FISHER -- Byler, Saloma J.
<u>Family records of John K. Fisher, 1854-1968</u>. Print   (A)
Shop. Gordonville, Pa., 1968.

FISHER -- Cummins, B. F.
<u>Fisher family of Chester County, Pennsylvania</u>.   (A)
Cherokee, Iowa, 1898, 1972.

FISHER -- Fisher, David M.
<u>Ancestors and descendants of Jesse Fisher of New Sewickley</u>
<u>Township, Beaver County, Pennsylvania</u>. Fisher. No city,
1974.

FISHER -- Fisher, the John M. family
<u>Descendants and history of Christian Fisher family</u>.   (A)
Amos Fisher. Ronks, Pa., 1957.

FISHER -- Fisher, Mayme E.
<u>Fisher families of Pennsylvania-Virginia-Kentucky</u>.   (A)
D.A.R. Sauk Trail Chapter. Chicago Heights, Ill., 1964.

FISHER -- Lybarger, Donald F. (from notes prepared
                    originally by his uncle William Fisher of
                    Harrisburg, Pa., in 1907, and from Pa.
                    archives, county histories, and other sources)
<u>Notes concerning the Fisher family of Fishing Creek Valley,</u>
<u>Newberry and Fairview Townships, York County, Pennsylvania</u>.
Cleveland? 1966.

FISHER -- Petersen, Florence Hepp & Elmore Petersen
<u>The Fisher-Stombaugh families and allied lineages of</u>
<u>Maryland and Pennsylvania, 1715-1949</u>. Boulder, Colo., 1950.

FISHER -- Smith, Anna Wharton
<u>Genealogy of the Fisher family, 1682 to 1896</u>. Philadelphia,
1896.

FITCH -- Lewis, Ailene Fitch
<u>Fitch, Crawford, Davis, Holderman, Francis, McFarland and</u>
<u>allied lines from Pennsylvania, Tennessee, Kentucky, North</u>
<u>Carolina, Illinois to Johnson County, Missouri; 1722-1976</u>.
Holden, Missouri, 1976.

FITLER -- Fitler, William W.
Genealogy of the Fitler and allied families. Being   (P)
the ancestry of Edwin Henry Fitler of Philadelphia
and of his wife Josephine R. Baker. Philadelphia, 1922.

FITZ RANDOLPH -- Du Bin, Alexander
Randolph family and collateral lines of Parry and Winslow.
Historical Pub. Society. Philadelphia, 1946.

FLEEK -- (Author unknown)
George Fleek and his descendants; a history of the Fleeks
and Maloneys of north-western Pennsylvania, with additional
notes on history of Little Cooley, Pa. Chatham?, N.J.,
1958.

FLEMING -- Fleming, Samuel
A record of the family and descendants of Robert Fleming,
who died at Hanover, Washington County, Pa., 1802.
Republican Job Print. Coldwater. Mich., 1868.

FLEMING -- Fleming, William A.
A Fleming family with colonial ancestors in Virginia,
Maryland, and Pennsylvania. Charleston, W. Va., 1947.

FLEMING -- Seaver, J. Montgomery
Fleming family records. Philadelphia, 1929.

FLICK -- Flick, Alexander C.
Captain Gerlach Paul Flick, 1728-1826; a Pennsylvania   (N)
pioneer. Philadelphia, 1929.

FLINT -- Bass, J. Lawrence
The Flint genealogy. Rewritten from Mr. Bass' "Flint
genealogy," in the New England historical and genealogical
register of 1860. Martin & Allardyce. Frankford, Pa.,
1912.

FLORY -- Bunderman, Walter Q.
Flory, Flora, Fleury family history, 1948. Church Center
Press. Myerstown, Pa., 1948.

FLORY -- Bunderman, Walter Q.
Flory-Flora-Fleury family history, 1948. Reading, Pa.,
1971.

FOELSCH -- Foelsch, Donald H.
A Foelsch family history. D. H. Foelsch. Williamsport,
Pa., 1981.

FOLLMER -- Wilson, Sarah E.
Follmers in Pennsylvania: descendants of Hans Jakob   (P)
Vollmar, 1698-1762. Gateway Press. Baltimore, Md., 1976.

FOOR -- Conover, George S.
The Foor family. Everett, Pa., 1962.

FOOS -- Bailey, Rosalie F.
The Foos family of Pennsylvania and Ohio, with appendix on
Griffith families of eastern Pennsylvania. The Genealogical
Society of Pennsylvania. Philadelphia, 1951.

FOOTE --Davenport, John Scott
A chronological streaming of the life of Conrad Foutz, an
immigrant to America in 1753, fom original records in
Pennsylvania, statements made by descendants appearing in
published biographies, temple records of the Latter-Day
Saints, and various historical sources. No city. No date.

FORBES -- Thomas, Amelia Forbes
Letters and journals of Waldo Emerson Forbes. Philadelphia,
Pa., 1977.

FORD -- Seaver, J. Montgomery
... Ford family records. American Historical-Genealogical
Society. Philadelphia, 1928?

FORNEY -- Bittinger, Lucy F.
The Forney family of Hanover, Pa., 1690-1893.   (A)
Pittsburgh, Pa., 1893.

FORNEY -- Folker, Howard O.
Sketches of the Forney family. Harper & Brother.
Philadelphia, 1911.

FORNEY -- Forney, John K.
Sketches and genealogy of the Forney family, from Lancaster
County, Pennsylvania, in part. Reflector Printing Co.
Abilene, Kansas, 1926.

FOSTER -- Morneweck, Evelyn Foster
Chronicles of Stephen Foster's family. Pittsburgh, Pa.,
1944.

FOSTER -- Seaver, J. Montgomery
Foster genealogical data; suggestions for a Foster family
association, and a national Foster family reunion.
American Historical-Genealogical Society. Philadelphia,
1928.

FOUCHE -- Howell, Mrs. J. G.
   Genealogy of Fouche, Penrod, Eshelman and allied   (A)
   families; American revolutionary soldiers of Pennsylvania,
   Massachusetts, Tennessee. D.A.R. Kansas City, Mo., 1948?

FOULKE -- Booth, Edwin Rhodes
   Genealogical tables, showing the descent of Edward and
   Eleanor Foulke, emigrants from Wales to Pennsylvania in
   1698, to which are added those of Jane and Hannah Jones,
   daughters of Owen and Susannah (Evans) Jones, who married,
   respectively Caleb and Amos Foulke. Also tables of the
   descendants of Edward and Eleanor Foulke, bearing the
   surname of Foulke, to the fifth generation, omitting those
   who are known to have died without issue. Loughead & Co.
   Philadelphia, 1898.

FOULKE -- Du Bin, Alexander
   Foulke family. The Historical Publication Society.   (N)
   Philadelphia, 1954.

FOX -- (Author unknown)
   Descendants of Henry Fox and Fanny Bauman, 1818-1968.
   Gordonville Print Shop. Gordonville, Pa., 1968.

FRANCIS -- Francis, Jay G.
   ... The Francis homeland and a bird's eye view of the   (P)
   family, with credits given in loco. J. G. Francis.
   Lebanon, Pa., 1936.

FRANCIS -- Francis, Jay G.
   ... Genealogical history of III. Thomas Francis of   (P)
   Coventry, Chester County, Pa. ... and How a Francis
   prevented an Indian war ... J. G. Francis. Lebanon,
   Pa., 1938.

FRANK -- Franks, Mrs. Harley A.
   The Michael Franks family history and genealogy. No
   city. No date.

FRANKLIN -- Jordan, John W.
   Franklin as a genealogist. Philadelphia?, 1899.

FRANTZ -- Frantz, E. Harold
   The genealogy of the Matthias Frantz family of Berks County,
   Pennsylvania. Boyer Printing Co. Lebanon, Pa., 1972.

FRAZER -- Frazer, Persifor
   General Persifor Frazer. A memoir principally from   (A)
   his own papers. Philadelphia, 1907.

FRAZEY -- Frazey, Hollis E.
    A list of descendants of Joseph Frazey of Burlington   (A)
County, New Jersey and Bedford County, Pa. New Rochelle,
N.Y., 1939.

FREED -- Freed, Eli A.
    History of the Freed family to the descendants of   (A)
John Freed to 1760. Sherman Print. Chester, Pa., 1920.

FREED -- Freed, Jacob A.
    Partial history of the Freed family and connecting families.
W. F. Goettler & Son. Souderton, Pa., 1923.

FREED -- Graff, Joyce Wilcox
    A Freed family history: ancestors and descendants of Walter
Curtin Freed and Dorothy Youngman Freed of Williamsport,
Pennsylvania. Gateway Press. Baltimore, Md., 1981.

FREELAND -- Focht, Harry A.
    A Freeland history, being a genealogical record of the
descendants of Mary (Pollock) Freeland of Carlisle,
Pennsylvania, 1746-1971. Hummelstown, Pa., 1971.

FRENCH -- French, Howard Barclay
    Genealogy of the descendants of Thomas French who came to
America from Nether Heyford, Northamptonshire, England,
and settled in the province and country of West New Jersey,
of which he was one of the original proprietors, together
with William Penn, Edward Byllynge, Thomas Olive, Gauen
Laurie and others, with some account of colonial manners
and doings ... together with one hundred and fifty picture
prints. Philadelphia, 1909-13.

FRETZ -- Fretz, A. J.
    A brief history of John and Christian Fretz and a complete
genealogical family register to the fourth generation with
accounts and addresses delivered at the Fretz family
reunions held at Bedminster, Pennsylvania, 1888, 1893,
1898, and 1903. Milton, New Jersey, 1904.

FRETZ -- Fretz, Abraham
    A genealogical record of the descendants of Abraham Fretz
of Bedminster, Pa. Stanhope Press. Stanhope, N.J., 1911.

FREY -- Frey, Samuel C.
    Ancestry and posterity (in part) of Gottfried Frey,   (P)
1605-1913. Dispatch-Daily Print. York, Pa., 1914.

FULMER -- Smith, Cecil M.
    Fulmer family, also Ruff family, of Bucks County,   (N)
Pennsylvania ... Brooklyn, 1942.

FULTON -- Craighead, Ernest Schwartz
    The Fulton family of Westmoreland County, Pennsylvania,
    1712-1772-1940; an account of the descendants of Abraham
    Fulton and Margaret Guthry, his wife, who emigrated from
    Articlave, Londonderry County, Ireland, in 1772 and
    settled in Westmoreland County, Pa. Together with
    genealogical notes on intermarried families of the earlier
    generations, including: Coe, Hartley, Sloan, Newlon,
    Robbins, Shaw, Boyd, Plumer ... E. S. Craighead. Edgewood,
    Pittsburgh, Pa., 1940.

FULTON -- Fulton, Hugh R.
    Genealogy of the Fulton family; being descendants of John
    Fulton, born in Scotland 1713. Emigrated to America in
    1753. Settled in Nottingham township, Chester County, Pa.,
    1762. With a record of the known descendants of Hugh Ramsey
    of Nottingham, and Joseph Miller, of Lancaster County, Pa.
    New Era Print. Lancaster, Pa., 1900.

FULTON --Fulton, William P.
    Brief sketch of David Campbell Fulton and Nancy Mayhew
    Fulton; their family and descendants. Philadelphia, 1920.

- G -

GABLE -- Allaben, Frank (for Percival K. Gable)
    <u>History of the Gable family</u>. Times Printing House.
    Norristown, Pa., 1903?

GABRIEL -- (Author unknown)
    <u>A history of the Gabriel family of southern Pennsylvania</u>
    <u>and their descendants</u>. Commercial Publishers. Parsons,
    Kans., 1960.

GAEDSCHALK -- Sperling, Jennie G.
    <u>Partial genealogical record of the Rev. Jacob</u>   (P)
    <u>Gaedschalk (Vander Heggen)</u>. Sperling. Lansdale,
    Pa., 1976?

GALBREATH -- Galbreath, Joseph W.
    <u>Galbreath; the descendants of Alexander of</u>   (N)
    <u>Campbelltown, Scotland, and York County, Pa., 1784-</u>
    <u>1930, also some notes on the Galbreaths of England and</u>
    <u>Scotland</u>. Warren, Ohio, 1930.

GALLEY -- Galley, Henrietta and J. O. Arnold
    <u>History of the Galley family with local and old-time</u>
    <u>sketches in the Yough region</u>. Press Philadelphia
    Printing and Publishing. Philadelphia, 1908.

GALLEY -- Galley, Nancy Ware
    <u>History of the Galley family with local and old-time</u>
    <u>sketches in the Yough region, by Henrietta Galley and</u>
    <u>J. O. Arnold - Rev. Ed</u>. C. Henry Print. Greensburg,
    Pa., 1968.

GARD -- Baer, Frank L.
    <u>Gard families of New Jersey, Pennsylvania, West Virginia</u>
    <u>and Ohio</u>. No city, 1963.

GARDNER -- Gardner, Ivan Orlo
    <u>The Gardner genealogy of Somerset County, Pennsylvania</u>.
    No city, 1973.

GARDNER -- Gardner, Lester Durand and Edgar Stanley Gardner
    <u>Captain Bernard Gardner of Lancaster County, Pennsylvania</u>
    <u>and his descendants</u>. No city, 1932.

GARDNER -- May, Lillian and Charles Morris Gardner
    <u>Gardner history and genealogy</u>. Erie Printing Co.
    Erie, Pa., 1907.

GARDNER -- Gardner, Ivan O.
Gardner genealogy of Somerset County, Pa. No City, 1972.

GARLING -- Garling, Paul Eugene
The Garling family from 1751 to 1953. Chambersburg?, Pa., 1954.

GARRETT -- Garrett, Martha H.
Family recollections ... read at an "ancestor (P) party" ... at the 83rd anniversary of the marriage of ... Thomas C. and Frances Biddle Garrett. Philadelphia, 1910.

GARRETT -- Hayden, Rev. Horace Hayden
Major John Garrett, slain July 3, 1778. A forgotten hero of the massacre of Wyoming, Pennsylvania. E. B. Yordy. Wilkes-Barre, Pa., 1895.

GARWOOD -- Kimble, Elizabeth L.
Garwood-Van Sciver genealogy: names, births, marriages, and deaths, with related family notes, 1628-1979. Fencor Enterprises. Philadelphia, 1979.

GASSERT -- Brossman, Schuyler C.
Notes on the Gosser-Gassert family of Berks and (A) Lebanon Counties, Pa. Rehresburg, Pa., 1975.

GAY -- Montgomery, Robert H.
John Gay of Sadsbury, Lancaster County, Pa. Genealogical Magazine. No city, September 18, 1951.

GAZZAM -- Mackenzie, A. De B.
History of the Gazzam family, together with a biographical sketch of the American branch of the family of De Beelen. C. F. Haage. Reading, Pa., 1894.

GEHMAN -- Gehman, Anna M.
The Gehman-Gayman family history. Mohnton, Pa., 1953.

GEHMAN -- Gehman, A. M.
Gehman-Gayman family history; a biographical and (A) genealogical history of the descendants of Christian Gehman from the time of his arrival in Pennsylvania down to the seventh generation. Mohnton, Pa., no date.

GEIGER -- Bair, Samuel F.
Sketch of children of Valentin Geiger, pioneer of the (A) Geiger family in America. Pottstown, Pa., 1922.

GEIGER -- Bell, Raymond Martin
Family record of Paul Geiger, born 1723, Berwangen, Baden-
Wurrtemberg, died 1798, Geigertown, Berks County, Pa.
Washington, Pa., 1967.

GELDER -- Gelder, Franklin Brown
Gelder --Brown, some ancestors and descendants of Frederick
Thomas Gelder, Jr. and Edith L. Brown. F. B. Gelder.
Scranton, Pa., 1982.

GERBERICH -- Gerberich, Kenneth Ryan
History of the Gerberich family in America (1613-1925).
Harrisburg, Pa., 1925.

GERNHARDT -- Gernerd, Jeremiah Meitzler Mohr
Heinrich Gernhardt and his descendants. Historical
facts and musings; cogitations on interesting
genealogical problems; records of births, marriages and
deaths of all branches of the family; brief sketches of
many of the members; and some interesting reminiscences
of the great civil war. Gazette and Bulletin.
Williamsport, Pa., 1904.

GETZ -- Sunday, O. E.
Getz (Gates) genealogy. Genealogical register of the   (P)
probable ancestor and of the actual descendants of
Henry Getz. Rebersburg, Pa., 1950.

GETZ -- Sunday, O. E.
Getz (Gates) genealogy. Philadelphia, 1961.

GIBBONS -- (Author unknown)
A Chester County family. John Gibbons and his   (P)
descendants. Prepared for the New historical work
of Hon. J. Smith Futhey and Gilbert Cope, on Chester
County. Chandler Printing House. Philadelphia, 1881.

GIBSON -- Roberts, Thomas P.
Memoirs of John Bannister Gibson, late chief justice of
Pennsylvania. With Hon. Jeremiah S. Black's eulogy, notes
from Hon. William A. Porter's Essay upon his life and
character, etc. etc. J. Eichbaum & Co. Pittsburg, Pa.,
1890.

GIFFEN -- Giffen, J. W.
Giffen. Genealogic family history of descendants of   (N)
Robert Giffen and Mary Bane Giffen, settlers at Big
Spring, Pa., in 1777, removed to Wheeling, Va., 1787.
Central Publishing House. Cleveland, Ohio, 1927.

GIFFIN -- (Author unknown)
Giffin family; pioneers in America prior to 1742; (A)
following the descent of Andrew Giffin I, from
Eastern Pennsylvania ... Giffin Reunion Assoc.
Canonsburg, Pa., 1933.

GIFT -- Gift, Aaron Kern
History of the Gift, Kern and Royer families. Harold
Printing and Publishing. Beaver Springs, Pa., 1909.

GILBERT -- Cope, Gilbert
Genealogy of the Gilbert family. W. Chester, Pa., 1864.

GILBERT -- Gilbert, Harold S.
Gilberts of Pennsylvania and allied families. (P)
San Francisco, Calif., 1953.

GILBERT -- Walton, William
A narrative of the captivity and sufferings of Benjamin
Gilbert and his family who were taken by Indians in the
spring of 1780. 3d ed., rev. and enl. To which is
prefixed, a short account of the Gilbert family who
settled at Byberry. And an appendix, giving some account
of the captives after their return. J. Richards.
Philadelphia, 1848.

GILLAM -- Crider, Edward C.
Genealogy of the Jonathan Gillam family, a Pennsylvania
soldier of the Revolution, to Indiana 1800, and many items
pertaining to the Gillams in general. Denver, Colo., 1954.

GILLINGHAM -- Gillingham, Harrold Edgar
Gillingham family, descendants of Yeamans Gillingham.
Patterson & White. Philadelphia, 1901.

GILLINGHAM -- Glenn, Thomas Allen
Ancestry of Joseph Gillingham, of Bucks County and
Philadelphia, Pa., and Rebecca, daughter of Samuel Harrold,
his wife. Gillingham, Taylor, Canby, Jarvis, Moon, Nutt,
Lucas, Scott, Harrold, Elliott, Smith, Croasdale,
Hathornwait, Wilson, Baker. Philadelphia, 1897.

GILLINGHAM -- Glenn, Thomas Allen
Descent of Joseph Eddy Gillingham, Esq. of Clairemont, (P)
Lower Merion, Montgomery County, Pennsylvania, from
Ellis Lewis. Norristown, Pa. No date.

GILLFILLAN - Gilfillan, Margaret
Alexander Gilfillan (1746-1836); Martha Boyd Gilfillan
(1759-1840). Pittsburgh, Pa., 1955.

GILPIN -- Gilpin, Thomas
    Memorials and reminiscences of the Gilpin family in   (P)
    England and America. T. K. and P. G. Collins.
    Philadelphia, 1852.

GILPIN -- Jackson, William
    The name, arms and crest of the family of Gilpin.
    Martin and Allardyce. Frankford, Pa., 1911.

GINGERICH -- Beachy, Nettie
    Family record of Daniel J. Gingerich and his   (N)
    descendants. Mennonite Publishing House.
    Scottsdale, Pa., 1930.

GINGERICH -- Miller, Emma J.
    Descendants of Joseph M. Gingerich. A. S. Kinsinger.   (A)
    Gordonville, Pa., 1964.

GIRARD -- Girard, Stephen
    Will of the late Stephen Girard, esq. ... with a short (A)
    biography of his life. T. and R. Desilver. Philadlephia,
    1832.

GIRARD -- (Author unknown)
    Will and codicil of the late Stephen Girard, Esq. ... (A)
    dated 1830. Chandler. Philadelphia, 1874.

GLEN -- Glenn, Thomas A.
    ... Genealogical notes regarding the family of Glen, (N)
    or Glenn. Philadelphia, 1912.

GLENN -- Glenn, Edwin S.
    The ancestors and descendants of James D. Glenn and (P)
    Hannah R. Thorn of Frankford, Pa. Philadelphia, 1936.

GLENN -- Glenn Thomas A.
    Descent of Sarah Catharine Glenn, wife of Edward Glenn, (P)
    Edquire, of Ardmore, Pa. ... from the families of Allen,
    Farthing, Lohra, Seyfried, Schmied, Knorr, Jones,
    Biederman, Zimmerman, Schonmayer. Philadelphia, 1901.

GLISON -- Glisan, Edith
    Genealogy and brief history of Thomas Glisan and the (A)
    John Glisan family. Uniontown, Pa., 1972.

GNAEGY -- Gnagey, Elias
    Complete history of Christian Gnaegi, and a complete (A)
    family register of his lineal descendants ... 1774
    to 1897 ... Mennonite Publishing. Elkhart, Ind.,
    1897.

GOAR -- Maze, K. G.
Looking backward. Evangelic Print. Harrisburg,
Pa., 1943.

GOBLE -- Boykin, Norman G.
The Goble family: descended fromThomas Goble of   (N)
Charlestown, Mass.: genealogy from 1634. Himes
Print Co. State College, Pa., 1976.

GOERING -- Guttendorf, Virginia L.
Our Allegheny ancestors: Goehring, Aeberli, Ruttkamp,   (A)
1865-1976. Guttendorff Printers. Pittsburgh, Pa., 1976.

GOOD -- Good, Mary Ellen Sappington
History of a Good family: descendants of Jacob & Mary
Bosley Good of Cambria Co., Pennsylvania, 1779-1978.
Gateway Press. Baltimore, Md., 1978.

GOOD -- Bell, P. G.
History and genealogical record of the Good and Hileman
families of Pennsylvania. Altoona Times. Altoona, Pa.,
1912.

GOODWIN -- Goodwin, John Samuel
The Goodwins of Delaware Water Gap, Pa., and Tompkins
County, N.Y. Chicago, Ill., 1898.

GOODWIN -- (Author unknwon)
Rooftrees; or, The architectual history of an American
family. England, MDCXXX-New England, MCMXXX.
J. B. Lippincott. Philadelphia, 1933.

GORDON -- Gordon, Cynthia
American origins: antecedants of Cynthia Laidlaw Gordon.
Gordon. Easton Pa., 1978.

GORDON -- Morgan, Kathryn L.
Children of strangers: the stories of a Black family.
Temple University Press. Philadelphia, 1980.

GORDON -- Russell, Virginia Gordon
Gordons of western Pennsylvania. Specialty Printers.
Cochranton, Pa., 1981.

GORGAS -- Goshow, Mildred
The Gorgas family. Descendants of John and Physche   (P)
Rittenhouse Gorgas of Germantown. Roxborough.
Philadelphia, 1966.

GORHAM -- Wood, Frederick
Genealogical chart of the American descendants of   (P)
James Gorham of Benefield, Northamptonshire, England
(1550-1576). Philadelphia, 1880-1930.

GORTON -- Gorton, Adelos
The life and times of Samuel Gorton ... with a genealogy
of Samuel Gorton's descendents to the present time.
Philadelphia, 1907.

GOSHORN -- Carter, Marjorie H.
Goshorn descendants of Johann Georg and Susannah Gransshorn
of Shade Valley, Pennsylvania. M. H. Carter. San
Francisco, Calif., 1981.

GOSHOW --Goshow, Mildred
The Goshow and allied families. Part I. the Hoshow   (P)
fam. of Philadelphia and Montgomery Co., Pa.
Part II ... the Humpstone fam., the Oliver fam.
(and) ... the Friesz ... Hallman ... Cotwals family.
Roxborough. Philadelphia, 1966-67.

GOSSER -- Brossman, Schuyler C.
Notes on the Gosser-Gassert family of Berks and Lebanon
Counties, Pennsylvania. Rehrersburg, Pa., 1975.

GOTTSHALL -- Godshalk, Abraham
A family record, and other matters which, is hoped, will
be good for the souls of men and women; the family back
to the first emigrant who came to this country and settled
at Germantown, then Philadelphia County, Pa. ... The
United Evangelical Press. Harrisburg, Pa., 1912.

GOTTSHALL -- Grubb, N. B.
A genealogical history of the Gottshall family,
descendants of Reverend Jacob Gottshall. Philadelphia,
1924.

GOTWALD --Gotwald, Luther Alexander
Testimony and trial-an autobiography. Davidsville, Pa.,
1973.

GOWER -- Gower, Irene May
Gauer-Gower family. Schlechter's. Allentown, Pa., 1939.

GOWER -- Kresge, Milton
Gower family. M. G. Roseberry. E. Stroudsburg, Pa.,   (A)
1934.

GRAFF -- Graff, Paul
   History of the Graff family of Westmoreland.
   Philadelphia, 1891.

GRAHAM -- Seaver, J. Montgomery
   Graham family records. Philadelphia, 1929.

GRANT -- Grant, William H.
   Ancestors and descendants of Moses Grant and Sarah
   Pierce ... Lebanon, Pa., 1930?

GRATZ -- Byars, William Vincent
   B. and M. Gratz, merchants in Philadelphia, 1754-1798;
   papers of interest to their posterity and the posterity
   of their associates. Hugh Stephens Printing Co.
   Jefferson City, Mo., 1916

GRAY -- Bloom, Raymond Roll
   Ancestors and descendants of John Calvin Gray (1841-1930)
   and his wife Ruth Ellen Patterson (1846-1917). York,
   Pa., 1970.

GRAY -- Price, Norma Adams
   From meeting house to statehouse, 1683-1783. Wallingford,
   Pa., 1976.

GRAY -- Williams, Garford F.
   Jonas Latham Gray and his wife, Lucy Spicer Gray;   (A)
   their ancestors (and) their descendants. Nicholson,
   Pa.?, 1956.

GRAY -- Iowa D.A.R.
   Diary of Henry Clay Terrell (1861-1868), with genealogical
   notes on his Gray lineage. Cedar Falls Chapter, D.A.R.,
   Cedar Falls, Iowa, 1973.

GRAYBILL -- Graybill, Henry B.
   Life story of Joseph and Susan Graybill. Heralds   (A)
   Print. Lancaster, Pa., 1974.

GRAYBILL -- Graybill, Kathryn R.
   A family history of William and Elizabeth Shelley   (A)
   Graybill and Rhoda E. Kauffman. Richfield, Pa.?,
   1964.

GRAYBILL -- Landis, James Clarkson
   A genealogy for the descendants of Peter Grebiel/Graybill,
   1734-1804 of Manheim Township, Lancaster County,
   Pennsylvania. J. C. Landis. Columbia, Pa., 1983.

GRAYDON -- Graydon, Alexander
     Memories of a life chiefly passed in Pennsylvania, within
     the last 60 years. Blackwood. Edinburgh, 1822.

GREEN -- Reed, Samuel C.
     The Green family, descendants of Jonathan Green   (P)
     (1816-1852). Paoli, Pa., 1972.

GREENE -- Sheppard, Walter L.
     Ancestry and descendants of Stephen Greene and Martha   (P)
     Mifflin Houston, his wife. Sheppard. Havertown, Pa.,
     1974.

GREGOR -- MacGregor, George B.
     Twenty-four wills needed to solve riddles vexing American
     Clan Gregor Society of Washington, D.C. for 45 years from
     1906 A.D. Newton, Pa., 1951.

GREINER -- Becker, Dorothy Robertson
     Some early related families of Lancaster County,
     Pennsylvania. Fort Worth, Tex., 1979.
GREINER -- Greiner, Maurice L.
     The Greiners of Amityville, Pennsylvania, 1700-1900.
     Pocatello, Idaho, 1981.

GRIER -- Coryell, T.
     Reminiscences of the Rev. J. Hays Grier, and the pupils of
     his schools of Pine Creek and Jersey Shore, Pa., from 1818
     to 1833. The Kerr and Finney schools of Milton, 1804-1808.
     Geology of the Grier divines, Recollection of citizens and
     events of Milton from 1804 to 1808, &c., &c.
     Williamsport, Pa., 1876.

GRIESEMERS -- Martindale, Ella Catherine Griesemer
     The Griesemers: origins of the family in Europe, also the
     history of John Valentine Griesemer and his family,
     colonial pioneers in Pennsylvania in 1730, and their
     descendants: in addition, other Griesemer families who
     came to the New World. Griesemer Family Association
     Mohnton, Pa., 1980.

GRIFFIN -- Streets, Thomas Hale
     Samuel Griffin of New Castle County on Delaware, planter;
     and his descendants to the seventh generation.
     Philadelphia, 1905.

GRIFFITH -- Glenn, Thomas Allen
The pedigree of William Griffith, John Griffith and Griffith Griffiths (sons of Griffith John, of the parish of Llanddewi Brefi, in the county of Cardigan, South Wales, Great Britain) who removed to the county of Chester, Pennsylvania, in the early part of the XVIIIth century). Philadelphia, 1905.

GRIFFITH - Seaver, J. Montgomery
... Griffith family records. Philadelphia, Pa., 1928?

GRIFFITTS -- Griffitts, Frank P.
Genealogical tables of the Griffitts family from 1752 to 1887. Daily Intelligencer. Lancaster, Pa., 1887.

GRIM -- Long, William Gabriel
History of the Grim family of Pennsylvania and its associated families including the following: Merkle, Greenawalt, Fertig, Zechman, Schaeffer, Smith, Felver, Conde, Garner, Robbins, Long, Kisling, Schartel, Manbeck, Giltner, Schreiner, Dreher, Kircher and Moyer families. Published by Mabel Estella Grim Smith, Jennie Lucretia Grim Long, Harry Heber Grim. Huntington Publishing Co. Huntington, W. Va., 1934.

GROFF -- Groff, Dorothy Strauss
The descendants of John Henry Groff (also known as Harry Groff) and his wife Lucretia Rebecca (Stoudt) Groff of Berks Co., Pa. Bernville?, Pa., 1972.

GROOME -- (Author unknown)
The Groome family and connections: a pedigree. With biographical sketches by Harry Connelly Groome. J. B. Lippincott. Philadelphia, 1907.

GROSS -- Hall, William C.
The Andrew Jackson Gross genealogy: being a history of Andrew Jackson Gross, born in Pa. and all his descendants from Hardin Co., Ohio to Iowa and thence to all parts of the United States. Hall. Nevada?, Iowa, 1978.

GROSS -- Klosek, Linda M. Gross
The Gross family history, 1754-1980. L.M.G. Klosek. Wescosville, Pa., 1980.

GRUBB -- Cope, Gilbert
The Grubb family of Pennsylvania and Delaware. West Chester, Pa., 1893.

GRUBB -- Grubb, Rev. A. Bertolet
    Traditions and some reminiscences in memory of my ancestors,
    and boyhood days. Issued on the occasion of a joint
    pilgrimage of the Montgomery and Berks County historical
    societies thru historical Frederick, September 24th, 1910.
    No city, 1910?

GRUBB -- Wanger, F. P.
    Descendants of John Grubb ... Pottstown, Pa., 1910.

GRUBB -- Wanger, F. P.
    Henry Grubb chart. Pottstown, Pa., 1910.

GRUBB -- Wanger, F. P.
    The Grubb families of America; John Grubb of Tenessee.
    Pottstown, Pa., 1910.

GRUBB -- Wanger, F.
    The Grubb families of America; John Grubb of Lancaster
    Co., Pa. Pottstown, Pa., 1913.

GRUBB -- Wanger, F. P.
    The Grubb families of America. the Irish family.
    Pottstown, Pa., 1913.

GRUBB -- Wanger, F. P.
    The Grubb families of America. Military service.
    G. F. P. Wanger. Pottstown, Pa., 1914?

GUTHERY -- May, Mary Sibyl (Gray)
    History of Lieutenant Colonel John Guthery of Greene
    County, Pennsylvania. Washington, D.C., 1969.

GUTHERY -- May, Richard Holman
    A supplement (including an index) to the History of
    Lieutenant Colonel John Guthery of Greene County,
    Pennsylvania, and allied families. Godfrey Memorial
    Library. Middletown, Conn., 1956.

GUTHRIE -- (Author unknown)
    America Guthrie and allied families. Chambersburg, Pa.,
    1933.

GUTHRIE -- Dunn, Harriet N. and Eveline Guthrie
    Records of the Guthrie family of Pennsylvania, Connecticut,
    and Virginia, with ancestry of those who have intermarried
    with the family. H. N. and S. L. Dunn. Chicago, Ill.,
    1898.

- H -

HAAS - Haas, Arthur Milton
Haas family history. Haas. Fogelsville, Pa., 1982.

HADOCK -- Wood, Charles R.
The Hadock family. Dauphin, Pa., 1974.

HAIN -- Swope, Frances Hain
History of the Hain family. Reading, Pa., 1969.

HAINES -- Cregar, William Francis
Ancestry of William Shipley Haines, with some account of
the descendants of John and Joseph Haines and Colonel
Cowperthwait. Philadelphia, 1887.

HAINES -- Haines, Mary Rhoads
Clovercroft chronicles, 1314-1893. J. B. Lippincott.
Philadelphia, 1893.

HAKE -- Hake, Amy Lemert
Hake and Robb families of Pennsylvania. No city, 1971.

HAKES -- Hakes, Harry
The Hake family; ... 2d ed.; with additions and corrections.
R. Baur & Son. Wilkes-Barre, Pa., 1889.

HALL -- Fering, Adele Smith
The Andrew Hall family of Cecil County, Maryland, and
Chester County, Pennsylvania, including related families:
Corkadel, Crowl, and Steel; tentative outline.
Washington, D.C., 1977.

HALL -- Johnson, Robert L.
American heritage of James Norman Hall, the woodshed   (A)
poet of Iowa and co-author of Mutiny on the Bounty.
Dorrance. Philadelphia, 1969.

HALL -- Weller, Eloise Barrick
Jonathon Hall of Pennsylvania and Ohio and his ancestors
and descendants. E. B. Weller. Evansville, Ind., 1984.

HALLER -- Behrens, Joan Erzer
The Haller family history: including the descendants
and ancestors of Frank A. Haller and Anna Bellentin Haller
of Erie, Pennsylvania. Behrens. Rancho Palos Verdes,
Calif., 1978.

HALLOWELL -- Hallowell, William Penrose
    Record of a branch of the Hallowell family including the
    Longstreth Penrose and Norwood branches. Philadelphia,
    1893.

HALLOWELL -- Hough, Mary Paul Hallowell
    The Hallowell-Paul family history; including the ancestry
    of the related families of Worth, Lukens, Jarrett, Morris,
    Scull, Stokes, Heath and others. Philadelphia, 1924.

HAMBLETON -- Hambleton, Chalkley J.
    Genealogical record of the Hambleton family,   (P)
    descendants of James Hambleton of Bucks County,
    Pennsylvania, who died in 1751. Chicago, Ill., 1887.

HAMER -- Hamer, Harry M.
    Hamer family tree. Johnstown, Pa., 1954.   (A)

HAMILTON -- Sener, S. M.
    Lancaster townstead. How, when and where laid out by
    the Hamiltons in 1730. The Hamilton ancestry and coat
    of arms. The ground rents, the market houses and the
    public spring. The population at various periods.
    Lancaster, Pa., 1901.

HAMM -- Hamm, Lee S.
    Genealogical record of the Ham, Hamm, Hamme family in
    America: genealogy and history beginning with the first
    family settlement in Pennsylvania more than 200 years
    ago, and comprising the record of the Peter Ham branch
    of the Daniel Ham family. No city, 1950.

HAMMER -- Parker, Wayne V.
    Hammers genealogy: the descendants of Peter Hammer,   (P)
    1757-1838, York and Greene Counties, Pa., a soldier
    of the Revolutionary War; also the family lines ...
    Linn-Lynn-Colborn-Skinner-Van Voorhees-Hanna.
    Wichita, Kan., 1972.

HAMMOND -- Jacob, Julian H.
    Lineage charts of the colorful families of Hammond,   (P)
    Howard, Boone, Ridgely, Westall, Orrick, Cockey,
    Humphrey and Jacob of Anne Arundel County, Md.
    Philadelphia, Pa., 1945.

HAMPTON -- Hampton, Vernon Boyce
    In the footsteps of Joseph Hampton and the Pennsylvania
    Quakers. The Bucks County Historical Society.
    Doylestown, Pa., 1940.

HAMRICK -- Hamrick, Mayme H.
   The Hamrick and other families; Indian lore.   Mennonite
Publishing. Scottsdale, Pa., 1939.

HANK -- Rudolph, Myra H.
   The Hank family in America. Luke Hank of Eastwood,
Notts, England and Chester County, Pa. and John Hank
of Ilkeston, Derbyshire, England. Warren?, Ohio, 1932.

HANKS --Baber, Adin
   The Hanks family of Virginia and westward; a genealogical
record from the early 1600s, including charts of families
in Arkansas, the Carolinas, Georgia, Illinois, Indiana,
Iowa, Kentucky, Missouri, Oklahoma, Ohio, Pennsylvania,
and Texas. A. H. Clarke & Co. Glendale, Calif., 1965.

HAND -- Dymond, Dorothy Hand
   Genealogy of the Hand family and related families.
Gateway Press. Baltimore, Md., 1982.

HAND -- (Author unknown)
   Commemoration of Lancaster County in the revolution at
"Indian Rock", Williamson park, near "Rockford", the
home of General Edward Hand, M.D., Fiday, P.M.
September 20, CMMXII ... L. B. Herr. Lancaster, Pa.,
1912.

HANNA --Barekman, June B.
   Francis Hannah, Revolutionary soldier of Greene County,
Pennsylvania, and his children ... Chicago, Ill., 1971
or 1972.

HANNIS -- Kirk, Henry Ivens
   Genealogy of the Hannis family of Philadelphia. No
city, 19__.

HANNUM -- Hannum, Curtis H.
   Genealogy of the Hannum family, descended from John and
Margery Hannum, settlers in Chester County, Pennsylvania.
With brief notices of other families allied with the
name, and abstracts of early wills. H. F. Temple.
West Chester, Pa., 1911.

HANNUM -- Williams, Dorothy C.
   Genealogy of George and Amanda Hannum of Worthington,
Jefferson Township, Greene County, Indiana; descendants
and allied families. No city, 1972.

HARAH -- Brownfield, R. L., Jr. and Rex Newlon Brownfield
Harah family chart, about seventeen hundred fity (1750)
of Chester County and Lancaster County, Pa.; genealogical
chart of Harah Gilchrist, and Long famalies (sic).
No city, 1910.

HARBAUGH -- Harbaugh, Rev. H.
Annals of the Harbaugh family in America, from 1736
to 1856. M. Kieffer & Co. Chambersburg, Pa., 1856.

HARDCASTLE -- (Author unknown)
Fiftieth anniversary of a marriage day. Dedicated to   (P)
the members and friends of the Hardcastle family.
Philadelphia, 1855.

HARDINGER -- Duncan, Alice Young
Hardingers of Bedford County Pennsylvania. No city,
1975.

HARDINGER -- Duncan, Alice Young
Hardingers of Bedford County, Pennsylvania: includes
some notes on the allied Dicken and Rice families as
related to the Hardingers of Bedford County, Pa.
A. Y. Duncan. Manhattan, Ks., 1980.

HARLAN -- Harlan, Alpheus H.
History and genealogy of the Harlan family, and particularly
of the descendants of George and Michael Harlan, who
settled in Chester County, Pa., 1687. Lord Baltimore
Press. Baltimore, Md., 1914.

HARLEY -- Witcraft, J. R.
The Heiligh and Harley family ... Dispatch Pub. House.
Frankford, Pa., 1914.

HARLLEE -- Harlee, William Curry
Kinfolks, a genealogical and biographical record of Thomas
and Elizabeth (Stuart) Harlee, Andrew and Agnes (Cade)
Fulmore. Benjamin and Mary Curry, Samuel and Amelia
(Russell) Kemp, John and Hannah (Walker) Bethea, Sterling
Clack and Frances (King) Robertson, Samuel and Sophia
Ann (Parker) Dickey, their antecedents, descendants, and
collateral relatives, with chapter concerning state and
county records and the derivation of counties of Alabama,
Florida, Georgia, Mississippi, North Carolina, Pennsylvania,
South Carolina, Tennessee, Texas and Virginia. Searcy &
Pfaff, Ltd. New Orleans, La., 1934-37.

HARNISH -- Harnish, Mrs. W. E. and Frederick S. Weiser
The Harnish Friendschaft (the Harnish family); a
collection of historical materials relating to descendants
of Martin Harnish of Conestoga Township, Lancaster County,
Pennsylvaia, 1729-1926 by W. E. (i.e. J. G.) Francis for
the Harnish Reunion Association. Gettysburg, Pa., 1955.

HARPER -- Harper, John W.
The Harper family of Centre County, Pa. Schenectady,   (P)
N.Y., 1953.

HARPER -- Leeper, Samuel
History of the descendants of Samuel Harper, James Purdy
and James Leeper. Philadelphia, 1894.

HARRINGTON -- Harrington, Ruth Haddox
Harrington-Heath heritage: ancestors and descendants
(1600-1984) of Oramel Warren Harrington and Martha C.
Heath. R. H. Harrington. Philadelphia, 1984.

HARRIS -- (Author unknown)
Record of the Harris family descended from John Harris,
born in 1680 in Wiltshire, England. G. F. Lasher.
Philadelphia, 1903.

HARRIS -- (Author unknown)
Notes on the ancestry of the children of Joseph Smith
Harris and Delia Silliman Brodhead. Allen, Lane & Scott.
Philadelphia, 1898.

HARRIS -- (Author unknown)
The collateral ancestry of Stephen Harris, born September 4,
1798 and of Marianne Smith, born April 2, 1805. G. F.
Lasher. Philadelphia, 1908.

HARRIS -- Chalmers, Mary Letitia
Our kith and kin; or, A history of the Harris family.
1754-1895. American Printing House. Philadelphia, 1895?

HARRIS -- Seaver, J. Montgomery
The Harris genealogy. Philadelphia, 1927.

HARRISON -- Harrison, William J.
Some descendants of William Harrison, engraver, born
London, England circa 1750, died Philadelphia, Pa.,
1803. Bloomfield, N.J., 1972.

HHARISON -- Harrison, William Welsh
The royal ancestry of George Leib Harrison of Philadelphia.
Philadelphia, 1914.

HARRISON -- Harrison, William Welsh
Harrison, Waples and allied families; being the ancestry
of George Leib Harrison of Philadelphia and of his wife
Sarah Ann Waples. Philadelphia, 1910.

HARRISON -- Keith, Charles Penrose
The ancestry of Benjamin Harrison, President U.S.A.,
1889-1893, in chart showing descendants of William
Henry Harrison, President, U.S.A. in 1841.
Philadelphia, 1893.

HARRISON -- Mervine, William M.
The genealogical register. Philadelphia, 1913.

HARROD -- Creighton, Isabelle Latimer
The Harrod's of Pennsylvania. No city, 1975.

HARSHBERGER -- Harshberger, John W.
The life and work of John W. Harshberger, Ph.D.
Philadelphia, 1928.

HART -- Davis, W. W. H.
History of the Hart family, of Warminster, Bucks County,
Pennsylvania. To which is added the genealogy of the
family, from its first settlement in America. W. W. H.
Davis. Doylestown, Pa., 1867.

HART -- Hart, Raymond Sagar
Supplemental record of the Hart family of Warminster,
Bucks County, Pennsylvania. Bethesda, Md., 1969.

HART -- Hart, Thomas
A record of the Hart family of Philadelphia. With a
genealogy of the family, from its first settlement
in America, augmented by notes of the collateral
branches. 1735-1920. Philadelphia, 1920.

HARTMAN -- Hartman, John Markley
Johannes Hartman of Chester County, Pennsylvania, and
his descendants. Mrs. L. M. Clapham. Philadelphia,
1937.

HARTMAN -- (Author unknown)
The families of Louis Hartman and Peter Rodenhauser of
Columbia, Lancaster County, Pennsylvania. Lancaster,
Pa., 1952.

HARTUNG -- Hartung, Henry Beck
Genealogy of the Hartung family of Wayne County, Pa.;
giving the descendants of John Henry Christian Hartung,
born about 1806 to 1962. Arlington, Va., 1962.

HARTZELL -- Hartzell, George Turner
A book of life: a Hartzell, Hertzel, Hirtzel, Hirzel
family history & genealogy. Hartzell. Fayetteville,
Pa., 1977.

HARTZELL -- Price, Charles H.
A Hartzell-Price family history and genealogy. Telford,
Pa., 1971.

HARVEY -- Devlin, Mrs. Dora H.
Leaves from the past. John C. Winston. Philadelphia,   (P)
1937.

HARVEY -- Harvey, M. B.
Journal of a voyage from Philadelphia to Cork in the   (A)
year of our Lord 1809 ... West Park Pub. Philadelphia,
1915.

HARVEY -- Harvey, Oscar Jewell
The Harvey book. Wilkes-Barre, Pa., 1899.

HARVEY -- Seaver, Jessie
Harvey family records. American Historical and   (A)
Genealogical Society. Philadelphia, 1929.

HARVEY -- Seaver, J. Montgomery
... Harvey family records. Philadelphia, 1928?

HAUPT -- Haupt, William H.
Descendants of Henry Haupt and his wife Anna   (N)
Margaretha (Schick) Haupt of Northampton County,
Pennsylvania, 1761-1798. Flourtown, Pa., 1931.

HAWKINS -- Hawkins, Carl H.
Hawkins genealogy; descendants of James Hawkins and   (A)
Martha Hollowell, married 1740 at Abingdon, Pa.
Richmond, Ind., 1975.

HAWLEY -- Hawley, Everett M.
The Chester County (Pa.) Hawley family. No city,   (P)
1957.

HAY -- Hay, Anna Margaret (Suppes)
Genealogical sketches of the Hay, Suppes, and allied
families. W. H. Raab. Johnstown, Pa., 1923.

HAYES -- Committee for the family
    Proceedings of the Bi-centennial gathering of the
    descendants of Henry Hayes at Unionville, Chester
    County, Pa., September 2nd, 1905, together with a
    partial genealogy and other material relating to the
    family ... West Chester, Pa., 1906.

HAYES -- Ewers, Mrs. Ernest
    Hayes records from New Garden Monthly Meeting of the
    Religious Society of Friends, Pennsylvania, 1725/26-
    1909, with a few entries from New Bedford Monthly
    Meeting records and Concord Monthly Meeting. Crete,
    Ill., 1964.

HAYES -- Seaver, J. Montgomery
    ... Hayes family records. American Historical-
    Genealogical Society. Philadelphia, 1929.

HAYNES -- Claussen, W. Edmunds
    Wyck: the story of an historic house, 1690 - 1970.
    M. T. Haines. Philadelphia, 1970.

HAYS -- Burnham, Walter J.
    Descendants of Robert Hays, born 1818 Ireland, settled in
    Armstrong Co., Pa., with other Hays. Pittsburgh, Pa.,
    1969.

HAZLEHURST -- Baer, Mabel Van Dyke
    Hazlehurst and allied families of Purviance and Latrobe;
    Pennsylvania, New Jersey and Maryland. No city, 1968.

HEACOCK -- Heacock, T. Reece
    The Heacock family. Jonathan and Ann Heacock who emigrated
    to America from England, and settled in Chester County,
    Pennsylvania in 1711, and their descendants. Lima, Pa.,
    1869.

HEATHCOTE - Heathcote, Charles William
    The Heathcote family, 1580-1924. Chambersburg, Pa., 1924.

HEFFELFINGER -- Heffelfinger, John Byers
    The Heffelfinter genealogy (through Philip Heffelfinger,
    the Revolutionary soldier, from Martin Heffelfinger,
    the Swiss immigrant, in Lancaster County, Pennsylvania,
    1740). With notes on some descendants of Philip.
    Newton?, Kans., 1951.

HEFFNER -- Heffner, Geo. H.
Family records of the descendants of Henry Heffner, 1754-1886 ... Also, the older generations of Johann Georg Haeffner (Rockland Stem,) 1733 -   , Yost-Heinrich Goerg (Herborn, Nassau, Germany, born 1707), Georg Spohn, (father of Conrad, born 1755), Adam Dietrch (born 1740), etc., with biographical and historical notes. Journal Steam Job Print. Kutztown, Pa., 1886.

HEFFNER -- Heffner, Wayne R.
Genealogical record and history of the Heffner families; descendants of Johan Georg Haeffner, 1733-1756. Reading?, Pa., 1956?

HEGE -- (Author unknown)
Genealogical register of the male and female descendants of Hans Hege; and also of the male and female descendants of Henry Lesher, and the relationship existing between the said two families. M. Kieffer. Chambersburg, Pa., 1859.   (A)

HEILMAN -- Heilman, Iva long
The Heilman source book; genealogical research of John Heilman, Eugene A. Heilman (and) Ruth Smith. York, Pa., 1968.

HEILMAN -- Heilman, S. P., M.D.
The name Heilman in European, American and Lebanon County history. Read before the Lebanon County Historical Society, November 2, 1917. Lebanon, Pa., 1917.

HEILMAN -- Heilman, U. Henry, A.M.
Descriptive and historical memorials of Heilman Dale; read before the Lebanon County Historical Society, April 16, 1909, Jonestown, Pa. ... Lebanon?, Pa., 1909.

HEINDEL -- (Author unknown)
The Heindel (Heindle-Haindel-Hindel-Heindell) family of Windsor Township, York County, Pennsylvania. Lancaster, Pa., 1953.

HEINECKE -- Heinecke, Rev. Samuel
Genealogy from Adam to Christ, with the genealogy of Adam Heinecke and Henry Vandersaal, from 1747 to 1881. To which is added a brief account of the author's travels in about sixteen years as an evangelist, and twelve sermons composed by himself. ... 2d ed. J. A. Hiestand. Lancaster, Pa., 1881.

HEINER -- Hensell, John
Chronicles of a German family; or, Heiners of Germany, (N)
Pennsylvania, Kentucky and Texas. J. Hensell. Houston,
Tex., 1958.

HEINLY -- Heinly, Harvey F.
The Heinly family in America, a history. Heinly Family
Association. Reading, Pa., 1944.

HEINTZ -- Proctor, John Clagett
Johannes Heintz and his descendants. Greenville, Pa., 1918.

HEISEY -- Heisey, John W.
Isaac T. Heisey and his family. York Springs?, Pa., 1960.

HEISEY -- Heisey, M. Luther
The Heisey family in America. Lancaster, Pa., 1941.

HELLER -- Heller, W. J.
Heller family history ... Genealogy of Christopher Heller
and his six sons. Easton, Pa., 1908.

HELM -- Bates, Martha Helms
Israel Helm, A Swedish settler of Pennsylvania and New
Jersey, 1627-1701/2. No city, 1963.

HELM -- Brownfield, Robert L.
Helm family of Lancaster County, Pennsylvania. No city,
1951.

HENCH -- Emig, Lelia Dromgold
Records of the annual Hench and Dromgold reunion held
in Perry County, Pennsylvania from 1897 to 1912; with
the genealogies of Nicholas Ickes, Johannes Hench,
Zachariah Rice, John Hartman, Thomas Dromgold.
Harrisburg, Pa., 1913.

HENDERSON -- Benson, E. A.
Henderson family of Salisbury Township, Lancaster (A)
County, Pa., and Maryland. Lancaster, Pa., 1959.

HENDERSON -- Henderson, Oren Vitellius
The descendants of Robert Henderson of Hendersonville,
Pennsylvania, Mercer County, born 1741 - died 1810.
Durham?, N.H., 1947?

HENDERSON -- Lloyd, Emma Rouse
Henderson family of Pennsylvania and Kentucky.
Cincinnati, Ohio, no date.

HENDERSON -- Seaver, J. Montgomery
... Henderson family records. American Historical-
Genealogical Society. Philadelphia, 1929.

HENDRICKS -- Hinds, Virginia Horner
Hendrickson, Capt. James Ridgeway, first burgess of
McKeesport, Allegheny County, Pennsylvania, 1812-1869,
some ancestors and descendants: family history, 1470-
1978, migration from Holland to New Amsterdam, New
Jersey, Pennsylvania, and points west: allied lines,
Bailey, Spielmyer, Implay, Lawrence, Cox, Stout, Lanen
Van Pelt, Polhemius, Ten Eyck, Vanderveer, DeMandeville.
Hinds. Waverly, Ohio, 1978.

HENDRICKS -- McConnell, Marie
Hendricksons of New York, New Jersey and Pennsylvania:
dealing mainly with the background, family and descendants
of William Hendrickson ("Wilm Hendricks"), but also, to
some extent, with others. University Microfilms International. Ann Arbor, Mich., 1979.

HENDRICKSON -- McConnell, Marie
Hendricksons of New York, New Jersey and Pennsylvania;
dealing mainly with the background, family and descendants
of William Hendrickson, 'Wilm Hendricks.' Lakeland,
Florida, 1965.

HENDRICKSON -- McConnell, Marie (Mrs. F. M.)
Hendricksons of New York, New Jersey, and Pennsylvania;
dealing mainly with the background, family, and descendants
of William Hendrickson ("Wilm Hendricks") but also, to
some extent, with others. Lakeland, Florida, 1972?

HENGST -- Hengst, Michael A.
The genealogy of Jacob and Margaret Hengst. M. A. Hengst.
Harrisburg, Pa...., 1981?

HENKEL -- (Author unknown)
... Henkel memorial dedicatory services ...   (P)
Germantown. Philadelphia, 1917.

HENKEL -- Stapleton, A.
The Henkel memorial; historical, genealogical and biographical. York, Pa., 1910-1919.

HENRY -- Clark, Martha B.
Henrys of Chester and Lancaster Counties, Pa., and   (A)
Detroit, Michigan. Lancaster, Pa., no date.

HENRY -- Henry, Jeanne Hand
My Henry family; Pennsylvania, Virginia, Tennessee, Alabama,
Mississippi and incidentally, Oklahoma. New Market,
Alabama, 1973.

HENRY -- Jordan, Francis, Jr.
Life of William Henry, of Lancaster, Pensylvania, 1729-1786,
patriot, military officer, inventor of the steamboat; a
contribution to revolutionary history. New Era Printing Co.
Lancaster, Pa., 1910.

HENRY -- Seaver, J. Montgomery
... Henry family records. American Historical-Genealogical
Society. Philadelphia, 1929.

HEPBURN -- Meginness, John F.
Genealogy and history of the Hepburn family of the
Sesquehanna Valley; with reference to other families
of the same name. Williamsport, Pa., 1894.

HEPLER -- Hepler, Bertha E.
Family record of Christopher (Stoffel) Hepler and his   (A)
descendants. Mennonite Pub. Scottdale, Pa., 1930.

HEPLER -- Swank, Ida H.
The Hepler family reunion and history of the family.   (P)
Record-American Print. Mahanoy City, Pa., no date.

HERBST -- Rowe, Mary
Jacob Herbst and his descendants. Gettysburg, Pa., 1957.

HERON -- Herron, William Alfred and William Herron Hezlep
Our Herron family of Allegheny, Pensylvania. Pittsburgh?,
Pa., 1960.

HERON -- O'Gorman, Mrs. Michael Martin
Some descendants of the immigrant Thomas Herron of
Armstrong County, Pennsylvania. Washington, D.C., 1935.
HERR -- Herr, Theodore W.
Lineage and family record of descendants of Reverend Hans
Herr from his birth A.D. 1639, made from the perfected
genealogical records of the pioneer settlers of Lancaster
County, Pennsyalvania, from A.D. 1709 to A.D.1729, and all
the lineal descendants of such pioneer settlers to the
present time. T. W. Herr. Denver, Colo., 1901.

HERRING -- Herring, Calvin A.
A history and genealogy of the Herring-Haring-Hering-   (P)
Harring family of Pennsylvania. Jacobs Press.
Allentown, Pa., 1962-66.

HERRMAN -- Glenn, Thomas A.
   <u>Bohemia manor and the Herrmans</u>. H. T. Coates.   (P)
   Philadelphia, 1899.

HERSHBERGER -- Bontrager, Amanda M. H.
   <u>Family record of Isaac J. Hershberger and Fannie J.</u>   (A)
   <u>Miller, 1850-1963</u>. A. S. Kinsinger. Gordonville, Pa.,
   1963.

HERSHBERGER --Miller, Valentine J.
   <u>Memorial history of Emanuel Hershberger; and a</u>   (A)
   <u>complete family register of his lineal descendants</u>
   <u>and those related to him by intermarriage ... 1811</u>
   <u>to 1968</u>. Gordonville, Pa., 1968.

HERSHEY -- Hershey, J. Eby
   <u>Hershey family history; (family record of Joseph and</u>   (A)
   <u>Fannie H. Hershey)</u>. Gordonville, Pa., 1959.

HERSHEY -- Hershey, Henry
   <u>Hershey family history</u>. Mennonite Pub. House.   (A)
   Scottdale, Pa., 1929.

HERSHEY -- Hershey, Scott Funk
   <u>History and records of the Hershey family from the year</u>
   <u>1600</u>. New Castle, Pa., 1909.

HERTZ -- Hill, Harry Segner
   <u>Conrad Hertz of Brecknock, soldier in the War of the</u>
   <u>Revolution. Documentary record and chronology of Conrad</u>
   <u>Hertz and of other Hertz (or Hartz) kin interred in the</u>
   <u>old cemetary of Allegheny Union Church (Alleghenyville,</u>
   <u>Brecknock Township, Berks County, Pennsylvania); also of</u>
   <u>their kin in other cemeteries of Pennsylvania</u>. Asbury
   Park?, N.J., 1953.

HESS -- Hess, Asher L.
   <u>Genealogical record of the descendants of Nicholas Hess,</u>
   <u>pioneer immigrant, together with historical and biographical</u>
   <u>sketches</u>. H. Ray Haas & Co. Allentown, Pa., 1912.

HESS -- Hess, John H.
   <u>A family record of the Hess family from the first</u>
   <u>emigrant to this country down to the present time</u>
   <u>as far as could be obtained. Mistakes excepted</u>.
   Sunbeam Print. Lititz, Pa., 1880.

HESS -- Hess, John R.
   <u>Hans Hess who died 1733 and some of his descendants</u>.   (A)
   White Horse, Pa?, 1957?

HESS -- Hess, John A.
(A) genealogy of the Hess family; from the first   (A)
emigrant to this country down to the present time ...
M. S. Hess. Lititz, Pa., 1963.

HESS -- (Author unknown)
Genealogical data. Hess - Brown, York and Bedford   (N)
Counties, Pa., and Columbus, Ohio. No city, 1916.

HIATT -- Johnson, William Perry
Hiatt-Hiett genealogy and family history, 1699-1949; being,
in particular, a record of John Hiett, Quaker, England to
Pennsylvania c. 1699, and upwards of ten thousand of his
descendants. Jesse Hiatt Family Association. Payson,
Utah, 1951.

HICKS -- Wilbur, Henry W.
The life and labors of Elias Hicks. Friends' General
Conference Advancement Committee. Philadelphia, 1910.

HIESTER -- Hiester, Isaac
The Hiester homestead in Germany; a paper before the
Historical Society of Berks County, by request of the
Council of the Society, March 12, 1907. Reading, Pa.,
1907.

HIESTER -- Valeria E. Clymer
A genealogy of the Hiester family. Reading Eagle Press.
Reading, Pa., 1941.

HIESTER -- Hill, V. E. C.
A genealogy of the Hiester family. Lebanon, Pa., 1903.

HIESTER -- Richards, Henry Melchior Muhlenberg
The Hiester family; prepared by authority of the
Pennsylvania-German Society. The Society. Lancaster,
Pa., 1907.

HILL -- Chetwynd, Janet Hill
Roger Enos Hills or Roger Hill and Elizabeth Farwell:
roots and branches: from the papers of Janet Hill
Chetwynd. L. M. Mohler. Washington, Pa., 1982.

HILL -- Smith, John Jay
Letters of Doctor Richard Hill and his children, also
Lloyd famly. Philadelphia, 1854.

HILLEGAS -- Du Bin, Alexander
Hillegas family and collateal lines of Nicholas-Smith-   (N)
Anthony-Kelly ... Historical Pub. Society.
Philadelphia, 1939.

HILLEGAS -- (Author unknown)
Hillegas family .... Historical Pub. Society.
Philadelphia, 1933.

HILLEGAS -- Whitney, Emma St. Clair
Michael Hillegas and his descendants. Pottsville,
Pa., 1892.

HILLIGOSS -- Hilligoss, Lillie A.
Hilligoss family of Pennsylvania, Fleming County,   (A)
Ky. and Rush County, Ind. No city, 1901.

HILLS -- Hills, Oscar A.
The golden wedding of Mr. and Mrs. Darwin T. Hills,   (P)
at Crawfordsville, Indiana ... Allegheny, Pa?. 1878.

HINCHILLWOOD --Hinchillwood, C. Milton
The descendants of John Hinchillwood of Philadelphia. (P)
South Pasadena, Calif., 1970.

HINCKLEY -- Cass, Earle Millard
Beulah Ball Cass, a descendant of Samuel Hinckley. New
Castle, Pa., 1945.

HINES -- Hines, Benjamin McFarland
Hines and allied families. Ardmore, Pa., 1981.

HINMAN -- Hoagland, Edward C.
John Hinman of Wysox, Pa., 1790, and some of his   (P)
descendants. Sacred Art Pess. Wysox, Pa., 1955.

HINMAN -- Hoagland, Edward Collbaugh
Some brief notes on the Hinman and Burrows families;
including a possible clue to the identity of Hannah,
wife of Edward Hinman, Jr., of Stratford, Conn.
Colportage Publishers. Wysox, Pa., 1946.

HINMAN -- Hoagland, Edward Coolbaugh
Twigs from family trees. Sacred Art Press. Towanda,
Pa., 19__.

HINSHILWOOD -- Hinshilwood, Charles M.
The descendants of John Hinchilwood of Philadelphia.
South Pasadena, Calif., 1970.

HIPPENSTIEL -- Hippenstiel, H. Franklin
The Hippenstiel families in America ... Bethlehem, Pa.,
1925.

HIRES -- Hires, William L.
The Hires family. Philadelphia, 1964.

HOAR -- Hoare, D. W.
   Genealogical data on some of the descendants of Robert   (P)
   Hoar of Lancaster County, Pa. Hoare. St. Petersburg,
   Pa., 1973.

HOBART -- Hobart, Donald Marcene
   The ancestors and descendants of John Sullivan Hobart.
   Bryn Mawr, Pa., 1951.

HOCH -- De Long, Dr. Irwin Hoch
   An early nineteenth century constitution of a union
   church, transcribed and edited with critical, historical
   and genealogical notes, and illustrated with a facsimile
   reproduction of a page of autograph signatures.
   Lancaster, Pa., 1931.

HOCH -- Stoudt, John B.
   The children and the children's children of Rudolph   (P)
   Hoch and Melchior Hoch, Swiss refugees who came to
   province of Pennsylvania in 1717 and settled in the
   Oley Valley. Hoch-High Family Reunion. No city, 1949.

HOCHSTETLER --Hostetler, Rev. Harvey, D.D.
   Descendants of Barbara Hochstedler and Christian
   Stutzman. Mennonite Publishing House. Scottdale,
   Pa., 1938.

HOCKLEY -- Goshow, Mildred
   The Hockley family of Chester County, Pennsylvania.   (P)
   Roxborough, Pa., 1960.

HOFFER --Hoffer, Isaac
   Genealogy of Matthias Hoffer and his descendants in the
   United States of America. J. R. Hoffer. Mount Joy,
   Pa., 1868.

HOFFMAN -- Huffman, Richard G.
   Jacob Huffman (Hoffman) family Unity Township,   (A)
   Westmoreland Co., Pennsylvania. Whitney, Pa., 1968.

HOLCOMB -- (Author unknown)
   Official program and report of the World Holcomb-e   (A)
   reunion, which was held at ... Philadelphia ...
   1926. The Council. Philadelphia, 1926.

HOLCOMB -- (Author unknown)
   The Holcombs. Some account of their origin, settlement
   and scatterment, as elicited at the first and second family
   reunions, held at LeRoy, Pa., October, 1879, and Mount
   Airy. N.J., August, 1886. G. H Hines Printer. Portland,
   Ore., 1887.

HOLCOMB -- Seaver, Jesse
    ... The Holcomb(e) genealogy; a genealogy, history and
directory ... of the Holcomb(e)s of the world, including
Holcombe descendants of William the Conqueror and King
Henry I, the ancient and modern English branch, the
American branches .... and others. American Historical-
Genealogical Society. Philadelphia, 1925.

HOLLAND -- Thrailkill, Fanny F.
    Holland notes. Philadelphia, 1946-47.   (P)

HOLLINGER -- Kauffman, Robert Terry
    The Hollinger family of Franklin County, Pennsylvania,
since 1736; a brief lineage of the children, grandchildren
and great-grandchildren of Daniel Hollinger and his wife,
Hannah Stephey Singer and their children Simon, Jacob,
John, Abraham, Lizzie, Ida, Laura and Hannah Alice.
Harrisburg, Pa., 1963.

HOLLINGSWORTH -- Jamar, Mary Hollingsworth
    Hollingsworth family and collateral lines of Cooch-Gilpin-
Jamar-Mackall-Morris-Stewart; early history and Cecil
County, Maryland, lines. The Historical Publication
Society. Philadelphia, 1944.

HOLLINSHEAD -- Hillary, William R.
    Some genealogical and historical facts about the   (N)
Hollinshead, Ridgway, Borton, Burr and Peacock
families. With photographs ... also charts and
facsimilies. Philadelphia, 1941-42.

HOLMES -- Seaver, J. Montgomery
    .... Holmes family records. Philadelphia, 1929?

HOLSINGER -- Holsinger, Paul G.
    Descendants of Rudolph Holsinger. Martingsburg, Pa., 1976.

HOLSTEIN -- Holstein, Mrs. Anna M.
    Swedish Holsteins in America from 1644 to 1892. Comprising
many letters and biographical matter relating to John
Hughes, the "stamp officer," and friend of Franklin, with
papers not before published relating to his brother of
revolutionary fame, Colonel Hugh Hughes fo New York. The
families of De Haven, Rittenhouse, Clay, Potts, Blackiston,
Atlee, Coates, and other descendants of Matthias Holstein of
Wicaco, Philadelphia, are included .... M. R. Wills
Printers. Norristown, Pa., 1892.

HOLSTEIN -- Holstein, Perry Floyd
    Some of my ancestry: Holsteins. Monroeville, Pa., 1972.

HOLT -- (Author unknown)
Holt happenings. Easton?, Pa., no date.

HOLTZLANDER -- Sandwick, Charles M.
The children and grandchildren of Nicholas Holtzlander and
Anna Magdalena Janewin. Easton?, Pa., 1959.

HOMBACH -- Adams, Pauline Homback and John Poist Keffer
Hombach family history; a history of Dr. Wilhelm Ludwig
Hombach who came from Germany to the United States of
America in 1836 and of his ancestors and descendants.
Bethlehem, Pa., 1968.

HOOD -- Hood, Rev. Geo.
Memorials of our father and mother. Also a family
genealogy. Collins Printer. Philadelphia, 1867.

HOOD -- Hood, George
A genealogy of Richard Hood, who came from Lynn in
England and settled at Lynn in Mass. about 1650.
Philadelphia, 1867.

HOOK --Hook, James William
Captain James Hook of Greene County, Pennsylvania. New
Haven, Conn., 1952.

HOOPES -- Bell, Albert Dehner
The Hoopes-Killough family Bible records, Chester &
Lancaster Counties, Pennsylvania. No city, 1948?

HOOPES -- (Author unknown)
The Holy Bible. M. Carey & Son. Philadelphia, 1818.

HOOPES -- Fuller, Gerald Ralph
The Hoopes family record: a genealogical record of the
Hoopes family, descendants of Daniel Hoopes of Westtown,
Chester County, Pennsylvania. Hoopes Family Organization.
Houston, Tex., 1983.

HOOVER -- Hoover, Harry M.
The Huber-Hoover family history ... A biographical and
genealogical history of the descendants of Hans Huber from
the time of his arrival in Pennsylvania down to the eleventh
generation. Mennonite Pub. House. Scottdale, Pa., 1928.

HOOVER -- Hoover, Mary Ruthrauff
A genealogical history of the descendants of Johannes or
John (Huber) Hoover and his wife Mary Watson who settled
in Lancaster County, Pennsylvania. Kansas City,
Mo., 1937.

HOPE -- Hope, Roy M.
Hope family tree. Merion Station, Pa., 1967.

HOPKINS -- Ball, Helen A.
Ezekiel and Sarah Hazzard Hopkins of Delaware, Maryland,
Pennsylvania and Bourbon County, Kentucky, including some
of their descendants and some related families. H. A. Ball.
East Lansing, Mich., 1978.

HOPKINS -- Ball, Helen A.
Ezekiel and Sarah Hazzard Hopkins of Delaware, Maryland,
Pennsylvania and Bourbon County, Kentucky, including some
of their descendants and some related families. -- 2nd ed.
H. A. Ball. East Lansing, Mich., 1980.

HOPKINS -- (Author unknown)
Hopkins; the name and the coat of arms. Martin and
Allardyce. Philadelphia, 1911.

HOPKINS -- Smith, William N.
Who's who in the Hopkinsfolk; a biographical record of (N)
Rt. Rev. John Henry Hopkins ... of Melusina Muller,
his wife, with all descendants, etc. to April, 1934.
Reading, Pa., 1934.

HOPKINS -- Smith, William N.
The 1945 Register of the Hopkinsfolk. A supplement to (N)
"Who's who in the Hopkinsfolk" of 1934. Reading, Pa.,
1945.

HORD -- Hord, Rev. Arnold Harris
Genealogy of the Hord family. J. B. Lippincott.
Philadelphia, 1898.

HORN -- Thompson, Ruth H.
The ancestors and descendants of Edward Traill Horn (P)
(1850-1915) - Harriet Chisolm ... Henry Hyster
Jacobs ... Laura Hewes Downing ... John C. Horn
Association. Huntingdon, Pa., 1976.

HORNER -- Bell, Jack Horner
Horner patriots of Pennsylvania. Gateway Press.
Baltimore, Md., 1980.

HORST -- Hurst, Frances W.
Descendants of Jacob M. Horst. J. W. Hocking. (A)
Ephrata, Pa., 1954?

HORST -- Horst, John E.
David H. Horst family: a short sketch of the ancestry of David H. Horst and the record of his lineage. Caslon Press. No city, 1976.

HORTON -- Alloway, Prof. Geo. W.
... Horton genealogy and history; descendants of Richard Horton (1727) and Elizabeth Harrison, and their nephew and niece, Deacon Nathaniel Horton (1741) and Rebecca Robinson, inluding a brief tracing of their ancestral line back to 1310. The Sheterom Printing Co. Saxton, Pa., 1929.

HORTON -- Horton, Byron Barnes, A.M.
The ancestors and descendants of Isaac Horton of Liberty, N.Y. Mohr Printery. Warren, Pa., 1946.

HORTON -- Horton, Geo. F., M. D.
... Horton genealogy; or, Chronicles of the descendants of Barnabas Horton, of Southold, L. I., 1640. Home Circle Publishing. Philadelphia, 1876.

HORTON -- Horton, Geo. F.
Addenda to: Horton genealogy ... Towanda, Pa., 1879.

HORTON -- (Author unknown)
Proceedings of the Horton family gathering and social reunion. Philadelphia, 1876.

HOSMER -- Penniman, Josiah H.
Address before the annual meeting of the Society of colonial wars in the commonwealth of Pennsylvania, March 12, 1931, at the Rittenhouse Club, Philadelphia. The Society. Philadelphia?, 1931.

HOSTETLER -- Hostetler, Harvey
Descendants of Barbara Hochstedler and Christian Stutzman. Scottdale, Pa., 1938.

HOSTETTER -- Hostetter, Richard L.
The Hostetter family. Gateway Press. Baltimore, Md., 1984.

HOSTLER -- Kilbourne, John Dwight
The Hostler family: the ancestry and descendants of Joseph Hostler of Fawn Township, York County, Pennsylvaia. No city, 1976.

HOTT -- Hamblin, John
Hott family genealogy, 1685-1936. No city, 1937.

HOUGH -- Hough, Orville Louis
Hough in Bucks County, Pennsylvania, 1683-1850. Hough.
Denver, Colo., 1975.

HOUGH -- Hough, Wallace Irwin
Early Hough families of Bucks County, Pennsylvania. A
paper read by Wallace Irwin Hough before the Bucks County
historical society at Doylestown, Pa., May 4, 1935.
Bristol Printing. Bristol, Pa., 1935.

HOUSE -- Fritchey, John A., II
Leonard and Clarissa (Brown) House and their descendants:
the Butts, Losey, Casbeer families. Harrisburg, Pa., 1968.

HOUSEHOLDER -- Rogers, Bessie R.
Householders of America; a genealogy of the descen-   (A)
dants of Jonathan Householder of Butler, Pa. Salt
Lake City, Utah, 1947.

HOUSEHOLDER -- (Author unknown)
Householders of America; a genealogy (!) of Johannes
Hausshalter, an early inhabitant of Maryland and
Pennsylvania, with families from Pennsylvania and
elsewhere of Householder, Housholder and Haushalter.
2d. ed., with corrections and additional (sic). Salt
Lake City, Utah, 1948.

HOUSEMAN -- Frazier, Harry Houseman
The Houseman family of Westmoreland County, Pennsylvania.
Advertiser Press. Tiffin, Ohio, 1937.

HOUSTON -- Huston, E. Rankin
History of the Huston families and their descendants
1450-1912; with a genealogical record. Carlisle Printing.
Mechanicsburg, Pa., 1912.

HOUSTON -- Houston, W. Willis
Ancestry of Charles B. Houston with origin and   (P)
history of the family name. Philadelphia?, 1903?

HOWE --Whitley, Olga Rolater
The Howe line, Pennsylvania, South Carolina, Kentucky;
with connections, Dunlap, McKenzie, Patrick, and Biggers.
Commerce?, Tex., 1967.

HUBBELL -- Hubbell, Walter
The Hubbell family. Philadelphia, 1879.   (P)

HUBER -- Hoover, Harry M.
The Huber-Hoover family history. Scottdale, Pa., 1928.

HUBER -- Huber, David A.
   John Michael Huber and his descendants. Pennsburg,
Pa., 1931.

HUBER -- Shetter, Jacob H.
   Genealogy of the Huber family. H. Horton.   (A)
Philadelphia, Pa., 1924.

HUFFMAN -- Huffman, Clifford B.
   Huffman, 1763-1967. Lancaster, Pa., 1967.   (A)

HUFFMAN -- Huffman, Richard G.
   The Jacob Huffman (Hoffman) family. Unity Township,   (P)
Westmoreland Co., Pa., 1767-1968 (and) related
families: Siegfried, Harmon, Uphouse, Stough,
Gettemy. Whitney, Pa., 1968.

HUFFNAGLE -- Anderson, John A. and Harry D. Paxson
   Springdale - the Huffnagle mansion and its collection.
Read at the fall meeting of the Bucks County historical
society, held at the Huffnagle mansion, New Hope, Penna.,
Saturday, October 28, 1916. No city, 1916.

HUFSTEDLER -- Glaser, Lean J. K.
   Hufstedler family and allied families (believed to be   (P)
descendants of Michael Hochstaedter of the ship Harle,
1736). Philadelphia, 1974.

HUGHES -- Griffith, Margaret
   Hughes of Pennsylvania and allied families of Lee and
Cherrington ... Comp. from ms. notes of May S.
Mansfield. San Francisco, Calif., 1949.

HUGHES -- Hughes, Nancy G. (C.)
   Lineage, genealogy and history: Hughes family origin   (A)
in western Pa., Aten or Eaton family origin in
Brooklyn, N.Y... western Pa.; Blackburn family origin
in western Pa.; Shultz family origin in Ohio. No
city, no date.

HUGHES -- Seaver, J. Montgomery
   ... The Hughes genealogy. American Historical-
Genealogical Society. Philadelphia, 1929?

HUGHES -- Hughes Family
   Hugh Hughes (1790 Garthbeibio, Montgomeryshire, Wales-
Ebensburg, Pa., USA 1866 and his descendants. No
City, 1984.

HUIDEKOPER -- Huidekoper, Edgar
    Huidekoper; Holland family, 1730-1924 .... Meadville,
Pa., 1924.

HULME -- Ely, Warren S.
    History of four famous old families of Lower Bucks   (P)
    County. Bristol, Pa., 1915.

HUMPHREY -- Humphrey, Arthur Luther
    The Arthur Humphrey genealogy, also Morgan, Orcutt,   (A)
    Field, Fendrick, Shannon, Hopkins, Millard families.
Pittsburgh, Pa., 1926.

HUMPHREYS -- Carson, Hampton L.
    The Humphreys family of Haverford and Philadelphia.   (P)
Wickersham Press. Lancaster, Pa., 1922.

HUNSBERGER -- Hunsberger, Byron K.
    The Hunsbergers ... B. K. Hunsberger. Norristown,
Pa., 1925.

HUNSBERGER -- Hunsberger, Byron K.
    The Hunsbergers; a portion of thre genealogical history
    of a few Swiss Hunspergers (also spelled Huntsberger,
    Honsberger, Huntzberger). Huntsberger-Hunsberger Family
Association. Norristown, Pa., 1941.

HUNSICKER -- (Author unknown)
    A sketch of the inquiry into the legitimacy of Wm. H.   (N)
    and Chas. F. Hunsicker, great grand-children of
    Frederick Eberhardt. Allentown, Pa?, 1893?

HUNSICKER -- Hunsicker, Henry A.
    A genealogical history of the Hunsicker family. J. B.
Lippincott. Philadelphia, 1911.

HUNTER -- Green, Seymour L.
    Genealogy of descendants of John Hunter (1667/8-1734   (A)
    and Margaret (Albin) Hunter. Haverford, Pa., 1964.

HUNTER -- Seaver, J. Montgomery
    .... Hunter family records. American Historical-
Genealogical Society. Philadelphia, 1929.

HURLEY -- Huntsberry, Thomas Vincent
    The descendants of Thomas George Hurley, Sr. and Ellen
    Maroney, of County Cork, Ireland, and Susquehanna,
    Pennsylvania, U.S.A. T. V. Huntsberry. Baltimore,
Md., 1982.

HUSTON -- Huston, James Archibald
Genealogy of some branches of the families of Huston,
Wilson, Wilkin, Holmes, Wells, Whitaker, Brown.
Sewickley, Pa., 1914.

HUTCHINSON -- Colket, Meredith B.
The English ancestry of Anne Marbury Hutchinson and
Katherine Marbury Scott ... Magee Press. Philadelphia,
1936.

HUTTON -- Hutton, C. Osborne
Descendants of the Quaker Huttons of Pensylvania.   (P)
Mentor, Ohio, 1965.

HUTTON -- Hutton, Samuel J.
Records of the direct family lines of Ulric Hutton,   (A)
1855-1929 and Mary Brooke (Janney) Hutton 1864-1947.
S.B. Hutton. West Grove, Pa., 1970.

HUYARD -- Martin, Luke S.
Demographic study of the Isaac Huyard family,   (A)
Lancaster County, Pa. Princeton Theological Seminary.
Princeton, N.J., 1968.

HUYETT -- Whittaker, William Alexander
The Huyetts and their kin. Altoona?, Pa., 1952.

- I -

IMBRIE -- Imbrie, Boyd Vincent
Genealogy of the Imbrie family of western Pennsylvania, descendants of James Imbrie, pioneer settler, and his wife Euphemia Smart, by Addison Murray Imbrie, Esq. Pittsburgh, Pa., 1953.

INGERSOLL -- Ingersoll, R. Sturgis
Our parents; a family chronicle. Boyertown Pub. Co. Boyertown, Pa., 1973.

INGHAM -- Ingham, Joseph F.
Early days of the Ingham family in Bucks County. (A)
No city, no date.

INNES -- Innis, James Robert
Francis Innis: pioneer of the Tuscarora Valley. Juniata County, Pennsylvania, and his descendants: being principally a genealogy (sic) of the family which arose from James Innis, son of Francis: from research papers of the late Iona Geraldine Innis Austin, and of the compiler and others. J. R. Innis, Jr. Cincinnati, Ohio, 1982.

INSKEEP -- Wallace, Henry E.
Sketch of John Inskeep, mayor, and president of the (P)
Insurance Company of North America. Philadelphia, 1904.

IRWIN -- Cathell, Ralph W.
Erwin history in Bucks and Steuben Counties. Cathell. Doylestown, Pa., 1977.

IRWIN -- Irwin, S. D.
The Irwin family. Sketch of Richard Irwin, of Chester County, Pa., and his descendants. Evening News Print. Franklin, Pa., 1893.

IRVINE -- Wainwright, Nicholas B.
(The) Irvine story. Historical Society of (A)
Pennsylvania. Philadelphia, 1964.

ISENBERG -- Isenberg, J. M. S.
An historical sketch and genealogical record of the (P)
Isenberg family of Pennsylvania. Spring City?, Pa., 1900.

- J -

JACKSON -- Jackson, Halliday
     Proceedings of the sesqui-centennial gathering of the
     descendants of Isaac and Ann Jackson. Philadelphia,
     1878.

JACKSON --
     Proceedings of the sesqui-centennial gathering of the
     descendants of Isaac and Ann Jackson, at Harmony Grove,
     Chester Co., Pa., eighth month, twenty-fifth, 1875.
     Together with the family genealogy... Published
     by the Committee for the family. Philadelphia, 1878.

JACKSON -- Smith, Margaret Allen Higgins
     The Jackson family. Fox Chapel, Pa., 1974.

JACOB -- Jacob, Julian H.
     The descendants of John Jacob, Maryland pioneers and   (P)
     some allied families. Philadelphia, 1943.

JACOB -- Jacob, Julian H.
     Jacob and allied families. Philadelphia, 1945.   (A)

JACOBS -- Davids, Richard Wistar
     Jacobs family, as described from "John Jacobs of
     Perkiomen" to the ninth generation in America.
     Spangler & Davis. Philadelphia, 1894.

JACOBS -- Knipe, James Lloyd
     The Jacobs family of Windsor Township, York County,
     Pennsylvania. Lancaster, Pa., 1955.

JACOBY -- Jacoby, Henry Sylvester
     The Jacoby family genealogy; a record of the descendants
     of the pioneer, Peter Jacoby of Bucks County, Pennsylvania.
     Lancaster Press. Lancaster, Pa., 1930.

JACOX -- Jacox, Marilyn E.
     The Jacox and Burlingame families of Central and   (A)
     Northern New York. Pittsburgh, Pa., 1959.

JAMES -- Stapleton, Harriet R.
     Bushrod Washington James, M. D.; a biography comp. from the
     notes of Dr. James. Provident Life and Trust Company.
     Philadelphia, 1921.

JAMES -- James, Wynne
     The James family of Wales and Bucks County, Pa.,   (P)
     1638-1974. No city, 1974?

JAMES -- Wynne, James, III
  The James family of Wales and Bucks County, Pa.,
  1638-1974. Arlington, Va., 1975.

JANNEY -- (Author unknown)
  Janney family, comp. from pub. records and from material
  furnished by living descendants. Historical Publication
  Society. Philadelphia, 1939.

JANNEY -- Janney, Samuel M.
  The Janney family tree. Nine generations of the descendants
  of Thomas Janney of Bucks County, Pennsylvania. No city,
  no date.

JANNEY -- Janney, Samuel M.
  Memoirs of Samuel M. Janney, late of Lincoln, Loudon
  County, Va. Philadelphia, 1881.

JANNEY -- White, Miles
  The Quaker Janneys of Cheshire and their progenitors.
  No city, no date.

JAQUETT -- Jaquett, Joseph
  Letter to his attorneys, 1845, and obituary notice of   (P)
  June 2nd, 1869. Philadelphia, no date.

JAQUETT -- Sellers, Edwin Jaquett
  Genealogy of the Jaquett family. Philadelphia, 1896.

JAQUETT -- Sellers, Edwin Jaquett
  Genealogy of the Jaquett family. Rev. Ed. Allen, Lane &
  Scott. Philadelphia, 1907.

JAQUETT - Sellers, Edwin Jaquett
  Supplement to genealogies. Allen, Lane & Scott,
  Philadelphia, 1922.

JAUDON -- Sellers, Edwin Jaquett
  An account of the Jaudon family. J. B. Lippincott.
  Philadelphia, 1890.

JEFFERIS -- Cope, Gilbert
  The Jefferis family. West Chester, Pa., 1869.   (P)

JEFFERYS -- (Author unknown)
  Jefferys of Worcestershire Nevis, Philadelphia. No
  city, 1939.

JEFFRIES -- Jefferys, Edward Miller
  Jefferys of Worcestershire, Nevis, Philadelphia ...
  Philadelphia, 1939.

JENKINS --
    <u>Jenkins family</u>. The Historical Publication Society.   (P)
    Philadelphia, 1932.

JENKINS -- Seaver, J. Montgomery
    <u>... Jenkins family records</u>. American Historical-
    Genealogical Society. Philadelphia, 1928?

JOHN -- John, William
    <u>John; descendants of Nicholas John who came from the</u>
    <u>province of Wales, Europe, to York County, Pennsylvania,</u>
    <u>A.D. 1648</u>. Riverside, Calif., 1903.

JOHNSON -- Horton , Lucien Ball
    <u>Johnson family ... based largely on the manuscipt</u>   (P)
    <u>of Roberta Stockton Benton Horton (Mrs. Lucien</u>
    <u>Ball Horton)</u>. The Historical Pub. Society.
    Philadelphia, 1933.

JOHNSON -- Johnson, Ralph Linwood
    <u>Genealogical studies of some Providence families</u>
    <u>(and their connections)</u>. Pennsburg, Pa., 1934.

JOHNSON -- Johnson, Ralph
    <u>A personal report on the Johnson-McGinnis family lineage</u>
    <u>of Washington and Greene County, Pa., 1605-1974</u>.
    Johnson. Philadelphia, 1975.

JOHNSON --Johnson, Robert W.
    <u>The ancestry of Rosalie Morris Johnson, daughter of</u>   (P)
    <u>George Calvert Morris ad Elizabeth Kuhn, his wife</u>.
    Ferris & Leach. Philadelphia, 1905-08.

JOHNSON -- Johnson, Robert Winder
    <u>The Johnson family and allied families of Lincolnshire,</u>
    <u>England</u>. Philadelphia, 1934.

JOHNSTON -- Johnston, A. R.
    <u>An incomplete directory of the descendants of my great-</u>
    <u>grandparents</u>. United Evangelical Church. Harrisburg,
    Pa., 1915.

JOHNSTON -- Parsons, N. Vincent
    <u>Johnston-Horning families: ancestors and descendants of</u>
    <u>Hugh Johnston, 1801-1847 & Jane L. Morrison, 1809-1866,</u>
    <u>John Horning, 1783-1851 & Elizabeth Vance, 1787-1828 of</u>
    <u>McVeytown, Mifflin County, Pennsylvania</u>. Holland,
    Mich., 1980.

JOLLIFFE -- Jolliffe, William
    Historical genealogical and biographical account of the
    Jolliffe family of Virginia, 1652 to 1893. Philadelphia,
    1893.

JONES - (Author unknown)
    Genealogical notes. Allegheny, Pa., 1910.

JONES -- (Author unknown)
    Genealogical notes: Joseph and Lydia (Roberts)   (P)
    Jones, of Gwynedd, Philadelphia County, Pennsylvania;
    John and Mary (Stall) Jones, of Vincent Township,
    Chester County ... Jesse and Elizabeth (Frick)
    Jones, of Vincent Township. Chester Co... Allegheny,
    Pa., 1910.

JONES -- Beale, Mrs. Ellen M.
    Genealogy of David Jones. Comp. by his great-great-
    granddaughter, Mrs. Ellen M. Beale. B. F. Owen & Co.
    Reading, Pa., 1903.

JONES -- Jones, E. R. (Mary)
    A genealogy of the family of Cereno Upham Jones of   (N)
    Weymouth, Nova Scotia (a descendant of Lewis Jones
    of Roxbury, Mass.). Allen, Lane. Philadelphia, 1905.

JONES -- Miles, George K.
    Descendants of Joseph and Lydia (Roberts) Jones, thru (P)
    son, Joseph Jones of Pikeland, Chester County, Pa.
    Allegheny, Pa., 1911.

JONES -- Rife, Lee Erasmus
    A record of the ancestors and descendants of Erasmus Jones
    and his wife, Mary Sellers Jones. Philadelphia, 1936.

JUKE -- Winship, A. E.
    Jukes-Edwards; a study in education and heredity.
    R. L. Myers & Co. Harrisburg, Pa., 1900.

- K -

KAGY -- Keagy, Franklin
A history of the Kagy relationship in America from
1715 to 1900. Harrisburg, Pa., 1899.

KALTREIDER -- Rohrbaugh, Nova Romaine Kaltreider
Urias Kaltreider family history. Kopy Kat Print.
Center. Hanover, Pa., 1972.

KANAGY -- Kanagy, Ezra J.
Family register of John H. (and) Gertrude (Yoder)   (A)
Kanagy (1817-1868) and his lineal descendants...
Berlin Pub. Berlin, Pa., 1964.

KAPROV -- Gillman, Joseph M.
The B'nai Khaim in America; a study of cultural change
in a Jewish group. Dorrance. Philadelphia, 1969.

KASTNER -- Castner, S.
The Kastner or Castner family of Pennsylvania.
Philadelphia, 1901.

KAUFFMAN -- Kauffman, Stanley Duane
Christian Kauffman, his descendants and his people.
Gateway Press. Baltimore, Md., 1980.

KAUFMAN -- (Author unknown)
The Kauffman family of Adams and Franklin Counties,
Pennsylvania, since 1800 A.D.; a brief lineage of the
children, grandchildren and great-grandchildren of
Leonard M. Kauffman, and his wife, Polly M. Carbaugh
through their son Isaac Martin Kauffman, and his wife,
Christina Naomi Baker and their children Elmira, Samantha,
Clara, Ida, Nettie, Murray, Harvey, Edward, Albert and
George. Harrisburg, Pa., 1963.

KAUFMAN -- Kauffman, Charles Fahs
A genealogy and history of the Kauffman-Coffman families
of North America, 1584 to 1937; including brief outlines
of allied Swiss and Palatine families who were among the
pioneer settlers in Lancaster and York Counties of
Pennsylvania from 1717 on; viz., Becker, Baer, Correll,
Erisman, Fahs, Kuntz, Kneisley, Hershey, Hiestand, Meyers,
Musselman, Neff, Martin, Ruby, Snavely, Shenk, Shirk,
Sprenkle, Witmer, and others. York, Pa., 1940.

KAUFMAN -- Kauffman, Robert Terry
     Lineages of the Murray M. Kauffman and Daniel Hollinger
     families of Adams and Franklin Counties, Pennsylvania,
     1696-1963. Harrisburg?, Pa., 1963.

KEAGY -- Keagy, Franklin
     A history of the Kagy relationship in America, from
     1715 to 1900. Harrisburg Publishing Co. Harrisburg,
     Pa., 1899.

KEAN -- (Author unknown)
     Autobiography of Captain John Kean of Harrisburg.
     Harrisburg Pub. Co. Harrisburg, Pa., 1888.

KEARNS -- Greene, David L.
     The Kearns family of Decatur and Derry Townships, Mifflin
     County, Pennsylvania. Demorest, Ga., 1979.

KEARSLEY -- White, Elmer L.
     The descendants of Jonathan Kearsley, 1718-1782, and his
     wife Jane Kearsley, 1720-1801, (from Scotland) who settled
     at Carlisle, Penna. Died at Shippensburg, Pa. and are
     buried at Middle Spring church yard, Cumberland County,
     Pa. Pittsburgh?, Pa., 1900.

KEATOR -- Keator, Alfred Decker
     Three centuries of the Keator family in America. American
     Historical Co. New York, N.Y., 1955.

KEATOR -- Keator, Alfred Decker
     Keator family in America. Harrisburg, Pa., 1961.

KEEN -- Keen, Gregory B.
     The descendants of Joran Kyn of New Sweden. The Swedish
     Colonial Society. Philadelphia, 1913.

KEIM -- Keim, De B. Randolph
     The Keim and allied families in America and Europe ...
     a monthly serial of history, biography, genealogy and
     folklore, illustrating the causes, circumstances and
     consequences of the German, French and Swiss emigrations
     to America during the 17th, 18th and 19th centuries.
     Harrisburg, Pa., 1899-(1900).

KELKER -- Kelker, Rudolph E.
     A record of the family of Kelker since their arrival
     in this country, in 1743. Harrisburg, Pa., 1883.

KELKER -- Kelker, Rudolph F.
Genealogisches verzeichniss de familie Kolloker von
Herrliberg, bezirk Meilen, kanton Zurich in der Schweitz,
abgefast in sommer 1849, durch John Jacob Hess...
(Translation of above) Genealogical record of the family
of Koelliker of Herrliburg, district of Meilen, canton
Zurich, Switzerland, completed in summer of 1849...
Added a record of the family of Kelker, since their
arrival in this country in 1743, comp. from authentic
sources, for the use of the members of the family.
L. S. Hart. Harrisburg, Pa., 1883.

KELLER -- Pierson, Susan Hewitt
Pennsylvania roots and spreading branches: genealogy of
allied lines, Keller, Leckenton, Page (Barge), 1721-1980.
Central Graphics. St. James, Mn., 1981?

KELLER -- Shumaker, Edward Seitz
Descendants of Henry Keller of York County, Pennsylvania and
Fairfield County, Ohio. E. S. Shumaker. Indianapolis,
Ind., 1924.

KELLEY -- Bell, Raymond Martin
James Kelly of Letterkenny Twp., Franklin Co., Pa., and
his descendants. Washington, Pa., 1973.

KELLEY -- Delaney, Edmund T. K.
The Kellys: printmakers of New York and Philadelphia
(1864-1881. Connecticut River Publications.
Chester, Conn., 1984.

KELLEY -- Lewis, Arthur H.
Those Philadelphia Kellys, with a touch of Grace. Morrow.
New York, N. Y., 1977.

KEMMERER -- Kemmerer Family Association
Two centuries of Kemmerer family history, 1730-1929.
Searle & Bachman Co. Allentown, Pa., 1929.

KEMPER -- McComb, Virginia M.
Kemper records. Chambersburg, Pa., 1946.

KEMPER -- McComb, Virgnia Mary
Kemper records (1946). A supplement to The Kemper
family (1899). Chambersburg?, Pa., 1946.

KENDERDINE -- Kenderdine, Thaddeus S.
The Kenderdines of America; being a genealogical and   (P)
historical account of the descendants of Thomas
Kenderdine of Montgomeryshire, Wales, who, two
hundred years ago, settled in Philadelphia County.
Doylestown Pub. Co. Doylestown, Pa., 1901.

KENNEDY -- Kennedy, Elias Davidson
History of the descendants of William Kennedy and his
wife Mary or Marian Henderson, from 1730 to 1880,
carried down by numbers. To which is added the meaning
of the name Kennedy, with some facts connected with their
history in Scotland and Ireland. H. B. Ashmead.
Philadelphia, 1881.

KENNEDY -- Kennedy, Russell
Genealogical descendants of David and Jane Greacen Kennedy,
1783-1919. Pittsburgh, Pa., 1919?

KENNEDY -- Seaver, J. Montgomery
The Kennedy family records. American Historical-
Genealogical Society. Philadelphia, 1929.

KENNER -- Cleveland, Paul Wood
Kenner; a compilation of family letters and data pertaining
to the Kenner and related families, their early life in
Virginia and subsequent years after migration to Ohio.
Erie, Pa., 1966.

KEPPEL -- (Author unknown)
Some early Keppel families: Keppel's of Pennsylvania,
Maryland, North Carolina. Various spellings: Keppel,
Keppele, Kepple, Kappel, Koeppel, Koppel, Copple,
Coppel, etc. Hollis, N. Y., 1952?

KERN -- Greene, David L.
The Kearns family of Decatur and Derry Townships,
Mifflin County, Pennsylvania. D. L. Green. Demorest,
Ga., 1979.

KERN -- Kern, Tilden H.
Kern family history. Mill Run, Pa., 1960.

KERR -- Kerr, Thomas B.
James Kerr, of Washington County, Pennsylvania, and his
descendants, 1782-1909. Englewood, N.J., 1909.

KERSHNER -- Kershner, George C.
History of the Kershner family. Berne, Pa., 1949.

KERSHNER -- Kershner, George C.
   History of the Kershner family.   Berne, Pa., 197?

KERSHNER -- Kershner, George C.
   History of the Kershner family (of Windsor Township,
   Berks County, Pennsylvania).   Kershner Family Association.
   Charlotte, N.C., 1983.

KEYSER -- Keyser, Charles S.
   ... The Keyser family; descendants of Dirch Keyser of
   Amsterdam.   W. F.Fell & Co.   Philadelphia, 1889.

KICHLINE -- Kichline, Thomas J.
   The Kichlines in America, prepared by Thomas J. Kichline,
   president of the Kichline family association and read by
   him before the Northampton County historical and
   genealogical society in Easton, Pa., under date of
   January 15, 1926, at 8 p.m., at the home of Frank C.
   Williams.   Easton?, Pa., 1926.

KIDDOO -- Simmons, Kiddoo P.
   A history of the Kiddoo family in the United States,   (N)
   1780-1938 ...   Grove City?, Pa., 1938?

KIEBLER -- Kiebler, Bertha A.
   Our Kieblers of Pennsylvania and auxiliary lines.
   B. A. Kiebler.   No city, 1984.

KIEFFER -- (Author unknown)
   Kieffer genealogy, descendants of Michael Kieffer who
   came to America in 1773 and settled in Pennsylvania.
   No city, no date.

KIMBALL -- Schneider, Mr. & Mrs. John H.
   Genealogy of Jacob Kimble of the Paupack settlements, Wayne
   and Pike County (sic) Pa., and his descendants with information on the allied families of Ridgway and Ansley.
   Accurate Law Print. Co.   No city, 1952.

KIMBER -- Kimber, Sidney A.
   The descendants of Richard Kimber. A genealogical history
   of the descendants of Richard Kimber, of Grove, near
   Wantage, Berkshire, England - Containing the families in
   the United States from the settlements in Pennsylvania and
   New York, the families in England, and the descendants in
   Australia.   S. A. Kimber.   Boston, 1894.

KING -- Chandler, Catherine Soleman
   A history of the King, Armstrong and allied families
   (Pennsylvania to Columbiana County, Ohio).   No city,
   1964.

KING -- King, Wilbur Lewis
<u>Genealogy: Jacob King (Konig) and Matheus King (Konig)</u>
<u>of Northampton County, Pennsylvania</u>. Bethlehem, Pa.,
1951 (i.e. 1952).

KING -- King, Wilbur Lewis
<u>Knauss genealogy; Luke Knauss (1633-1713) of Delsheim,</u>
<u>Germany, and his American descendants</u>. Bethlehem, Pa.,
1930.

KING -- Shue, Richard
<u>The Kings of York County: pioneers, patriots, and</u>
<u>paper-makers</u>. York?, Pa., 1959-1960.

KINGSBURY -- Kingsbury, Joseph Addison
<u>... A pendulous edition of Kingsbury genealogy, gathered</u>
<u>by Rev. Addison Kingsbury ...</u> Murdoch-Kerr Press.
Pittsburgh, Pa., 1901.

KINSINGER -- Kinsinger, Paul J.
<u>Family record of Peter Kinsinger and his descendants</u>   (A)
<u>as of April 1, 1974</u>. Meyersdale, Pa., 1974.

KIRK -- Cope, Gilbert
<u>Genealogy of the Kirk family, descended from John</u>   (P)
<u>Kirk of Alfreton, Derbyshire and Darby, Pa.</u> West
Chester, Pa., no date.

KIRK -- Johnston, William H.
<u>The descendants of John (1774-1841) & Tibatha Kirk</u>   (P)
<u>(1789-1882) of Abington Township, Montgomerty County,</u>
<u>Pennsylvania</u>. Skippack, Pa., 1972.

KIRK -- Roberts, Miranda S.
<u>Genealogy of the descendants of John Kirk, born 1660, at</u>
<u>Alfreton, in Derbyshire, England. Died 1705, in Darby</u>
<u>Township, Chester (now Delaware) County, Pennsylvania</u>.
Press of the Intelligencer. Doylestown, Pa., 1912-13.

KIRK -- Stubbs, Charles H. M.D.
<u>Historic-genealogy of the Kirk family, as established</u>
<u>by Roger Kirk, who settled in Notingham, Chester</u>
<u>County, province of Pennsylvania, about the year 1714 ...</u>
Wylie & Griest. Lancaster, Pa., 1872.

KIRKPATRICK -- (One of the descendants)
<u>Major Abraham Kirkpatrick and his descendants</u>. J. P.
Durbin. Pittsburgh, Pa., 1911.

KIRKPATRICK -- Bigham, Kirk Q.
   Major Abraham Kirkpatrick and his descendants.
   Pittsburgh, Pa., 1911.

KIRKPATRICK -- Blackburn, Rev. Wm. M.
   The Kirkpatrick memorial; or, Biographical sketches of
   father and son, and a selection from the sermons of the
   Rev. Jacob Kirkpatrick, Jr., the sketches by the Rev.
   George Hale, D.D. Westcott & Thompson. Philadelphia,
   1867.

KIRKPATRICK -- Hale, George
   The Kirkpatrick memorial. Philadelphia, 1867.

KITZMILLER -- (Author unknown)
   Descendants of John Kitzmiller, of Lancaster County,   (A)
   Pa. and John Jacob Kitzmiller, of York County, Pa.
   Muscatine, Iowa, 1953.

KITZMILLER -- Bishop, Jerome C.
   The Kitzmiller family in Pennsylvania before 1800.   (A)
   Muscatine, Iowa, 1959.

KITZMILLER -- Rettew, Edward W.
   Genealogy of the Emanuel Kitzmiller branch of the   (P)
   Kitzmillr family. Reading, Pa., 1961.

KLAUDER -- Klauder, Alexander L. A.
   Genealogy of the Klauder family, Rhenish-German and   (P)
   American branch. Malone, N.Y., or Philadelphia, 1929.

KLECKNER -- (Author unknown)
   The Klechner-Fessler families in Berks, Schuylkill,
   Northampton, and Lancaster Counties, Pennsylvania.
   No city, 1957.

KLEE -- Shaw, Don C.
   A genealogy and history of some of the descendants of
   Johan Nicholas Klee of Bern Township, Berks County,
   Pennsylvania; Clays of Pennsylvania Dutch ancestry.
   Chicago, Ill., 1968.

KLEINGINNA -- Seeley, Ralph M.
   Johannes Kleinjenni (Kleinginna) of Berks County, Pa.   (N)
   and some of his descendants. Candor, N.Y., 1959.

KLEPPINGER -- Kleppinger, Carl T.
   Johann Georg Kloppinger von Pfungstadt. Kleppinger.   (A)
   Allentown, Pa., 1963.

KLEPPINGER -- Kleppinger, Stanley J.
Kleppinger-Clippinger family history. Bethlehem Printing
Co. Bethlehem, Pa., 1928.

KLEPPINGER -- Jeremiah, Stabley

KLINE -- Historical Society (H. J. Young, Genealogist)
Kline and Little families of York and Adams Counties, (A)
Pennsylvania. The Society. York, Pa.?, 1934.

KLINGER -- Bowman, Mary E.
Records of the Klinger Church, Dauphin County, (P)
Pennsylvania; including the Bowman and Klinger
families. The Bookmark. Knightstown, Ind., 1975.

KLUNK -- Wood, Charles R.
The Klunk (Clunk) family. C. R.Wood. Coatesville,
Pa., 1979.

KNARR -- Reeser, Nellie Wallace
Daniel Knarr and Lucinda Ault? York, Pa., 1955.

KNAUER -- Helfferich, Anna Knauer
The Knauerton story. A. K. Helfferich. Knauerton,
Pa., 1982.

KNEASS -- Magee, Miss Anna J.
... Memorials of the Kneass family of Philadelphia.
No city, no date.

KNEISLY -- Kneisly, Harry Loren
Kneisly genealogy, copyright ... Including the names of
685 descendants, and relatives of the earliest residents
in America of whom records have been obtained, and
references to 150 others believed to be related ...
Miller Printing and Lithographing. Reading, Pa., 1932.

KNEPP -- Wagler, Mary (K.)
Family record of Abraham Knepp and his descendants. (A)
Print Shop. Gordonville, Pa., 1973.

KNEPPER -- Knepper, Laura M.
Knepper families in Pennsylvania. San Diego, Calif.,
1950.

KNICKERBOCKER -- Martin, George Castor
The Knickerbacker or Knickerbocker family. Martin &
Allardyce. Frankford, Pa., 1912.

KNIGHT -- Knight, Charles W.
A genealogy of all the descendants of Ephriam Knight through John Knight. Philadelphia?, 1956.

KNIPE -- Knipe, James Lloyd
Early Knipe families of Pennsylvaia (including the male line of descent to the present generation). Lancaster, Pa., 1949.

KOCH -- (Author unknown)
Thirty ancestors of Richard Henry Koch, 1939. J. F. Seiders Printing. Pottsville, Pa., 1939.

KOHL -- Foster, Mary K.
The three sisters. Philadelphia, 1978.

KOLB -- Cassel, Daniel Kolb
A genealogical history of the Kolb, Kulp, or Culp family and its branches in America. Norristown, Pa., 1895.

KOLLOCK -- Hill, J. Bennett
The New England descendants of Cornelius Kollock   (P)
of Delaware. Wynnewood, Pa., 1961.

KOLLOCK -- Sellers, Edwin Jaquett
Genealogy of the Kollock family of Sussex County, Delaware, 1657-1897. J. B. Lippincott. Philadelphia, 1897.

KOONTZ -- Smith, Ione R. Card
Germany, Baden-Wurrtemberg (i.e. Wurttemberg) Catholic church vital records: Reichenbach (Busenbach), 1762-1869, Pfaffenrot (Burbach, Marxwell), 1810-1869, Schielberg (Frauenalb), (includes a few Evangelical records from Bretten): Kun(t)z families, several to Cambria County, Penn. I. C. Smith. Elkhorn, Neb., 1984.

KORNMAN -- Cornman, Charles Albert
Genealogical record of descendants of Ludwig Kornman, Sr., in America. The Sentinel. Carlisle, Pa., 1916.

KORNS -- Korns, Charles Byron
The genealogy of Michael Korns, Sr., of Somerset   (P)
County, Pennsylvania. Berlin Publishing Co. Berlin, Pa., 1949.

KRAMER -- Kramer, William E. (and) Joseph J. Kramer
The Kramer clan; a genealogical (sic) and biographical
record of its families in the State of Pennsylvania,
beginning in the year 1732, with the first German
Kramer pioneers. No city, 1961.

KRAMM -- Patton, Alfreda
David Kramm. York, Pa., 1978.

KRAYBILL -- Kraybill, Spencer L.
History of the Kraybill family in America, 1754-1972.   (A)
Essinger Print. Adamstown, Pa., 1972.

KREADY -- Kready, Norman B.
Genealogy of the Kready from the first emigrant to   (P)
this country to the present time ... Kready.
Manheim, Pa., 1976.

KRESGE -- Kunkle, E. T.
The Kresge family. Stroudsburg, Pa., 1926.

KRIDER -- Hewlett, Joseph M.
The Krider (Grieder) family of Philadelphia. The   (P)
ancestors and descendants of Margaret (Grieder)
Rorer, John Krider, Martin Grieder. Wyncote, Pa.,
1959.

KRINER -- Hege, Jacob W.
History of the Kriner family. Williamson, Pa., 1913.   (A)

KRESSEN -- Von Frank, Karl F.
Die Kressen... Amerikanischen Biographien von   (P)
Charles R. Roberts. Allentown, Pa., no date.

KRETZ -- Gretz, Julius
Kretzenbuch; Familiengeschichte der Kretz, Gretz,   (A)
Kratz, Gratz und verwandter Linien ... Bruchsal ...
1933.

KRETZING -- Wright, Jeffrey L.
History of the Kretzing and Lyons families of   (P)
Perry County, Pa. ... Perry Co., Pa., 1970.

KRUG -- Krug, Paul William
Krug history. Hanover, Pa., 1975.

KRUMBHARR -- (Author unknown)
Krumbharr family; one of the series of sketches to   (P)
be embraced in the "Old Philadelphia families." ...
The Historical Publications Society. Philadelphia,
1932.

KRUMREIN -- Kocher, Frank
    <u>The family of Johann Stephen Krumrein</u>. State   (P)
    College, Pa., 19__.

KRUSE -- Krebs, Ebba Victoria
    <u>Family sketches</u>. J. B. Lippincott. Philadelphia, 1924.

KUHN -- (Author unknown)
    <u>Kuhn families of York County, Pa.</u> Wichita, Kansas,   (A)
    1945.

KUHN -- Black, Helen K. (J.)
    <u>Kuhn (Coon) family of Allegheny Co., Pa.; with</u>   (A)
    <u>reprint of History and genealogy of the Kuhn family,</u>
    <u>by David Kuhn, 1910 ... and Statler and Sites ancestry</u>.
    Audibon, Iowa, 1956.

KUHN -- Venable, Clara
    <u>Peter Kuhn</u>. Harrisburg, Pa., 1953.

KUHN -- McTeer, Frances Davis
    <u>Coon-Gohn descendants from Chanceford Township, York</u>
    <u>County, Pennsylvania</u>. McTeer. Holiday, Fla., 1979.

KULP -- (Author unknown)
    <u>Kulp family, descendants of Samuel and Catherine</u>   (A)
    <u>(Kolb) Kulp</u>. Feroe Print. Pottstown, Pa., 1966.

KULP -- Cassell, Daniel Kolb
    <u>A genealogical history of the Kolb, Kulp or Culp</u>
    <u>family, and its branches in America, with biographical</u>
    <u>sketches of their descendants, from the earliest</u>
    <u>available records from 1707 to the present time,</u>
    <u>including Dielman Kolb in Germany ...</u> M. R. Wills.
    Norristown, Pa., 1895.

KUNKEL -- Shannon, David Theodore
    <u>The Conkles of German Solitude</u>. Shannon. Hatborough,
    Pa., 1979.

KURTZ -- Kinsinger, Ray S.
    <u>Family record of John H. Kurtz and his descendants</u>.   (A)
    Berlin Pub. Co. Berlin, Pa., 1952.

KURTZ -- Redcay, Ruth K. (M.)
    <u>Descendants of Jacob S. and Lydia Mast Kurtz</u>.   (A)
    Elverson, Pa., 1970.

KYN -- Keen, Gregory B.
    <u>The descendants of Joran Kyn of New Sweden</u>.   (P)
    Historical Society of Pa. Philadelphia, 1878-1883.

- L -

LAIDLAW -- Gordon, Cynthia
 <u>American origins</u>. Easton, Pa., 1978.   (P)

LAMB -- Lamb, James B.
 <u>What is known about the direct line of the Lamb</u>   (P)
 <u>family from Pearce Lamb to John Emerson Lamb and</u>
 <u>his descendants to the present year ... 1962</u>.
 Philadelphia, 1962.

LAMBERT -- Rathgeber, John F.
 <u>Biography and family record of John Michail Lambert</u>.   (P)
 Freemansburg, Pa., 1893.

LAMBING -- By a member of the family
 <u>Michael Anthony and Anne Shields-Lambing; their</u>
 <u>ancestors and their descendants</u>. Fahey & Co.
 Pittsburgh, Pa., 1896.

LAMBORN -- Lamborn, Samuel
 <u>The genealogy of the Lamborn family</u>. Philadelphia, 1894.

LAMBORN -- Rowe, Richard L.
 <u>Records and memories of the Lamborn genealogy</u>.   (A)
 Philadelphia?, 1925.

LAMM -- Lamm, Sterling
 <u>Lamm family</u>. Reading, Pa., 1970?   (A)

LAMONT --La Mont, James H.
 <u>Genealogy of the La Mont family from 1755</u>.   (A)
 Granville Centre, Pa?, 1903.

LANCASTER -- Lancaster, Harry Fred
 <u>The Lancaster family. A history of Thomas and Phebe</u>
 <u>Lancaster, of Bucks County, Pennsylvania, and their</u>
 <u>descendants, from 1711 to 1902. Also a sketch on the</u>
 <u>origin of the name and family in England ...</u>
 A. J. Hoover. Huntington, Ind., 1902.

LANDES -- Landes, Henry S.
 <u>Descendants of Jacob Landes of Salford Township,</u>
 <u>Montgomery County, Pennsylvania</u>. Soudertown, Pa.,
 1943.

LANDIS -- Landis, D. B.
The Landis family of Lancaster County, a comprehensive
history of the Landis folk from the martyrs' era to the
arrival of the first Swiss settlers, giving their
numerous lineal descendants; also, an accurate record
of members in the rebellion, with a sketch of the start
and subsequent growth of Landisville and Landis Valley,
and a complete dictionary of living Landis adults ...
Lancaster, Pa., 1888.

LANDIS -- Landis Family Reunion Assoc.
Reunion of the Landis family. 1st - 1911-. Lancaster,
Pa., no date.

LANDIS -- Landis, Ira D.
The Landis family book. Lancaster, Pa., 1950, 1954.

LANDIS -- Landis, Norman A. and H. K. Stoner
The Landis genealogy, with an historical outline by
James B. Landis. Berlin Pub. Co. Berlin, Pa., 1935.

LANDRETH -- Leach, Frank W.
Landreth family; one of the series of sketches   (P)
written by Frank Willing Leach for the Philadelphia
North America, 1907-1913, and brought down to date.
The Historical Pub. Soc. Philadelphia, 1933.

LANMAN -- Stone, Don Charles
The Lanman family; the descendants of Samuel Landman of
Boston, Massachusetts, 1687, with data on the Boylston
family in England and America. Lancaster, Pa., 1968.

LAPP --Blosser, Sadie E.
Family history of Isaac and Elizabeth Lapp. S. E.
Blosser. Pennsylvania?, 1979.

LAPSLEY -- Froehlich, Dean
Thomas Lapsley: a 1772 settler in southwestern
Pennsylvania. D. Froehlich. No city, 1983.

LARGE -- Armstrong, W. C.
Albert Large, the hermit naturalist of Bucks Co.,   (A)
Pa. J. Heidingsfeld. New Brunswick, N.J., 1932.

LARGE -- Cook, Lewis D.
Ancestors and descendants of John B. and Sarah W.   (P)
(Meade) Large of Philadelphia. No city, 1948.

LARIMER -- Mellon, Rachel H. L.
   The Larimer, McMasters and allied families, also Sheakley,
   McCurdy, Creighton, Hughey, King, McLaughlin, Irwin,
   families. Philadelphia, 1903.

LA RUE -- Davis, William W. H.
   The La Rue family, Bucks County, Pennsylvania.   (P)
   Lewis Pub. Co. No city, 1805 (i.e. 1905).

LARZELERE - Du Bin, Alexander
   Larzelere family and collateral lines of Elkinton,
   Stockton, Brigham, Carpenter. Historical Publication
   Society. Philadelphia, 1950.

LASHELLS -- Ault, Alden
   Lashells of Conewago and Buffalo Valley, Pennsylvania:
   descendants of George Lashells (1756-1844). Ruth
   Foster Viggers. Decorah, Iowa, 1985.

LATTA -- Nassau, Robert Hamill
   Crowned in palm-land. A story of African mission life ...
   J. B. Lippincott. Philadelphia, 1874.

LAUDER -- Lauder, Margaret E.
   The Lauder family in America: a history of the   (A)
   decendants of Adam and Janet (Davidson) Lauder of
   Roxboroughshire, Scotland and of Schenectady County,
   New York ... Lauder. Ridgway, Pa., 1975.

LAUFFER -- Lauffer, Joseph A.
   The Lauffer history. Greensburg, Pa., 1906.

LAUGHLIN -- Laughlin, Mary A.
   History of the Prather, Shank, Royer, Laughlin   (A)
   families. Greencastle, Pa., 1955.

LAUX -- Laux Family Association
   ... Two hundred and first anniversary of the founding   (N)
   of the Laux family in America. York, Pa., 1911.

LEA -- Lea, James Henry
   The ancestry and posterity of John Lea. Philadelphia,
   1906.
LEDLIE -- Laughlin, Ledlie I.
   Joseph Leslie and William Moody. Pittsburgh, Pa., 1961.

LEE -- Dean, Cynthia A.
   "My Lee family of Fayette County, Pennsylvania", currently
   back to 1812: ancestors of Christian Renee Dean-Schnaible.
   C. A. Dean. Santa Clara, Calif., 1982.

LEE -- Lee, Edmund Jennings
Lee of Virginia, 1642-1892. Philadelphia, 1895.

LEE -- Lea, James Henry and George Henry Lea
The ancestry and posterity of John Lea, of Christian
Malford, Wiltshire, England, and of Pennsylvania in
America, 1503-1906. Lea Brothers & Co. Philadelphia,
1906.

LEE --
Memoir of Benjamin Lee. Address to his grandchildren by his
son Alfred Lee .... J. B. Lippincott. Philadelphia, 1875.

LEE -- Seaver, J. Montgomery
The Lee genealogy. Philadelphia, 194_.

LEE -- Smith, Earl Lee
Descendants & ancestors of Charles & Fanny Crandall Lee:
a Lee tree. E. L. Smith. Middleburg, Pa., 1985.

LEEDOM -- Eachus, Sara Ann Leedom
The Leedom family. Bryn Mawr, Pa., 1982.

LEEDOM -- Lefferts, Arthur Francis
Leedom genealogy; descendants of John Leedom and Elizabeth
Potts of Pennsylvania, from 1824 to 1953. Jenkintown?,
Pa., 1953.

LEEDS -- Leeds, Benjamin Franklin
Thomas Leeds, an Englishman, settled at Shrewsbury, N.J.,
probably 1677. Philadelphia, 1886.

LEESE -- Leese, Charles
The Lawrence Leese family history; two centuries in
America (1741-1941); a biographical and genealogical
history of Lawrence Leese and his descendants from the
time of his arrival in the city of Philadelphia through
a period of two hundred years down to the ninth
generation. Roberts Printing Co. Frankfort, Ky., 1941.

LEFEVRE -- Le Fevre, George Newton
The Pennsylvania Le Fevres. Le Fevre Cemetery and
Historical Association. Strasburg, Pa., 1952.

LEFFERTS -- Lefferts, Arthur F.
The Old York Road branch of the Lefferts family tree.
Jenkinstown?, Pa., 1952.

LEHMAN -- Thomas R.
　　A tree in a forest: Linneaus Sheetz Lehman (1862-1918)
　　and Alice Baseshore Brandt (1865-1947): their ancestors
　　and descendants. T. R. Lehman. Pennsylvania?, 1985.

LEHMAN -- Spessard, Howard L.
　　A brief history of the Lehman family and genealogical (P)
　　register of the descendants of Peter Lehman of Lancaster
　　County, Pennsylvania... Hagerstown, Md., 1961.

LEIBENSPERGER -- Leibensperger, Elmer I.
　　History and genealogy of the Leibensperger family,
　　descendants of John George Leipersberger and Catherine.
　　Leibensperger Family Association. Kutztown, Pa., 1943.

LEIBY -- Leiby, Blanche
　　Leiby genealogy. Tamaqua, Pa., 1956.

LEIBY -- Rupp, Margaret Leiby Glanding
　　The Leiby-Lambert lineage. York, Pa., 1952-1953.

LEIDY -- (Author unknown)
　　Leidy family ... Historical Pub. Soc. Philadelphia,　　(N)
　　1934.

LEIDY --
　　Lieut. Col. Jacob Reed; proceedings at the dedication
　　of the monument erected to his memory in Franconia
　　Township, Pennsylvania, under the auspices of the
　　Historical Society of Montgomery County, Pennsylvania,
　　October 8, 1901. Norristown, Pa., 1905.

LEIGHTY -- Leighty, Floyd Harold
　　The genealogy of the Jacob Leighty family in Fayette
　　County, Pennsylvania. F. H. Leighty. Tulsa, Okla.,
　　1980.

LEINBACH -- Veazie, I. W.
　　Genealogy of the Leinbach-Lineback families:
　　Pennsylvania section. I. W. Veazie. Summit, N.J., 1977.

LEININGER -- Bailer, Sophia L. Bailer
　　Leininger family; one of the oldest in the state and　　(A)
　　nation, reunion July 13, 1930. Tremont, Pa., 1930.

　　- Same. Tremont, Pa., 1947.　　　　　　　　　　　　　　(P)

LEIPER -- Robins, Robert P.
　　A short account of the first permanent tramway in
　　America; a biographical sketch of its projector, Thomas
　　Leiper (with genealogy). Philadelphia, 1886.

LEIPHAM -- Stang, William Henry
    History and genealogy of the family of Peter Leipham
    and his wife Catherine Berger of Russell Hill, Penn'a.
    and Vacation reminiscences. Wilkes-Barre, Pa., 1927.

LEMMEN -- Lemmon, Lawrence Clifton
    John Lemmon and wife, Elizabeth Mickey: pioneer settlers
    of colonial Pennsylvania: ancestors and descendants, with
    a short history of their Scotch-Irish background.
    Gateway Press. Bowie, Md., 1983.

LENHART -- (Author unknown)
    The Lenhart family of Greenwich and Albany Twps., Berks
    County, and York County, Pa. No city, 1937.

LEONARD -- Russell, Mildred Huffman
    Some of the descendants of Joseph Leonard of Washington
    County, Pennsylvania and Delaware County, Ohio. No
    City, 1958.

LERCH -- (Author unknown)
    History of the Lerch family, 1560-1942. Smith OK   (A)
    Print. Allentown, Pa., 1942?

LESH -- Rupp, Margaret Leiby Glanding
    Meet the Lesh family. York, Pa., 1956.

LESHER -- Hess, Lydia R.
    John Lesher famly; a short sketch of the ancestry of   (A)
    my great-grandfather John Lesher and the record of his
    lineage. L. R. Hess. Marion, or Chambersburg, Pa.,
    1939.

LESLIE -- Lesley, Allen
    The Leslies: Counts of the Austrian Empire. Lesley.   (P)
    Philadelphia, 1974.

LEVERS -- McCracken, George E.
    Col. Robert Levers of Pennsylvania. No city,   (P)
    no date.

LEVICK -- (Author unknown)
    Life of Samuel J. Levick, late of the city of   (A)
    Philadelphia .... W. H. Pile's Sons Print.
    Philadelphia, 1896.

LEVERING -- Jones, Horatio Gates
    The Levering family. Philadelphia, 1858.

LEVERING -- Jones, Horatio Gates
The Levering family; or, A genealogical account of Wigard
Levering and Gerhard Levering, two of the pioneer settlers
of Roxborough Township, Philadelphia County ... and their
descendants; and an appendix, containing brief sketches
of Roxborough and Manayunk. King & Baird. Philadelphia,
1858.

LEWIS -- Barnes, Harriet Southworth (Lewis)
Lewis, with collateral lines: Andrews, Belden, Bronson,
Butler, Gillett, Newell, Peck, Stanley, Wright, and
others; ancestral record of Henry Martyn Lewis.
Philadelphia, 1910.

LEWIS -- Lewis, Harry W.
Lewis and Lewises. Erie, Pa., no date.

LICHTENWALNER -- Lichtenwalner Re-Union.
Committee for the Pennsylvania Branch
Lichtenwalner-Lichtenwalter family history. Eastob, Pa.,
1950.

LILLY -- Park, Percival David
Some descendants of John A. Lilly (1827-1891) and
Irene Foster Lilly (1824-1908) of Franklin County,
Pennsylvania. P. D. Park. Atlanta, Ga., 1984.

LINCOLN -- Egle, William H.
Pennsylvania ancestry of President Lincoln.   (A)
(Manuscript copy from the original in the possession
of Robert T. Lincoln, of Chicago, copied by Harriet
Henton, 1902).

LINCOLN -- Gwynne, Jacob M.
The cousin connection and genealogy of Abraham   (P)
Lincoln, 16th president of the United States and
Abraham Lincoln of Fayette County, Pennsylvania.
Gwynne. Willingboro, N.J., 1976.

LINDBERGH -- O'Brien, P. J.
The Lindberghs; the story of a distinguished family.
International Press. Philadelphia, 1935.

LINDSAY -- Wood, Forest Patrick
The Lindsay-Lindsey family of Pennsylvania, Virginia,
Kentucky and Indiana. Seattle, Wash., 1966.

LINDSEY -- Cooke, Margaret Watson
The Hezekiah Lindsey family (Lindsay, Lindsey) of
Westmoreland County, Pennsylvania, Cleremont County,
Ohio. No city, 1963.

LINN -- Hull, Margarett Virginia
Genealogical history of the family of William Linn.
Scottdale, Pa., 1932.

LINN -- Linn, George W.
A history of a fragment of the clan Linn and a   (P)
genealogy of the Linn and related families.
Report Print. Lebanon, Pa., 1905.

LINTON -- Linton, Morris
A genealogy of the descendants of John Linton (1662-   (P)
1708) and Rebecca Relf and their "in-laws."
Swarthmore, Pa., 1938.

LINTON -- (Author unknown)
Linton-Lacock, 1831-1881. Philadelphia, 1881.

LIPPINCOTT -- Lippincott, Charles, Cinnaminson
A genealogical tree of the Lippincott in America,
from the ancestors of Richard and Abigail ...
New Jersey. J. L. Smith. Philadelphia, 1880.

LIPPINCOTT -- Lippincott, James S.
The Lippincotts in England and America. Philadelphia,
1909.

LITTLE -- Baer, Mabel Van Dyke
Little-Colehouse families of Maryland & Pennsylvania.
No city, 1974.

LITTLE -- Winters, J. Lytle
Descendants of Edward Little (Lytle) of   (A)
Pennsylvania ... 1959. No city, no date.

LIVEZEY -- Smith, Charles Harper
The Livezey family. Philadelphia, 1934.

LIVEZEY -- Smith, Charles H.
Supplement to the Livezey family, 1934-1954.   Times   (A)
Chroncile Co. Jenkintown, Pa., 1945-.

LIVINGSTON -- Glenn, Thomas A.
Clermont and Livingstons. H. T. Coates. Philadelphia,
1897.

LLEWELLYN -- Cooke, Morris Llewellyn
Morris Llewellyn of Haverford, 1647 (!)-1730.
Philadelphia, 1935.

LLOYD -- Foster, Sandys B.
     The pedigrees of Lloyd of Dolobran, Montgomeryshire, the
     Wordsworth family ... Foster, late of Le Court, Hants ...
     Hanbury of Holfield grange, Essex ... Wakefield of Sedgwick
     house, Kendal ... Wakefield of New Zealand and So.
     Australia ...   W. H. and L. Collingridge. London, 1890.

LLOYD -- Glenn, Thomas A.
     Lloyd manuscripts. Lancaster, Pa., 1912.

LLOYD -- Glenn, Thomas Allen
     Genealogical notes relating to the families of Lloyd,
     Pemberton, Hutchinson, Hudson and Parke, and to others
     connected directly or remotely with them from the
     original manuscript of James P. Parke and Townsend Ward,
     with notes, additions and corrections, ed. at the request
     of Charles Hare Hutchinson ... E. Stern & Co., Inc.
     Philadelphia, 1898.

LLOYD -- Lucas, E. V.
     Charles Lamb & the Lloyds; comprising newly discovered
     letters of Charles Lamb, Samuel Taylor Coleridge, the
     Lloyds, etc. J. B. Lippincott. Philadelphia, 1899.

LLOYD -- Lloyd, Howard Williams
     Lloyd manuscripts. Genealogies of the families of
     Awbrey-Vaughan, Blunston, Burbeck, Garrett, Gibbons,
     Heacock, Hodge, Houlston, Howard, Hunt, Jarman, Jenkin-
     Griffith, Jones, Knight, Knowles, Lloyd, Newman, Paschall,
     Paul, Pearson, Pennell, Pitt, Pyle, Reed, Sellers, Smith,
     Thomas, Till, Williams, Wood. New Era Printing Co.
     Lancaster, Pa., 1912.

LOBB -- Lobb, Hugh Rowland
     Genealogy of the family of Lobb of America and   (A)
     England. Pennsylvania?, 195_?

LOCKE -- Locke Family Association
     Records of meetings, constitution and by-laws,   (N)
     also ...list of members. Walther Print House.
     Philadelphia, 1894.

LOCKWOOD -- Downs, Arthur Channing
     Rev. Clark Lockwood, 1805-1892. Primros?, Pa., 195_.

LOCKWOOD -- Holden, Frederic A. and E. Dunbar Lockwood
     Descendants of Robert Lockwood. Colonial and revolutionary
     history of the Lockwood family in America, from A.D. 1630.
     Philadelphia, 1889.

LOGAN -- Burkett, Mrs. William H.
    Logan families of Pennsylvania. No city, 1880.

LOGAN -- The Historical Society of Pennsylvania
    Memoir of Dr. George Logan of Stenton, by his widow
    Deborah Norris Logan, with selections from his
    correspondence, ed. by their great-granddaughter,
    Frances A. Logan; with an introduction by Charles J. Stille.
    Philadephia, 1899.

LOGUE -- Buchanan, Jane Gray
    John Logue of North Carolina: history and hypothesis:
    Logue and related families of Delaware, Maryland,
    Pennsylvania, Virginia, and Tennessee. Buchanan.
    Oak Ridge, Tenn., 1980.

LONG -- Brownfield, Robert L., Jr. and Rex Newlon Brownfield
    Long family records, Lancaster County, Pennsylvania.
    No city, 1951.

LONG -- Ely, Warren Smedley
    Long family of Drumore Township, Lancaster County,
    Pennsylvania. Doylestown?, Pa., 1909.

LONG -- Long, George E.
    John Long of Lancaster County. Pennsylvania and   (P)
    some of his descendants. Polyanthos. New Orleans,
    1974.

LONG -- Long, Theodore K.
    Emigre saga, a tale of early America. Carson Long
    Institute. New Bloomfield, Pa., 1943.

LONG -- Long, William Gabriel
    History of the Long family of Pennsylvania.
    No city, 1930.

LONG -- Ogier, Lois M.
    Longs and Leedys - pioneers; a chronological record   (A)
    of the Long and Leedy families of Maryland, Pennsylvania,
    Ohio and points West. Barberton, Ohio, 1962.

LONG -- Royer, Nellie Viola (Geiger)
    Pertinent biographical and genealogical (!) data
    concerning the descendants of Christian Long and
    Hannah Ellen Atkinson, assembled for submission to
    William Gabriel Long, historian, for culling material
    in future editions of the Long history in Pennsylvania
    including some briefed data from the (1) to (6)
    generation. Chambersburg?, Pa., 1904.

LONGACRE -- Longacre-Longaker-Longenecker Re-Union Association
   History of the Longacre-Longaker-Longenecker family.
   Philadelphia, 1899.

LONGSTRETH -- Taylor, Agnes Longstreth
   The Longstreth family records. Ferris & Leach.
   Philadelphia, 1909.

LORD -- Lord, Edward L.
   The Lord-Locke genealogy. E. L. Lord. Glenside,   (P)
   Pa., 1956.

LOTT -- Daughters of the American Colonists,
       Manor of Maske Chapter, Pa.
   Berlin-Ferree-Lott. Gettydburg, Pa., 1954.   (N)

LOUGHRY -- Jewett, Julia A.
   A brief genealogy of the Loughry family of Pennsylvania.
   St. Louis, Mo., 1923, 1924.

LOWE -- Weslager, Clinton Alfred
   Notes about the families of William Lowe and Eliza (Perry)
   Lowe of Pittsburgh, Pa. Hochessin, Del., 1971.

LOWER -- Lower, Rev. Joseph Leany
   Some account of the Lower family in America, principally
   of the descendants of Adam Lower, who settled in
   Williamsburg, Pa., in 1779. Monfort & Co. Cincinnati,
   1913.

LUDWICK -- Bowersox, Anna H.
   It's a long story ... the Ludwick family history.   (P)
   No city, 1969.

LUDWIG -- Guldin, Isaac W.
   History and genealogy of the Ludwig family from 1700   (A)
   to 1905. Reading, Pa., 1905.

LUDWIGS -- Virdin, Donald O.
   The Ludwigs (Ludwicks) and related Pennsylvania families,
   also Gordon E. Halter, Ludwick, Leis, Best, Schaeffer, Reef,
   Gordon, Halter, Bowersox, Anna Hankey families.
   Alexandria, Va., 1980.

LUKENS -- Lukens, Lewis N.
   Family memoranda, an essay upon the Lukens family.   (P)
   Haverford, Pa., 1927.

LUTTON -- McGilvray, Suzanne Flick
<u>Benjamin Lutton , Sr. of Pittsburgh, Pennsylvania, and</u>
<u>Cecil County, Maryland and his family</u>. Silver Spring,
Md., 1986.

LYBARGER -- Lybarger, Donald F.
<u>A brief history of the Lybarger family ...</u> Reading,
Pa., 1915.

LYLE -- Ewing, Thomas
<u>The Lyles of Washington County, Pa., 1681 to 1886,</u>   (A)
<u>with an account of the centennial reunion, June 18,</u>
<u>1884</u>. Jos. Eichbaun. Pittsburgh, Pa., 1886.

LYLE -- White, Alvin Dinsmore
<u>The Lyles of Washington County, Pennsylvania</u>.
Carlisle, Pa., 1934.

LYLE -- White, Alvin Dinsmore
<u>The Lyles of Washington County, Pennsylvania</u>.
Burgettstown, Pa., 1963.

LYLE -- White, Alvin D.
<u>(The) Lyles of Washington County, Pennsylvania,</u>   (A)
<u>being an account of the origin, migrations and</u>
<u>generations of the family. (Ed. 3)</u>. Enterprise Press.
Burgettstown, Pa., 1963.

LYMAN -- Lyman, Robert R.
<u>Life and times of Major Isaac Lyman, founder of</u>   (A)
<u>Potter County, Pennsylvania</u>. Potter Co. Hist. Society.
Coudersport, Pa., 1969.

LYNN -- Lynn, Eliza B. Lynn
<u>Genealogy of Colonel Andrew Lynn, Jr. and Mary Ashercraft</u>
<u>Johnson and their descendants</u>. The Uniontown Print Co.
Uniontown, Pa., 1912.

LYNN -- Linn, Dr. George Wilds
<u>A history of a fragment of the clan and a genealogy of</u>
<u>the Linn and related families</u>. Report Print. Lebanon,
Pa., 1905.

LYNN -- Hull, Margarett Virginia
<u>Genealogical history of the family of William Linn who</u>
<u>came from Belfast, Ireland, in 1771</u>. Mennonite Pub.
House. Scottsale, Pa., 1932.

LYON -- Goldsborough, Robert R.
Lyon memorial book IV: Bicentennial issue, 1776-1976.
Lyon(s) Families Assoc. of America. State College,
Pa., 1976.

LYTLE -- Lytle, Leonard
The descendants of William Lytle and his wife Jane of
Washington County, Pennsylvania and Clermont County,
Ohio. Royal Oak, Mich., 1951.

LYTLE -- Winters, John L.
The descendants of Edward Lytle of Pennsylvania,   (P)
Butler County, Ohio and Indiana. West Newton?,
Ind., 1959.

- M -

MACGREGOR -- (Author unknown)
 <u>The Bard's notes</u>. American Clan Gregor Society.
 Pittsburgh, Pa., 1932-5.

MACK -- Ankrum, Rev. Freeman, A.B.
 <u>Alexander Mack, the Tunker, and descendants</u>. Herald
 Press. Scottsdale, Pa., 1943.

MACKENZIE -- Linsey, Charles
 <u>(The) life and times of Wm. Lyon MacKenzie. With</u>   (A)
 <u>an account of the Canadian rebellion of 1837 ...</u>
 J. W. Bradley. Philadelphia, 1862.

MACKEY -- Sanner, Wilmer Mackey
 <u>Record of Robert Mackey and William Mackey and their</u>
 <u>descendants who lived mostly in Pennsylvania and/or</u>
 <u>Maryland, about 1729 to 1973</u>. Sanner. Ellicott City,
 Md., 1974.

MACLAY -- Aurand, A. Monroe, Jr.
 <u>The genealogy of Samuel Maclay, 1741-1811. A brief sketch</u>
 <u>of a prominent citizen and public official and a genealogy</u>
 <u>of the Maclay family in America from the year 1734</u>.
 Aurand Press. Harrisburg, Pa., 1938.

MACDONALD -- Macdonald, Reginald Henry
 <u>Notes on the house of Macdonald of Kingsburgh and Castle</u>
 <u>Camus</u>. Pittsburgh?, 1962.

MACDONALD -- Seaver, J. Montgomery
 <u>... MacDonald, McDonald family records</u>. American
 Historical-Genealogical Society. Philadelphia, 1929.

MADDEN -- Madden, Dutton
 <u>History of the Maddens</u>. Smith Printing Co.   (N)
 Reedsville, Pa., 1896.

MACGINNIS -- Meginness, John F.
 <u>Origin and history of the Magennis family, with sketches</u>
 <u>of the Keylor, Swisher, Marchbank and Bryan families ...</u>
 Heller Bros. Printing House. Williamsport, Pa., 1891.

MAGEE -- Stevenson, Robert Ashley
 <u>Additions and corrections to The Magee family</u>.
 Stevenson. New Castle, Pa., 1977.

MALLERY -- Mallery, Ira D.
American lineage of the Mallery family of Wayne County,
Pennsylvania. No city, 1962.

MALLET -- Mallett, Anna S.
John Mallet, the Huguenot, and his descendants, 1694-
1894. Harrisburg Pub. Co. Harrisburg, Pa., 1895.

MAN -- Lloyd, Richard W.
The Man family. Haverford, Pa., 1923.

MANN -- Moyer, Reba Mann
Genealogy of Mann-Diehl, Ruth-Fluck families. Perkasie,
Pa., 1951.

MANN -- Needles, Samuel Hambleton
Record of the Man, Needles (Nedels), and Hambleton families,
with others affiliated thereunto. A.D. 1495 to A.D. 1876,
et seq. E. Deacon. Philadelphia, 1876.

MANN --
The autobiography of Robert Mann, with reminiscences of
the Mann family in the counties of Centre, Mifflin, and
Clinton, Pennsylvania. J. B. Lippincott. Philadelphia,
1897.

MARIS -- (Author unknown)
The Maris annual. (v. 1 - 1886 -). West Chester,   (P)
Pa., 1886-.

MARKEY -- (Author unknown)
Genealogy and history of the Jacob Markey family of York
County, Pennsylvania, 1750-1961. No city, 1961?

MARKLEY -- Dotterer, H. S.
Descendants of Jacob Markley of Shippack, Montgomery
County, Pennsylvania. No city, 1884.

MARKLEY -- Markley, Joseph M.
The history of the Markley relationship. Canton,
Ohio, 1922-1924.

MARR -- Marr, W. P.
Marr family of Pennsylvania. Racine, Wisc., 1918.

MARRS -- Wheeler, Harriette Marr
William Marr of Northampton County, Pennsylvania, and
his six children. H. M.Wheeler. Grosse Pointe,
Mich., 1983.

MARSH -- Baer, Mabel Van Dyke
Marsh and allied families and O'Neill of New York,
Pennsylvania and Indiana. No city, 1970.

MARSHALL -- Cormack, Maribelle
History and genealogy of the Michael Marshall family of
Hartstown, Pennsylvania. Providence, R.I., 1940.

MARSHALL -- Marshall, Joseph B.
Marshall family of Pennsylvania. Wilmette, Ill., 1952.

MARSHALL -- Marshall, O. S.
The Marshall family. Kittanning, Pa., 1884.

MARSHALL -- Marshall, Oscar S.
The Marshall family. A history of the descendants of   (P)
William Marshall (1722-1796). Reichart Print.
Kittaning, Pa., 1884.

MARSHALL -- Stein, Thomas S.
The Marshalls of Berks and Lebanon Counties,   (P)
Pennsylvania. Hiester Print. Annville, Pa., 1915.

MARTIAU -- Stoudt, John Baer
Nicolas Martiau. Norristown, Pa., 1932.

MARTIN -- Bell, Raymond Martin and John Martin Stroup
The descendants of Samuel Martin, 1775-1842, of
Mifflin County, Pennsylvania. Washington, Pa.,
1967.

MARTIN -- Bird, Lucien
Reminiscences of James Martin and famly. Penfield,
Pa., 1908.

MARTIN -- Martin, George Castor
The Martin family. Vol. I. Martin & Allardyce.
Philadelphia, 1911-.

MARTIN -- Martin, Richard B.
Family history of Nathaniel Z. Martin, 1841-1971.   (A)
Print Shop. Gordonville, Pa., 1971.

MARTIN -- Mohler, Louise Martin
The Martin family of Ohio. L. M. Mohler.
Washington, Pa., 1978-1982.

MARTIN -- Risser, John D.
Family record of Abraham Martin and his descendants.   (A)
Mennonite Pub. House. Scottdale, Pa., 1940.

MARTIN -- Seaver, J. Montgomery
The Martin genealogy. Philadelphia, 1923.

MARTIN -- Seaver, J. Montgomery
... Martin family records. American Historical-
Genealogical Society. Philadelphia, 1929.

MARTIN -- Weiler, Emma M.
Eli W. Martin family and descendants of Henry K.   (A)
Martin, 1691-1971. Ensinger Print. Adamstown,
Pa., 1972.

MARTZ -- Martz, Hannibal L.
The family of William Martz, 1739-1803, of Somerset
County, Pennsylvania: allied families Gaumer, Kenell,
Shroyer, Shumaker, Sturtz, Troutman. Ruby Martz.
Aurora, Ill., 1984.

MARVIN -- Marvin, Francis M.
Biography of John Huston Marvin. Bartonsville, Pa., 194_?

MASON -- Brooks, Rubylee S.
John Mason (Johannes Maurer) 1730-1812, founder of
Masontown, Pennsylvania and some of his descendants.
Pittsburgh, Pa., 1980.

MASON -- Mason, Harrison D.
Archibald Dale Mason; his life, ancestry and descendants.
Pittsburgh, Pa., 1921.

MATHER -- Lippincott, Horace Mather
The Mather family of Cheltenham, Pennsylvania.
Philadelphia, 1910.

MATHER -- Lippincott, Horace Mather, PH.B.
The Mather family of Cheltenham, Pennsylvania; being an
account of the descendants of Joseph Mather, comp. from
the records of Charles Mather of Jenkintown. L. J.
Levick. Philadelphia, 1910.

MATHIAS -- Mathias, Joseph
Bucks County, Pennsylvania, Mathias family. -- Genealogical
record book of the Rev. Joseph Mathias to which supplementary information by other Mathias family members has
been added. Reproduction from microfilm of holograph:
microfilm produced at Doylestown, Pa. by the Genealogical
Society. Salt Lake City, Utah, 1960.

MATHIAS -- Seale, Dorothy Weiser
Mat(t)hias milestones: the genealogy & biographical
history of Daniel Mathias, Senior (a soldier of the
Revolution) of Westmoreland County, Pennsylvania &
Stark County, Ohio, with a related appendix, the life
of Michael Sanor (a soldier of the Revolution).
Westview Press. Boulder, Colo., 1984.

MAULE -- Maule, James Edward
The history and genealogy of the Maules. J. E. Maule.
Carlisle, Pa., 1981.

MAULE -- Nicholson, Richard L.
Genealogy of the Maule family, with a brief account of
Thomas Maule, of Salem, Massachusetts ... Philadelphia,
Pa., 1868.

MAULEVERER -- Marshall, Charles
The descent of Anne Mauleverer (Abbott) and   (P)
Rebecca Humphrey (Owen) from the Sureties for the
observance of the Magna Charta, 1215 A.D. Times
Printing House. Philadelphia, 1904?

MAULEVERER -- Thompson, John J.
Mauleverer (genealogical chart). Philadelphia, no   (P)
date.

MAURER -- Dunkelberger, George Franklin and Enid Eleanor Adams
The Maurer family, Pennsylvania pioneers; a brief history
of the family, with records of all known descendants of
Jacob Maurer, 1791-1863, and his wife, Maria Polly
Hilbisch, 1793-1861, of Snyder County, Pennsylvania.
Seattle, 1954.

MAY -- Kee, Raph M.
David May of Mifflin County, Pennsylvania and his
descendants. Kee. Springfield, Va., 1980.

MAY -- Mase, Catharine A.
Mace, Maize, Mase, Mays, Maze: family history. Mase.
Lebanon, Pa., 1978.

MAYER -- Mayer, Brantz
Memoir and genealogy of the Maryland and Pennsylvania
family of Mayer. Baltimore, Md., 1878.

MAXWELL -- Maxwell, Henry D.
The Maxwell family. Descendants of John and Ann Maxwell,
1701-1894. With appendix containing sketch of the Maxwell
family and biographical sketches. Easton Express Print.
Easton, Pa., 1895.

McAFEE -- McAfee, Joseph E.
You are a McAfee; for the descendants of John Armstrong (A)
McAfee and Anna Waddell Bailey McAfee. Evangelical
Print. Harrisburg, Pa., 1935.

McALLISTER -- Reed, H. P.
Nathaniel McAllister (1836-1926). Wernersville, Pa.,
1975.

McCABE -- Mecabe, William H.
A genealogy of some of the descendants of Owen and (N)
Catherine (Sears) McCabe, who settled in Tyrone on the
Juniata River in Sherman's Valley, Perry County, Pa.
Watertown, Conn., 1972.

McCALL -- McCall, Max
McCall history; an account of the history and lineage (A)
of the McCalls particularly ... in Indiana County,
Pa. Indiana, Pa., 1965.

McCANDLESS -- Ferree, Joseph A.
The McCandless and related families: pioneers of
Butler County, Pennsylvania. Joseph A. Ferree, Jr.
Natrona Heights, Pa., 1977.

McCANDLESS -- Morgan, Olive Jane McCandless
The McCandless families of Center and Franklin Townships,
Butler County, Pennsylvania, 1929. Bridgeville, Pa.,
1929.

McCAUSLAND -- Casanova, Jessie McCausland
A McCausland family of Lancaster County, Pennsylvania.
No city, 1936.

McCHESNEY -- Schultz, Katherine
The descendants of Robert McChesney of Monmouth County,
N.J. Annville, Pa., 1966.

McCLENAHAN -- Henderson, John McClenahan
The John McClenahan folk. The United Presbyterian Board
of Publication. Pittsburgh, Pa., 1912.

McCLENAHEN -- Bell, Raymond Martin
The McClenahen family (with some Dorman notes).
Washington, Pa., 1963.

McCLENAHEN -- Bell, Raymond Martin
The McClenahen family: Mifflin County, Pennsylvania.
Washington, Pa., 1977.

McCLINTOCK -- Mervine, W. M.
McClintock genealogy; reprinted from volume one of   (A)
the Genealogical Register. Philadelphia, 193.

McCOMB -- McComb, P. H. K.
A genealogical register of the McComb family in America,
compiled from records furnished by the individual families,
and public records, etc. 1912-1942 record and notes
compiled by Virginia M. McComb. Chambersburg, Pa., 1942.

McCOMB -- McComb, Peter Hathaway Kemper
A genealogical register of the Mccomb family in America.
Chambersburg, Pa., 1942.

McCONAHEY -- McConahey, Samuel C.
The narrative of a family, Thomas Mitchell   (P)
McConahey - Nancy Jane McCune, 1844-1953.
Wilkinsburg, Pa., 1958.

McCONNELL -- McConnell, Joy L.
Ancestors and descendants of Myron and Bessie McConnell:
the story of Myron and Bessie McConnell of Monroe Township,
Kosciusko County, Indiana: ancestors from Wayne, Stark,
and other counties of Ohio, New Jersey, New York, and
Pennsylvania, descendants scattered from coast to coast.
J. L.McConnell. Salem, Oregon, 1985.

McCONNELL -- McConnell, R. Kirk
McConnell family in history. Smith Bros. Pittsburg,   (A)
Pa., 1936.

McCORMICH -- McCormick, Drucilla Mary
The Henry McCormick family with ancestors Green, Allen,
Rogers, Williams, Garnsey and allied families in Hanover
Township, Dauphin County, Pennsylvania and Saratoga and
Monroe Counties, New York. No city, 1979.

McCRACKEN -- MacCracken, Constable
A record of the descendants of John McCracken, born Central
Pennsylvania, 1776, died Xenia, Ohio, 2 Jan. 1828.
Gateway Press. Baltimore, Md., 1979.

McCULLOUGH -- McCullough, John, III.
Genealogy of the McCullough family and other sketches.
Telegraph Printing Co. Harrisburgh, Pa., 1912.

McCULOUGH -- McCullough, Sarah
Historical reminiscences of the McCulloughs.
Philadelphia, 1860.

McCURDY -- (Author unknown)
   Biographical sketch of the McCurdy families, Lewistown, Pa., 1761-1924. Lewistown, Pa., 1924.

McCURLEY -- McCurley, James B.
   McCurley (or Curley) of Pennsylvania (1779).   (P)
   McCurley. Chevy Chase, Md., 1975.

McDONALD -- Vining, Elizabeth G.
   Flora: a biography. Lippincott. Philadelphia, 1966.   (A)

McFARLAN -- Stern, Cyrus
   Our kindred. West Chester, Pa., 1885.

McFARLAND -- Bell, Raymond Martin
   Three central Pennsylvania families: McFarland of Blair Co., Weston of Huntingdon Co. (and) Gates-Getz of Centre Co. Washington, Pa., 1948.

McFARQUHAR -- Reed, Alexander P.
   Colin McFarquhar (1728-1822) pastor of Donegal   (P)
   Springs Presbyterian Church, Pa. and his descendants. Pittsburgh, Pa., 1960.

McGARRY -- McGeary, George D.
   The genealogy of the McGeary-McGary-McGarey-McGara family of Pennsylvania. Mag Fhearadhaigh Press. Bend, Oregon, 1981.

McGAUGHEY -- Sutton, Polly Rachel McGaughey
   Descendants of William and Margaret McGaughey: (settled in York County, Pa., 1740. Quintella Print Co. Oklahoma City, Okla., 1984.

McGINNESS -- McGinness, Samuel W.
   McGinness and Scott families and their branches. Pittsburgh, Pa., 1892.

McINTIRE -- McIntire, Robert Harry
   Descendants of Philip McIntire, a Scottish Highlander who was deported by Oliver Cromwell following the battle of Dunbar, September 3, 1650, and settled at Reading, Mass., about 1660. Lancaster Press. Lancaster, Pa., 1941.

McKEAN -- Buchanan, Roberdeau
   Genealogy of the McKean family of Pennsylvania, with a biography of the Hon. Thomas McKean, LL.D. ... with an introductory letter by the Hon. Thomas F. Bayard, LL.D. Inquirer Print. Lancaster, Pa., 1890.

McKEE -- McKee, George Wilson
The McKees of Virginia and Kentucky. Pittsburgh,
Pa., 1891.

McKEE -- McKee, James V.
A history of the descendants of David McKee of Anahlt.
Philadelphia, 1802.

McKEEVER -- Bushfield, Bernice Bartley
The McKeevers and allied families of West Middletown,
Washington County, Pennsylvania. Toronto, Ohio, 1959.

McKELVEY -- Mabon, Ellen J.
Story of the McKelveys in America. New Florence,   (A)
Pa., 1928.

McKINLEY -- Hewlett, Joseph M.
The McKinley family; the Sloan family; the Campbell   (P)
family of Northern Ireland and the United States.
Wyncote, Pa., 1962.

McKINLEY -- (Author unknown)
Ancestors ofWilliam McKinley. Phil. Print. No city,   (A)
1897.

McKINNEY -- Swope, Belle McKinney Hays
History of the families of McKinney - Brady - Quigley.
Newville, Pa., 1905.

McMAHAN -- McMahan, Samuel
History of the McMahan family. Milton, Pa., 1899.

McMASTERS -- Horan, John P.
The McMaster family of Pennsylvania. No city,   (P)
no date.

McMILLAN -- Bennett, Daniel M.
Life and work of Rev. John McMillan, D.D., pioneer,
preacher, educator, patriot, of western Pennsylvania.
Bridgeville, Pa., 1935.

McMILLAN -- McMillan, Robert H., Jr. and Gladys Green McMillan
Record of McMillan and allied families. Peninsular Pub.
Co. Tallahassee, Fla., 1973.

McMILLAN -- Weaver, Ruth Clarke
Supplement (1935-1981) to life and work of Rev. John
McMillan, D.D., pioneer, preacher, educator, patriot,
of western Pennsylvania by Daniel M. Bennett, 1935.
Genealogical Committee of the McMillan Clan.
Canonsburg, Pa., 1981.

McMURTRIE -- McMurtry, Richard K.
McMurtry; ancestors and descendants of Joseph McMurtry
(1764-1846) of New Jersey and Pennsylvania, including the
arrival and early history of the family in America.
MacMurtrie Clan-Family Historical Records Worldwide.
Lexington, Ky., 1968.

McPHERSON -- McPherson, Edward
List of the descendants of Robert and Janet McPherson,
the former of whom died near Gettysburg, Pennsylvania,
December 25, 1749, aged 60 years, and the latter
September 23, 1767, aged 78 years. Gettysburg, Pa.,
1869.

McTEER -- McTeer, Frances Davis
The McTeer-Mateer families of Cumberland County,
Pennsylvania. Holiday, Florida, 1975.

McWHIRTER -- Keim, Ethel Smith
History of the McWhirter clan. Latrobe, Pa., 1937.

MEAD -- Mead, Spencer P.
History and genealogy of the Mead family of Fairfield
County, Connecticut, eastern New York, western Vermont,
and western Pennsylvania. New York, N.Y., 1901.

MEANS -- Sinnett, Charles N.
Ancestor Samuel Means of Pennsylvania and descendants.   (N)
Carthage, S.D., 1926?

MEANS -- Sinnett, Charles N.
The Means families of Pa., the South, Illinois, etc.   (P)
Complete index to the names. Fertile, Minn., no date.

MEARS -- Mears, John W.
Biographical notice of Henry Haller Mears, Sr. to   (P)
which is appended a genealogy of the Mears family.
J. B. Rodgers Co. Philadelphia, 1873.

MEGGS -- Meigs, Samuel E.
Meggs, of Bradford-Peverel ... Copied from ... Bible   (P)
which belonged to the late Dr. Charles D. Meigs.
Philadelphia, 1904.

MEISSER -- Meiser, Joseph, Jr.
A genealogy of the Meisser family (Meiser, Miser,
Mizar, Mizer, Myser): from the founding in America
by immigrant ancestors to the present time. Meisser
Genealogy Association. Lancaster?, Pa., 1975.

MEISSER -- Mizer, Lloyd E.
A genealogy of the Meisser family (Meiser, Miser,
Mizer, Myser). Lancaster, Pa., 1966.

MELLON -- Denton, Frank Richard
The Mellons of Pittsburgh. Newcomen Society of England,
American Branch. New York, N.Y., 1948.

MELLON -- Mellon, Thomas
Thomas Mellon and his times. W. G. Johnston.   (A)
Pittsburgh, Pa., 1885.

MELLON -- Mellon, William Larimer
Judge Mellon's son. Pittsburgh?, Pa., 1948.

MELLON -- O'Connor, Harvey
Mellon's millions, the biography of a fortune; the life
and times of Andrew Mellon. The John Day Co. New York,
N.Y., 1933.

MELSHEIMER -- Prowell, George R.
Frederick Valentine Melsheimer, a pioneer entomo-   (A)
logist, and a noted clergyman and author.
Historical Society of York Co., Pa., 1897.

MENSCH -- Mensch, Frank W.
The Mensch genealogy. Philadelphia, 1921.

MENDENHALL -- Jacobs , Lillian Mendenhall Powell
Ancestors and descendants of Jacob H. Mendenhall and
his wife Hannah W. Newlin from the first emigrants,
Benjamin Mendenhall, England, and Nathaniel Newlin,
Ireland, to Chester County, Pensylvania, 1683.
L. M. P. Jacobs. Sarasota, Fla., 1983.

MEREDITH -- (Author unknown)
Meredith genealogies. A collection of biographical   (P)
sketches of Philadelphia Merediths. No city, no date.

MEREDITH -- Graham, S. Meredith
A short history of the three Merediths. Tunkhannock,   (P)
Pa., no date.

MERRITT -- Merritt, Gilbert S.
Whence came these stones: a compilation of Merritt family
data. G. S. Merritt. Damascus, Pa., 1982.

MERRYMAN -- Tracy, Elsie Howlett
Merrimans (Merrymans) and Tracy (Traceys): pioneer
community builders, from Maryland 1756 through
Pennsylvania to Ohio from 1814-1820, to family
migrations after 1828 to Michigan, Indiana, Illinois,
and points west. E. H. Tracy. LaJolla, Calif., 1976.

MERSHON --
Mershon news bulletin, the Association of the descendants
of Henry Mershon, Inc. Philadelphia, no date.

METHENY -- Metheny, William Blake
Metheny family: origin of the seigneures de Methenay ...
Philadelphia, Pa., 1937.

MEYER -- Fretz, Abraham James
A genealogical Record of the descendants of Christian and
Hans Meyer. Harleysville, Pa., 1896.

MEYER -- Meyer, Abraham J.
A genealogical record of the descendants of Christian   (N)
and Hans Meyer and other pioneers .... News Print House.
Earlysville, Pa., 1896.

MICHENER -- Shaddinger, Anna E.
More Micheners in America. Doyleston, Pa., 1970.

MICHIE -- Michie, Thomas
The Michies. Pittsburgh, Pa., 1942?

MICKLEY -- Hicks, Ada Bonebrake
A genealogy of the Mickley family. Hicks. Wayneboro,
Pa., 1980.

MIDDLETON -- Coleman, Ruth M.
James Middleton of Centre County, Pennsylvania, circa
1800-1820, and some of his descendants who migrated to
Ross County, Ohio. R. M. Coleman. No city, 1977.

MIDDLETON -- Herndon, John Goodwon
Robert Middleton (ca. 1651 - ca. 1707) of Charles and
Prince Georges Counties, Maryland, and numerous
descendants of his. Haverford, Pa., 1954, 1955.

MIDDLETON -- Middleton, William J.
Aaron Middleton of Philadelphia, Pa., 1730-1820.   (P)
T. J. Middleton. Somers Point, N.J., 1914.

MIFFLIN -- DuBin, Alexander
Mifflin. Philadelphia?, 193?

MIFFLIN -- Leach, Frank Willing
Mifflin family; one of a series of sketches written (P)
by Frank Willing Leach for the Philadelphia North
American, 1907-1913, and brought down to date, 1932.
The Historical Publication Society. Philadelphia,
1932.

MILES -- Banes, Charles H.
Annals of Miles ancestry in Pennsylvania and story of
a forged will. G. H. Buchanan. Philadelphia, 1895.

MILHAM -- Thacher, Elwood James
The Millham's family reunion, Laceyville, Pennsylvania,
July 29, 1972. Thacher. Winter Haven, Fla., 1977.

MILHOUS -- Bell, Raymond Martin
West with the Milhous and Nixon families; a story of
the forebears of Richard Milhous Nixon. Washington,
Pa., 1954.

MILLARD -- Millard, Julian
The Millard family in Pennsylvania. No city, no date. (P)

MILLER -- (Author unknown)
The David and Anna Miller story. Scottdale, Pa., 1979.

MILLER -- Darby, Milton M. and Clarence A. Miller
... The lineage of the Miller family and allied families
of Fayette County, Pennsylvania, and Frederick County,
Maryland. No city, 1930.

MILLER - Miller, David A.
Christian Miller, an American pioneer; his descendants (P)
through the families of David A. Millrr and Samuel P.
Miller. Allentown, Pa., 1959.

MILLER -- Miller, Jacob J.
Descendants of Eli J. Miller and wives, Mary Weaver (A)
and Elizabeth Miller. Print Shop. Gordonville, Pa.,
1969.

MILLER -- Miller, Milo H.
A history and genealogy of the Miller family, 1725-1933.
Pittsburgh, Pa., 1933.

MILLER -- Miller, N. C.
John H. Miller and his descendants. Gettysburg, Pa., 1939.

MILLER -- Miller, Reuben
The Miller family. Pittsburgh, Pa., 1914. (P)

MILLER -- Miller, Victor H.
Miller family record, 1830-1936. Coopersburg?, Pa.,
1937?

MILLER -- Miller, William H.
Brief history of Yost (Joseph) and Jeremiah Miller   (A)
and their descendants. Benshoff Print. Johnstown,
Pa., 1930?

MILLER -- Miller, William H.
A brief history of Yost (Joseph) and Jeremiah Miller
and their descendants. Johnston, Pa., 1937.

MILLER -- Newton, Eliabeth M.
Dear Palatines and Switzers: Nicholas Miller and
allied families: Mauss, Meyer, Hefflefinger,
Wolfersberger, Eichholtz, 18th century immigrant
settlers in Heidelberg Twp., Lancaster Co., Pa.,
ancestors of Ludwig Miller & Philip Hefflefinger
of Cumberland Co., Pa. E. M. Newton. Kutztown,
Pa., 1983.

MILLER -- Pursel, Vida Miller
Genealogy of the Miller and Pursel families. Smith
Print Shop. Bloomsburg, Pa., 1939.

MILLER -- Stone, Mary M. Besecker
A brief sketch of the ancestry and life of Stephen
Miller. Edella, Pa., 1901.

MILLER -- Yoder, Loretta J.
Descendants of Joseph Miller and Christian Eicher.   (A)
Print Shop. Gordonville, Pa., 1970?

MILLIKEN -- Smith, Sarah Augusta
Milliken and Milligan (family of Pennsylvania and Ohio).
Columbus, Ohio, 1921.

MILLS -- Goddard, Thomas H.
The Mills, Cope, and related families of Georgia.
Dunlap Print. Philadelphia, 1962.

MILLS -- Kirkbride, Mabelle Mills
The Mills, Payton, Mott, and Butler families; my grand-
parents and their ancestors, showing the lines of
connection with the families who married into them.
Chancellor Press. Bridgeport, Pa., 1963.

MILNE -- Du Bin, Alexander
Milne family. Historical Publ. Society. Philadelphia,
1948.

MINIER -- Finch, Jesse Howell
The Minier family of Pennsylvania and New York. No city, 1943.

MISCHLER -- Mishler, John Milton
History of the Mishler families and their descendants ...
Press of E. Pengelly & Bro. Reading, Pa., 1921.

MITCHELL -- Massey, George Valentine, II
The Mitchells and days of Philadelphia, with their kin.
New York, N., 1968.

MITCHELL -- Massey, George V.
The Mitchells and Days of Philadelphia. With their   (P)
kin: Dr. S. Weir Mitchell and Helena Mary Langdon
(Mitchell) and Kenneth Mackenzie Day. I. A. Hermann.
New York, N.Y., 1968.

MITCHELL -- Seaver, J. Montgomery
... Mitchell family records. American Historical-
Genealogical Society. Philadelphia, 1929.

MITCHELL -- Seaver, J. Montgomery
The Mitchell genealogy. Philadelphia, 1929.

MOAK -- Moak, Lennox Lee
The Moak and related families of South Carolina and
Mississippi, 1740-1960; with notes as to members of
the family in Tennessee and Illinois and also notes
as to other Moak families in New York, Pennsylvania,
Maryland, and Virginia. Fort Washington, Pa., 1960.

MOHLER -- (Author unknown)
The Mohler family of Ohio, descendants of Jacob Mohler,
grandson of Ludwig Mohler of Lancaster County,
Pennsylvania. Beaver Falls, Pa., 1958.

MONTGOMERY -- Du Bin, Alexander
The family of Montgomery. The Historical Pub. Society.
Philadelphia, 1943.

MONTGOMERY -- Forster, John Montgomery
A sketch of the life of the Rev. Joseph Montgomery.
Harrisburg, Pa., 1879.

MONTGOMERY -- Montgomery, David B.
History of the Montgomery family. Argus Book and   (P)
Job Print. Milton, Pa., 1886.

MONTGOMERY -- Montgomery, Thomas H.
    History of the family of Montgomerie from its earliest
    record in Normandy in the ninth century ... to the
    eldest male branches now settled in America.
    Philadelphia, 1961.

MONTGOMERY -- Montgomery, Thomas Harrison
    A genealogical history of the family of Montgomery,
    including the Montgomery pedigree.   H. B. Ashmead.
    Philadelphia, 1863.

MONTGOMERY -- Montgomery, Thomas H.
    Memoir of Thomas H. Montgomery ... together with
    extracts from his personal notes on his parents.
    Harris & Partridge. Philadelphia, 1905.

MOOMAW -- Coleman, Mildred Moomaw
    Moomaw; an account of some of the descendants of
    Lenhart Mumma, b. circa 1690, d. 1770, who arrived
    in Philadelphia Sept. 9, 1732. With a detailed
    account of the descendants of Benjamin Franklin
    Moomaw, 1814-1900. Richmond?, 1964?

MOOMAW -- Huffman, Richard Glenn
    Genealogy of the George Muma family, Westmoreland County,
    Pennsylvania: Mumma, Mumaw, Moomaw, Mumau. Huffman.
    Whitney, Pa., 1971.

MOORE -- Moore, Clara Jessup
    Ancestry of Clarence Bloomfield Moore of Philadelphia.
    Washington, D.C., 1940.

MOORE -- Moore, James W.
    Rev. John Moore of Newtown, Long Island, and some of his
    descendants. Chemical Pub. Co. Easton, Pa., 1903.

MOORE -- Norris, G. Heide
    A history of Col. James Moore of the Revolutionary Army,
    together with an account of his ancestors and descendants
    and the distribution of his estate, eighty-seven years after
    his death, in the case of Hopkins vs. Moore, Supreme Court
    of Pennsylvania, March term, 1814, no. 82, and undet the
    order of the Orphan's court of Philadelphia, April term,
    1891, no. 177. Times Printing House. Philadelphia, 1893.

MOORE -- Passmore, John Andrew Moore
    Ancestors and descendants of Andrew Moore.   1612-1897.
    Wickersham Print.Co. Philadelphia, 1897.

MOORE -- Seaver, J. Montgomery
... Moore family record. American Historical-Genealogical
Society. Philadelphia, 1929.

MOORHEAD -- Moorhead, Elizabeth
Whirling spindle; the story of a Pittsburgh family.
University of Pittsburgh Press. Pittsburgh, Pa., 1942.

MORELAND -- Moreland, Edna (Robertson)
Thanks for yesterday; the Moreland family history (1796-
1956). Greenville?, Pa., 1956.

MORRIS -- Du Bin, Alexander
The Morris family ... Historical Pub. Society.   (N)
Philadelphia, 1948.

MORRIS -- Hart, Charles H.
Mary White - Mrs. Robert Morris ... Collins. Philadelphia,
1878.

MORRIS -- Johnson, R. Winder
The ancestry of Rosalie Morris Johnson, daughter of
George Calvert Morris and Elizabeth Kuhn, his wife.
Ferris & Leach. Philadelphia, 1905-08.

MORRIS -- Moon, Robert C.
The Morris family of Philadelphia. Philadelphia, 1898-1909.

MORRIS -- Moon, R. C.
The Morris family of Philadelphia; descendants of
Anthony Morris, born 1654 - 1721 died. R. C. Moon.
Philadelphia, 1898-1909.

MORRIS -- Morris, Anthony S.
Genealogical chart of the Morris family. F. Bourguin.
Philadelphia, 1896.

MORRIS -- Morris, Anthony Saunders
A lithogrtaphed tree chart of the descendants of
Anthony Morris, 2d born at St. Dunstans Stepney of
London, Aug. 23, 1654 and his wife Mary Jones.
F. Bourquin & Co. Philadelphia, 1861.

MORRIS -- Morris, Edward Shippen
Descendants of Samuel Morris, 1734-1812. Philadelphia,
1959.

MORRIS -- Morris, James R.
Morris family history. News Pub. Co. Punxsatwaney,
Pa., 1922.

MORRIS -- Morris, Robertt
Deeds. Heirs of Robert Morris to Robert S. Paschall;   (N)
and Robert S. Paschall to John Moss. Quinn & Swan.
Philadelphia, 1854.

MORRIS -- Seaver, J. Montgomery
... Morris family records. American Historical-Genealogical
Society. Philadelphia, 1929?

MORRISON -- Haag, Mary Helen Morrison
Samuel Morrison of Bucks County, Pa. and some of his
descendants. M. H. M. Haag. Dayton, Ohio, 1981.

MORRISON -- Sage, E. J. P.
Samuel Morrison of Bucks and Lycoming Counties,
Pennsylvania. Rutland, Vermont, 1936.

MORROW -- Wolfe, Alice Houseworth
The Morrow sept and the MacPherson clan of Bradford
County, Pennsylvania. No city, 1971.

MORTON -- McKenney, Ruby Griffin
Genealogical records of John Morton and his descendants
of Pennsylvania, Virginia, North Carolina, Georgia, and
Florida. No city, 1961.

MOSELEY -- Mousely, Franklin
Moseley-Mousley index to genealogy. The Historical
Society of Pennsylvania. Philadelphia, 1942.

MOTT -- Harris, Edw. Doubleday
The descendants of Adam Mott Hempstead, Long Island,
N.Y. A genealogical study. The New Era Print. Co.
Lancaster, Pa., 1906.

MOUNTAIN -- MacPike, Eugene Fairfield
... Notes on the Mountain, Drake and MacPike families.
Philadelphia, 1928.

MOYER -- Fretz, Rev. A. J.
A genealogical record of the descendants of Christian
and Hans Meyer and other pioneers, together with
historical and biographical sketches ... News
Printing House. Harlysville, Pa., 1896.

MOYER -- Moyer, H.
A family history (genealogical record) of Bishop Jacob
Meyer (I), Henry Abraham Moyer (IV), and their descendants to date; with a short history of other Meyer
pioneers. E. G. Crist Co. Allentown, Pa., 1973.

MUHLENBERG -- Heyer, W. C.
A brief monograph with reference to the mother of
the leading family in the American life of the epoch
which inaugurated freedom and independence for the
American people and government, and for the church
and word of the Lord Jesus in government, and for the
church and word of Lord Jesus in America. The Leader
Pub. Co. Shamokin, Pa., 1916.

MUHLENBERG -- Hocker, Edward W.
The fighting parson of the American revolution; a
biography of General Peter Muhlenberg, Luthern
clergyman, military chieftan, and political leader.
Philadelphia, 1936.

MUHLENBERG -- Reichmann, Felix
The Muhlenberg family, a bibliography compiled from the
subject union catalog (of) Americana-Germanica of the
Carl Schurz memorial foundation. Carl Schurz Memorial
Foundation. Philadelphia, 1943.

MUHLENBERG -- Richards, Henry Melchior Muhlenberg
Descendants of Henry Muhlenberg. Pennsylvania-German
Society. Lancaster, Pa., 1900.

MUHLENBERG -- Wallace, A. W.
The Muhlenbergs of Pennsylvania. Books for Libraries
Press. Freeport, N.Y., 1970, c. 1950.

MUHLENBERG --
In memoriam. Henry Melchior Muhlenger, 1711, 1742, 1787.
Commemorative exercies held by the Susquehanna synod of
the Evangelical ·Lutheran church, at Selinsgrove, Pa.,
October 18 and 19, 1887. Lutheran Publication Society.
Philadelphia, 1888.

MUHLENBERG --
Muhlenberg bicentennial, 1742-1942: for God and   (A)
country, the epic story of the heroic Muhlenberg
family, Muhlenberg College ... 1942. The College.
Allentown, Pa., 1942.

MUMA -- Huffman, Richard Glenn
Genealogy of the George Muma family. Whitney,
Pa., 1971.

MUNDELL -- Barry, Ruby M.
 The Mundell (Mundle) family, descendants of James   (A)
 Mundell and his wife, Margaret (Garrett) Mundell
 of New Castle County, Delaware, and Greene County,
 Pa. And the migrations of their children into
 Kentucky, Ohio, West Virginia ... and other Western
 states. Kansas City, Mo., 1968.

MURDOCK -- Murdock, Anna Virginia
 The Murdocks of Washington, Pa.; the story of my
 family. No city, 1973.

MURDOCK -- Murdock, Joseph B.
 Murdock genealogy, Robert Murdock, of Roxbury,
 Massachusetts, and some of his descendants, with
 notes on the descendants of John Murdo of Plymouth,
 Massachusetts, George Murdock of Plainfield, Conn.,
 Peter Murdock of Saybrook, Conn., William Murdock
 of Phialdephia, Pa., and others. C. E. Goodspeed
 & Co. Boston, Mass., 1925.

MURRAY -- Seaver, J. Montgomery
 ... Murray family records. American Historical-
 Genealogical Society. Philadelphia, 1930.

MURRAY -- Seaver, Jesse
 Murray family history. American Historical-
 Genealogical Society. Washington, D.C., 1972.

MURROW -- (Author unknown)
 The genealogy of the Murrow family. Philadelphia?,
 194_?

MUSSER -- (Author unknown)
 History of the Musser family, also the reunion of the
 descendants of Benjamin Engle Musser, 1810-1884.
 Bulletin Print. Mt. Joy, Pa., 1927?

MUSGRAVE -- Shartle, Stanley Musgrave
 A history of a Quaker branch of the Musgrave family of
 the north of Ireland, Pennsylvania, North Carolina,
 Illinois, and elsewhere, with selected papers relating
 to the ancient and landed Musgraves of England.
 Indianapolis, Ind., 1961.

MYERS -- Myers, Forrest D.
 Sam Myers, 1805-1883 and Lydia Horner, 1833-1907:
 their ancestors and descendants. A. E. Myers.
 Harrisburg, Pa., 1979.

- N -

NAGEL -- Kaup, Paul Edwin
The Adolph Karl Gustav Nagel families: this is an
account of their origin in America and their generations.
Kaup. Pittsburgh, Pa., 1980.

NAUGLE -- Baer, Mabel Van Dyke
Naugle family of Pennsylvania, Virginia and Indiana.
No city, 1972.

NEALE -- Neill, Edward Duffield
John Neill, of Lewes, Delaware, 1739, and his descendants.
Collins Print. Philadelphia, 1875.

NEEL -- Neel, Gregg L.
The ancestors of Gregg Livingstone. Pittsburgh, (P)
Pa., 1973.

NEEL -- Neel, William Trent
The Neel-Dickson genealogy. Rev. to Jan 1, 1949.
Bryn Mawr, Pa., 1953?

NEFF -- Neff, Elizabeth Clifford
A chronicle, together with a little romance regarding
Rudolf and Jacob Npaf, of Frankford, Pennsylvania,
and their descendants, including an account of the Neffs
in Switzerland and America. Cincinnati, Ohio, 1886.

NEFF -- Neff, Elmer Ellsworth
A memorial of the Neff family. Altoona, Pa., 1931.

NEFF -- Ramsey, Ruthanna Schomp
Jacob Neff (1761-1839). No city, 1966.

NEILL -- Neill, Edward D.
John Neill of Lewes, Delaware, 1739, and his descendants.
Philadelphia, 1875.

NEILL -- Shippen, Edward
Memoir of John Neill, M.D., late emeritus professor of (P)
clinical surgery in the University of Pennsylvania.
Collins. Philadelphia, 1880.

NELSON -- Seaver, J. Montgomery
... Nelson family records. American Historical-Genealogical
Society. Philadelphia, 1929.

NESBIT -- Hartman, Blanche T.
A genealogy of the Nesbit, Ross, Porter, Taggart families
of Pennsylvania. Pittsburgh, Pa., 1929.

NESBIT -- Nesbit, Charles Frances
An American family. Washington, D.C., 1932.

NEUENSCHWANDER -- Longyear, Peter R.
A short history and genealogy of the Swiss family   (NP
Neuenschwander who reached America in 1754 and
settled in Lancaster County, Pennsylvania. Bern,
1953.

NEWBOLD -- Newbold, Joseph
The American descendants of Anthony Newbold: a record of
the children of Anthony Newbold and their families.
Newbold. Philadelphia, 1976.

NEWBOLD -- Platt, Charles
Newbold Genealogy in America. New Hope, Pa., 1964.

NEWCOMER -- Mallett, Manley William
The Newcomer families of Pennsylvania. M. W. Mallett.
Largo, Fla., 1983.

NEWHARD -- Roberts, Charles R.
History of the Newhard family of Pennsylvania.   (P)
Allentown, Pa., 1915.

NEWKIRK -- Newkirk, Adamson Bentley
... The van Nieukirk, Nieukirk, Newkirk family. Hall
of the Historical Society of Pennsylvania. Philadelphia,
1934.

NEWLIN -- Du Bin, Alexander
Newlin family and collateral lines. The Historical
Publication Society. Philadelphia, 1942.

NEWSOME -- Newsome, Samuel H.
The descendants of James Newsome and his wife   (P)
Rebecca Illingworth in the United States of America
(to which they came in 1856). Under the auspices
of the Delaware County Historical Society. Chester,
Pa., 1976.

NICHOLAS -- Peter, Jerry F.
The Nicholases of Pennsylvania in the Civil War
1861-1865. Wilmington, Del., 1968.

NICHOLSON -- (Author unknown)
<u>Nicholson, the name and the arms</u>. Martin and Allardyce.
Frankford, Pa., 1910.

NICHOLSON -- Jacob, Caroline N.
<u>Nicholson family history</u>. West Chester, Pa., 1970.   (A)

NICHOLSON -- Nicholson, James B.
<u>Nicholson, Bruner and Getz family history</u>.   (P)
Philadelphia, 1930.

NICHOLSON -- Nicholson, William H.
<u>My ancestors, 1675-1885</u>. A. C. Leeds. Philadelphia,   (P)
1897.

NICHOLSON -- Taylor, Rebecca N.
<u>A family history of the residence of Rebecca and Sarah</u>
<u>Nicholson, Haddonfield, New Jersey, built 1799-1800 by</u>
<u>John Estaugh Hopkins</u>. Innes & Sons Printers.
Philadelphia, 1917.

NIXON -- Bell, Raymond Martin
<u>The Nixon chart</u>. Washington, Pa., 1954.

NIXON -- Bell, Raymond Martin
<u>From James to Richard; the Nixon line</u>. Washington,
Pa., 1957.

NIXON -- Bell, Raymond Martin
<u>From James to Richard; the Nixon line, 2d. ed.</u>
Washington, Pa., 1969.

NIXON -- Bell, Raymond Martin
<u>The ancestry of Richard Milhous Nixon</u>. Washington,
Pa., 1970.

NIXON -- Bell, Raymond Martin
<u>The ancestry of Richard Milhous Nixon</u>. Washington,
Pa., 1972.

NOBLET -- Noblit, John Hyndman
<u>Genealogical collections relating to the families of</u>
<u>Noblet, Noblat, Noblot and Noblets, of France; Noblet</u>
<u>and Noblett, of Great Britain; Noblet, Noblett, Noblit</u>
<u>and Noblitt, of America; with some particular account</u>
<u>of William Noblit of Middletown Township, Chester</u>
<u>County (now Delaware county), Pennsylvania, U.S.A.</u>
Ferris & Leach. Philadelphia, 1906.

NOEL -- Noel, Charles A.
    <u>The Noel tree: "a history of the Noel and allied families</u>
    <u>of Pennsylvania, including Fevrier, Fritz, Dickey, Stepp,</u>
    <u>and others."</u> Southwest Pennsylvania Genealogical
    Services. Laughlintown, Pa., 1978.

NOLT -- Zimmerman, Enos N.
    <u>Nolt's family history, 1771-1969, containing over</u>   (A)
    <u>3700 families</u>. Print Shop. Gordonville, Pa., 1970.

NOOKES -- Cope, Gilbert
    <u>Nookes family</u>. West Chester, Pa., 1869.

NORRIS -- Harrison, Marjorie B.
    <u>Pennsylvania descendants of Thomas Norris of Maryland,</u>   (P)
    <u>1630-1959 and allied families</u>. Edwards. Ann Arbor,
    Mich., no date.

NORTH -- North, Dexter
    <u>John North of Farmington, Connecticut, and his descen-</u>
    <u>dants; with a short account of other early North families</u>.
    Washington, D.C., 1921.

NORTH -- North, Dexter
    <u>The Caleb North genealogy, descendants of Caleb North</u>
    <u>who came from Ireland to Philadelphia in 1729</u>.
    Washington, D.C., 1930.

NORTON -- Morton, David
    <u>The Nortons of Russellville, Ky., reminiscences</u>.   (A)
    Lippincott. Philadelphia, 1891.

NOVINGER -- McNamara, Elizabeth W.
    <u>The Novinger family of Dauphin County, Pennsylvania</u>
    <u>and Adain County, Missouri</u>. Fort Thomas, Ky., 1978.

- O -

OBERHOLTZER -- Loomis, Elisha S.
Some account of Jacob Oberholtzer, who settled, about
1719, in Franconia Township, Montgomery County,
Pennsylvania, and from some of his descendants in
America. Cleveland, Ohio, 1931.

OBERHOLTZER -- Oberholtzer, Levi N.
Oberholtzer family history, 1802-1968. Ensinger   (A)
Print. Adamstown Pa., 1968.

OBERHOLTZER -- Overholser, Charles E.
An account of the Oberholtzer family. Terre Hill,
Pa., 1906.

OBERTEUFFER -- Oberteuffer, Reece M.
Oberteuffer genealogy. Philadelphia, 1916.   (P)

OGDEN -- Ogden, Charles Burr
The Quaker Ogdens in America; David Ogden of ye goode
shipe "Welcome" and his descendants 1682-1897; their
history, biography, and genealogy. J. B. Lippincott.
Philadelphia, 1898.

OGDEN -- Wheeler, William Ogden
The Ogdens of South Jersey; the descendants of John
Ogden of Fairfield, Conn., and New Fairfield, N.J.
Philadelphia, 1894.

OGDEN -- Wheeler, William Ogden
The Ogden family in America, Elizabethtown branch, and
their English ancestry; John Ogden, the Pilgrim, and
his descendants, 1640-1906, their history, biography
& genealogy. J. B. Lippincott. Philadelphia, 1907.

OLIVER -- Hayden, Rev. Horace Edwin
Oliver genealogy; a record of the descendants of Joseph,
Reuben, and Levi Oliver of New York, Pennsylvania, and
Delaware 1727-1888, and of Pierre Elisee Gallaudet,
M.D. of New Rochelle, New York 1711-1888. J. J. Little
& Co. New York, N.Y., 1888.

OLIVER -- Oliver, Captain Frederick L.
Descendants of John Oliver, born 1811 in England,   (N)
died 1864 at Mechanicville, N.Y. Pittsburgh,
Pa., 1944.

OLMSTEAD -- Hoagland, Edward Coolbaugh
    Some brief notes on the Olmstead family. Hoagland.
    Wysox, Pa., 1955.

OLMSTEAD -- Stone, Rufus Barrett
    Arthur George Olmstad, son of Pennsylvania pioneer;
    boy orator of Ulysses; for the freedom of the slave;
    defense of the Union; development of the northern tier;
    citizen, jurist, statesman. The John C. Winston Co.
    Philadelphia, 1919.

OLP -- Knipe, James L.
    The Olp family of Shrewsbury Township, York County, Pa.
    Lancaster, Pa., 1952.

O'MALLEY -- (Author unknown)
    Genealogy of the O'Malleys of the Owals.   (P)
    Philadelphia, 1913.

ORMSBY -- Barlow, Claude W.
    Ormsby families of Connecticut prior to 1800. Easton,
    Pa., 1965.

ORMSBY -- Page, Oliver Ormsby
    A short account of the family of Ormsby of Pittsburgh.
    Albany, N. Y., 1892.

ORNDORFF -- Orndorff, John Barclay
    John Orndorff, Pennsylvania pioneer and his ancestors.
    Graysville, Pa., 1953.

ORWIG -- Wagenseller, George W.
    The descendants of Gottfried Orwig, 1719-1898.
    Middleburgh, Pa., 1898.

OSBORN --
    The pastor of the old stone church. Mr. Hotchkin's
    memorial, Judge Elmer's eulogy, and Mr. Burt's
    address, commemorative of Rev. Ethan Osborn ...
    W. S. and A. Martien. Philadelphia, 1858.

OSTRANDER -- (Author unknown)
    A genealogical history of the Stephen Ostrander branch
    of the Ostrander family in America, 1660-1902.
    Danville, Pa., 1902.

OWEN -- Owen, Ralph Dornfeld
    Descendants of John Owen of Windsor, Connecticut
    (1622-1699); a genealogy. Philadelphia, 1941.

- P -

PAGE -- Lawrence, Schuyler
Page family of Ipswich, County Suffolk, England.   (N)
A photostat of materials relating to this family
from Suffolk collections in the British Museum,
London ... with a brief pedigree ... showing
branches in Norfolk and Pennsylvania. Towanda,
Pa., 1945.

PAINTER -- Painter, J.
Our ancestors ... (Descendants and relatives of Samuel
Painter of Phila., Pa., 1707, with allied families,
being the ancestors of the author, J. Painter).
Lima, Pa., 1869.

PAINTER -- Painter, Orrin Chalfant
Genealogy and biographical sketches of the family of
Samuel Painter, who came from England and settled in
Chester County, Pennsylvania, about the year 1699.
J. S. Bridges & Co. Baltimore, Md., 1903.

PALMER -- Fell, Sarah M.
Genealogy of the Palmer family in America; descended   (A)
from John and Christian Palmer, who settled in Bucks
County, Pa., 1683. Wilmington, Del., 1902.

PALMER -- Palmer, Alexander M.
A history of the Quakers in Stroudsburg, with some   (P)
special reference to the Walton, Palmer and other
families. Stroudsburg, Pa., 1929.

PALMER -- Palmer, Lewis
A genealogical record of the descendants of John and Mary
Palmer. Philadelphia, 1875.

PALMER -- Palmer, Lewis
A genealogical record of the descendants of John and Mary
Palmer, of Concord, Chester (now Delaware) Co., Pa.,
especially through their son, John Palmer, Jr., and
sons-in-law, William and James Trimble. With notes of
ancestry, or information, of many of the families with
whom they married. J. B. Lippincott. Philadelphia,
1875.

PALMER -- Palmer, Lewis
A genealogical record of the descendants of John and
Mary Palmer of Concord, Chester (now Delaware) Co.,
Pa. in two divisions - Palmer-Trimble. Palmer division,
embracing also, largely, the surnames: Almond, Arment,
Baker ... and others. New ed. Press of Chester Times.
No city, 1910.

PANGBURN -- McClure, Cicero P.
Randolph-Pangburn. William Pangburn and his wife,   (A)
Hannah Fitz Randolph; their ancestry an descendants,
1620-1909. The Society of Allegheny County, Pa.
Pittsburgh, Pa., 1909.

PARDEE -- Du Bin, Alexander
Pardee and Ives families. Historical Publication
Society. Philadelphia, 1950.

PARDEE -- Foulke, C. Pardee
Calvin Pardee, 1841-1923: his family and his enterprises.
Pardee Company. Philadelphia, 1979.

PARISH -- Wharton, Susanna Parrish
The Parrish family (Philadelphia, Pennsylvania) including
the related families of Cox, Dillwyn, Roberts, Chandler,
Mitchell, Painter, Pusey, by Dillwyn Parrish, 1809-1886.
With special reference to Joseph Parrish, M.D., 1779-1840,
with sketches of his children, by members of the family
and others. George H. Buchanan Company. Philadelphia,
1925.

PARK -- (Author unknown)
Park family of Washington Co., Pennsylvania.
Washington, D.C., 1922?

PARK -- (Author unknown)
Simon Parke of Franklin, Pa., and descendants.
Washington, D.C., 1922?

PARK -- Jacobus, Donald Lines
The ancestry of Rev. Nathan Grier Parke & his wife Ann
Elizabeth Gildersleeve. Woodstock, Vt., 1959.

PARK -- Parks, Frank Sylvester
Parks and Park in the census of 1790. (First census of
the United States). Washington, D.C., 1922.

PARK -- Stanton, John M.
Ancestors and descendants of Joel Parke of East Troy,
Pa. Elmira, N.Y., 1923.

PARKE -- Parks, Frank Sylvester
Genealogy of Arthur Parke of Pennsylvania. Washington, D.C., 1922.

PARKER -- De Long, Irwin Hoch
The lineage of Malcolm Metzger Parker from Johannes De Lang. Lancaster, Pa., 1926.

PARMLY -- Brown, Lawrence Parmly
The greatest dental family. Philadelphia, 1923?

PARRISH -- (Author unknown)
The Parrish family, Philadelphia. A reunion held at Dormy house, Pine Valley, New Jersey, May 18th, 1929. No city, no date.   (P)

PARRISH -- Wharton, Susanna Parrish
The Parrish family, Philadelphia, Pennsylvania. Philadelphia, 1925.

PARRY -- (Author unknown)
Parry family records. D. C. Ryan. Philadelphia, 1877.

PARRY -- Rubincam, Milton
The family of Henry Parry of Pittsburgh, Pennsylvania. No city, no date.

PARSONS -- Parsons, John A.
Eli Parsons of Enfield, Connecticut and Columbia Township, Bradford County, Pennsylvania. Troy, Pa., 1924.

PARTHEMORE -- Parthemore, E. W. S.
Genealogy of the Parthemore family, 1744-1885. L. S. Hart. Harrisburg, Pa., 1885.

PARVIN -- Parvin, Richard H.
A genealogy of the descendants of Francis Parvin of Berks County, Pennsylvania, 1700-1978. Parvin. Woodland Hills, Calif., 1978.

PATTERSON -- Patterson, Mary L.
History of the Patterson family of Cross Creek Township, Washington County, Pa. Davis. Pittsburgh, Pa., 1924.   (A)

PATTERSON -- (Author unknown)
A record of the families of Robert Patterson (the elder), emigrant from Ireland to America, 1774; Thomas Ewing, from Ireland, 1718; and Louis Du Bois, from France, 1660; connected by the marriage of Uriah Du Bois with Martha Patterson, 1798. Part first containing the Patterson lineage ... J. C. Clark. Philadelphia, 1847.

PATTON -- Patton, John W.
Family record of John Patton, born in Ireland, and his descendants from 1700, the approx. time of his arrival at Carlisle, Pa., to 1954. Los Angeles, Calif., 1954.   (P)

PAUL -- Paul, N. Alice
History of descendants of James Paul of Northern Ireland. Washington, Pa., 1939?   (A)

PAUL -- Paul, Henry N.
Joseph Paull of Ilminster, Somerset, England and some of his descendants who have resided in Philadelphia, Pennsylvania. Philadelphia, 1933.

PAUL -- Shultz, Lawrence W. (and many members of the Paul family)
Paul family record, 1763-1963. Including the 1917 record of the descendants of Henry and Susannah Brumbaugh Paul of Martinsburg, Pennsylvania; and one earlier generation of Daniel Paulus; and the data of generations since 1917, edited by Herman Taylor. Light and Life Press. Winona Lake, Ind., 1963.

PAWLING -- Kitts, Mrs. Katherine (Wallace)
Henry Pawling and some of his descendants. Sharon Hill, Delaware County, Pa., 1903.

PAWLING -- Pawling, Albert Schoch
Paweling genealogy. Lewisburg, Pa., 1905.

PAXSON -- Scarborough, Henry W.
Genealogical data of the Paxson, Harding, and allied families ... from a notebook kept by Hugh P. Paxson. Philadelphia, 1923.

PAXTON -- Paxton, W. M.
The Paxtons: their origin in Scotland, and their migrations through England and Ireland, to the colony of Pennsylvania, whence they moved South and West, and found homes in many states and territories ... Landmark Print. Platte City, Mo., 1903.

PEACHEY -- Yoder, Mary E. P.
Family record of Jonas Z. Peachey and Amelia (Yoder)   (A)
Peachey and their descendants. Berlin Pub. Berlin,
Pa., 1957.

PEACHY -- Peachey, Samuel M.
A memorial history of Peter Bitsche, and a complete family
register of his lineal descendants and those related to him
by intermarriage, from 1767 to 1892. Chronologically
arranged. With an appendix of those not received in time
for their proper place. J. Baer's Sons. Lancaster, Pa.,
1892.

PEARSON -- Armstrong, William C.
Crispin Pearson of Bucks County, Pennsylvania, 1748-1806;
a genealogy compiled and published by Annie Pearson Darrow.
J. Heidingsfeld Co. New Brunswick, N.J., 1932.

PECK -- Roberts, George Braden
Genealogy of Joseph Peck and some related families,
including the Bordens, the Fowles, the Winters, the
Grovers, the Carpers, the Clays, the Chapmans, the
Staffords, the McClures, the Meeks, the Molletts (and)
the Osbornes. State College, Pa., 1955.

PECK -- Weyburn, S. Fletcher
History of a distinctive family of Scranton and Lackawanna
County, Pennsylvania. Scranton, Pa., 1929.

PECK -- (Author unknown)
The Peck coat of arms. Martin & Allardyce.   (N)
Philadelphia, 1910.

PEDRICK -- Shoemaker, Hubert B.
A genealogical and biographical record of the Pedrick
family of New Jersey, 1675-1938. Temple Typecrafters.
Philadelphia, 1938.

PEIRPOINT -- Stickney, Alpheus Beede
Lucy & Oliver, some West Virginia genealogy: Peirpoint,
Smell, Jones, Fetty. Pittsburgh, Pa., 1953.

PEMBERTON -- Pemberton, Phineas
Annals of the Pemberton family, with notes respecting
some of their contemporaries. Philadelphia, 1835.

PEMBERTON -- Price, Eli K.
The diary of John Pemberton, for the years 1777 and 1778.
A paper read before "The Numismatic and antiquarian society
of Philadelphia" ... July 5, 1866. H. B. Ashmead.
Philadelphia, 1867.

PENFIELD -- Penfield, Florence Bentz
     The genealogy of the descendants of Samuel Penfield.
Reading, Pa., 1960.

PENFIELD -- Penfield, Florence Bentz
     The genealogy of the descendants of Samuel Penfield,
with a supplement of Dr. Levi Buckingham line, and the
Gridley, Dwight, Burlingham, Dewey, and Pyncheon
collateral lines. Harris Press. Reading, Pa., 1963.

PENN -- (Author unknown)
     William Penn, proprietary of Pennsylvania, his ancestry
and descendants. Philadelphia, 1852.

PENN -- (Author unknown)
     Articles, wills and deeds creating the entail of
Pennsylvania and three lower counties upon Delaware
in the Penn family. Philadelphia, 1870.

PENN -- (Author unknown)
     A short account of Penn of Pennsylvania and his family.
The Historical Register Pub. Co. Philadelphia, 1895.

PENN -- Chidsey, A. D.
     The Penn patents in the forks of the Delaware. John S.
Correll Co. Easton, Pa., 1937.

PENN -- Coleman, James
     A pedigree & genealogical notes, from wills, registers,
and deeds, of the highly distinguished famly of Penn,
of England and America, designed as a tribute to the
memory of the great and good William Penn. J. Coleman.
London, 1871.

PENN -- Conner, P. S. P.
     Sir William Penn, knight, admiral, and general-at-sea;
great-captain-commander in the fleet. J. B. Lippincott.
Philadelphia, 1876.

PENN -- Hogg, Oliver F. G.
     Further light on the ancestry of William Penn.
Harrington Gardens, London, 1964.

PENN -- Ingraham, Edward D.
     Portraits and scenes of the Penn family.   (N)
Philadelphia, 1850.

PENN -- Jenkins, Howard M.
     The family of William Penn founder of Pennsylvania,
ancestry and descendants. Philadelphia, 1899.

PENN -- Lea, J. Henry
Genealogical gleanings, contributory to a history of the
family of Penn. J. B. Lippincott. Philadelphia, Pa.,
1890.

PENN -- Lea, J. Henry
Genealogical gleanings contributory to a history of the
family of Penn. Boston, Mass., 1900.

PENN -- Pound, Arthur
The Penns of Pennsylvania and England. The Macmillan Co.
New York, 1932.

PENN -- Rawle, William Brooke
The general title of the Penn family to Pennsylvania, an
abstract by the Honorable John Cadwalader ... deceased,
continued to the present time. Philadelphia, 1900.

PENN -- Smith, John J.
The Penn family (paper read before the Historical Soc.
of Pa., Nov. 1867). No city, no date.

PENN -- Smith, John Jay
The Penn family. Philadelphia, 1870.

PENN -- Smith. John Jay
The Penn Family (from Lippincott's magazine).
J. B. Lippincott. Philadelphia, 1870.

PENN -- Webb, Maria
The Penns & Peningtons of the seventeenth century in their
domestic and religious life, illustrated by original family
letters, also incidental notices of their friend Thomas
Ellwood, with some of his unpublished verses.
H. Longstreth. Philadelphia, 1868.

PENNINCK -- Penninck, James
Result of investigation in West Virginia regarding   (N)
properties belonging to "Gerrit Penninck" residing
in Philadelphia, 1784. New York, N.Y., 1919.

PENNOCK -- Massey, George V.
The Pennocks of Primitive hall, written for the   (A)
Chester County Historical Soc. Chester County
Historical Society. West Chester, Pa., 1951.

PENNOCK --
Map of the descendants of Christopher Pennock,   (P)
Caroline Pennock, delineator. J. T. Bowen.
Philadelphia, no date.

PENNOYER -- Lounsbury, Raymond H.
   <u>Pennoyer brothers: colonization, commerce, charity in
   the 17th century</u>. Dorrance. Philadelphia, 1971.

PENROSE -- Leach, Josiah Granville
   <u>History of the Penrose family of Philadelphia</u>. D.Biddle.
   Philadelphia, 1903.

PENROSE -- Penrose, George H.
   <u>A genealogical chart ... being a supplement to the</u>   (P)
   <u>Penrose family (pub. in Philadelphia in 1903)...</u>
   The Knickerbocker Press. New York, N. Y., 1929?

PENROSE -- Waters, J. Wesley
   <u>Biography of the late Boies Penrose and family,</u>
   <u>copyright ...</u> The Sumner Printing Press. Philadelphia,
   1939.

PENNYPACKER -- (Author unknown)
   <u>The Pennypacker reunion, October 4, 1877</u>. Bavis &
   Pennypacker Printers. Philadelphia, 1878,

PENNYPACKER --(Author unknown)
   <u>The descent of Samuel Whitaker Pennypacker ... from</u>
   <u>the ancient counts of Holland. With authorities in</u>
   <u>proof, Philadelphia, 1898</u>. No city, no date.

PENNYPACKER -- Pennypacker, Samuel W.
   <u>The pedigree of Samuel Whitaker Pennypacker, Henry Clay</u>
   <u>Pennypacker, Isaac Rusling Pennypacker, James Lane</u>
   <u>Pennypacker, of Philadelphia, sons of Isaac Anderson</u>
   <u>Pennypacker and Anna Maria Whitaker</u>. Globe Printing
   House. Philadelphia, 1892.

PENNYPACKER -- Penypacker, Hon. Samuel W.
   <u>Hendrick Pannebecker, surveyor of lands for the Penns.,</u>
   <u>1674-1754, Flomborn, Germantown and Shippack</u>.
   Philadelphia, 1894.

PERDUE -- Perdue, Robert Hartley
   <u>Descendants of Dr. William Perdue, who settled in Chester</u>
   <u>County, Pennsylvania, in 1737-38, and his wife, Susanna</u>
   <u>(Pim) Perdue. Part II. Ancestors of Lucinda Maria (Smith)</u>
   <u>Perdue giving Smith, Potter and Hamilton lines. John</u>
   <u>Purdue, founder of Purdue University</u>. Cleveland, Ohio,
   1934.

PERSHING -- Pershing, Edgar Jamison
   <u>The Pershing Family in America</u>. Philadelphia, 1924.

PFAUTZ -- Pfautz, John Eby
 <u>A family record of John Michael Pfautz, a native of
 Switzerland, Europe, who emigrated from the Palatinate
 to America, about the year 1707, and his posterity down
 to the year 1880</u>. J. Baer's Print. Lancaster, Pa.,

PFAUTZ -- Pfautz, John E.
 <u>Family record of John Michael Pfautz ... and his</u>   (A)
 <u>posterity down to the year 1880</u>. Comp. Print.
 Gettysburg, Pa., 1916.
 1881.

PFEIFFER -- Sellers, Edwin Jacquett
 <u>Genealogy of Dr. Francis Joseph Pfeiffer of Philadelphia,
 Pennsylvania, and his descendants. 1734-1899</u>. J. B.
 Lippincott. Philadelphia, 1899.

PICKETT -- Pickett, Warren E.
 <u>Family ancestors of Edward Pickett (1865-1899) and</u>   (A)
 <u>Mary Agnes Updike (1864-1894)</u>. Washington, Pa.,
 1942.

PIKE -- Pike, Alfred John
 <u>The Pike family in southeastern Pennsylvania</u>. No city,
 1950.

PIKE -- Pike, Alfred J.
 <u>The Pike family in Southeastern Pennsylvania</u>. No city,
 1956.

PINNELL -- Pinnell, N. A.
 <u>Short history or biography of the Pinnell family</u>   (A)
 <u>from the XVI century to 1903-7</u>. Erie Print.
 Erie, Pa., 1907.

PIPER -- Piper, Marshall C.
 <u>History of the descendants of John and Margaret</u>   (A)
 <u>Piper who lived near Mill Creek, Pennsylvania,</u>
 <u>125 or more years ago</u>. Milesburg, Pa., 1937.

PLATT -- (Author unknown)
 <u>Notes upon the ancestry of John Platt, born in Burlington
 County, N.J., Aug. 13, 1749; died near Wilmington, Del.,
 Dec. 1823, and also, a list of his descendants</u>.
 Philadelphia, 1896.

PLATT -- Platt, Charles
 <u>Platt genealogy in America</u>. New Hope, Pa., 1963.

PLATT -- Platt, Franklin
     Notes upon the ancestry of John Platt. Philadelphia,
1896.

PLEASANTS -- Du Bin, Alexander
     Pleasants family ... Historical Publication   (N)
Society. Philadelphia, 1950.

PLEASANTS -- Leach, Frank Willing
     Pleasants family. One of a series of sketches   (P)
written by Frank Willing Leach for the Philadelphia
North American, 1907-1913, and brought down to date.
The Historical Pub. Society. Philadelphia, 1939.

PLUMB -- Plumb, H. B.
     The Plumbs. Peely, Pa., 1893.

PLUMER -- Smith, George P.
     Genealogy of the descendants of Francis Plumer of   (A)
Newbury. Mainly those who remained in New England.
Philadephia, 1875?

PLUMMER -- Palmer, Edgar Z.
     Plummers of Harmony Grove, Pa. Friends United Pr.   (A)
Richmond, Ind., 1974.

POLLOCK -- (Author unknown)
     Pollock: a record of the descendants of John, James,
Charles, and Samuel Pollock, who emigrated from
Ireland to Pennsylvania about 1750 ... Harrisburg,
Pa., 1884.

POLLOCK -- Griffith, Helen Coloa (Pollock) &
             Captain Edwin T. Pollock
     David Pollock of Westmoreland County, Pennsylvania, and
his descendants. No city, 1936?

POLLOCK -- Hayden, Rev. Horace Edwin
     Pollock genealogy. A biographical sketch of Oliver
Pollock, esq., of Carlisle, Pennsylvania, United
States commercial agent at New Orleans and Havana,
1776-1784. With genealogical notes of his descendants.
Also genealogical sketches of other Pollock families
settled in Pennsylvania. L. S. Hart Printer.
Harrisburg, Pa., 1883.

POLLOCK -- Pollock, Jessie M.
     Family record of Adam, James and Robert Pollock of Erie
County, Pennsylvania. No city, 1939.

POMEROY -- Pomeroy, Edwin Moore
    History and genealogy of the Pomeroy family and collateral
    lines, England, Ireland, America; comprising the ancestors
    and descendants of George Pomeroy of Pennsylvania.
    W. McL. and J. N. Pomeroy. Philadelphia?, 1958.

POORBAUGH -- Calder, Treva E. G.
    Burbach-Poorbaugh-Purbaugh family history, 1771-1974.   (A)
    Poorbaugh-Purbaugh Assoc. Somerset County, Pa.,
    1976.

PORTER -- Smyth, Samuel G.
    Scotch-Irish pioneers of the Schuykill Valley, Pa.,   (P)
    with notes relating to the Porter family. Recorder
    Print. Conshohocken, Pa., 1901.

POTTER -- Potter, William A.
    Potter family; a collection of historical and   (A)
    genealogical data ... traditions, legends and
    military records. Wilmerding, Pa., 1971?

POTTS -- Du Bin, Alexander
    Potts family. Historical Pub. Society. Philadelphia,
    1948.

POTTS -- Potts, Thomas M.
    A short biographical sketch of Major James Potts,   (A)
    born 1752, died 1822, and two ancestral charts.
    Canonsburg, Pa., 1877.

POTTS -- Potts, Thomas Maxwell
    Our family ancestors. Canonsburg, Pa., 1895.

POTTS -- Potts, Thomas M.
    The arms of Pott or Potts. Canonsburg, Pa., 1900.   (P)

POTTS -- Potts, Thomas Maxwell
    Historical collections relating to the Potts family in
    Great Britain and America, with a historic-genealogy of
    the descendants of David Potts, an early Anglo-Welsh
    settler of Pennsylvania, including contributions by the
    late William John Potts. Canonsburg. Pa., 1901.

POWELL -- Powell, Alfred R.
    Genealogy of the Powell and Montzheimer families.   (P)
    The ancestors, descendants and other relatives of
    William Alfred Powell (1867-1927) and Marie
    (Montzheimer) Powell (1861-1951). Pittsburgh,
    Pa., 1962.

POWELL -- Powell, W. Bleddyn
Genealogy and descent of the family of Powel of Castle   (P)
Madoc and of Wm. M. Powell of Philadelphia, Pa. From
the reguli of England and Wales. No city, 1895-1899.

POWELL - Smith, Leonard H.
Some descendants of William Powell of Mifflin County,
Pennsylvania. Smith. Clearwater, Fla., 1980.

PRESCOTT -- Ticknor, George
Life of William Hickling Prescott. J. B. Lippincott.
Philadelphia, 1903.

PRESTON -- Belsterling, Charles Starne
William Preston of Newcastle-upon-Tyne, England and
Philadelphia, Pennsylvania and allied families.
The Dolphin Press. Philadelphia, 1934.

PRICE -- (Author unknown)
The golden wedding of Benjamin and Jane Price. With brief
family record ... J. B. Lippincott. Philadelphia, 1870.

PRICE -- (Author unknown)
Rev. Jacob Price chart. Pottstown, Pa., 1910.

PRICE -- Price, Eli K.
Biographical sketches of James Embree, Philip Price,   (P)
and Eli K. Price. Reprinted from the "History of
Chester County, Pa. L. H. Everts. Philadelphia, 1881.

PRICE -- Price, Violet (Hallett)
The Price family of Barrett Township, Montoe County,
Pennsylvania. Christopher Pub. House. Boston, 1948.

PRICE -- Seaver, J. Montgomery
... Price family history. American Historical-
Genealogical Society. Philadelphia, 1927?

PRICE -- Wanger, Geo. F. P.
A genealogy of the descendants of Rev. Jacob Price,
evangelist, pioneer. The Evangelical Press.
Harrisbyrg, Pa., 1926.

PRIEST -- Russell, George Ely
Priest genealogy: Part 1, Pennsylvania, 3d ed. Bowie,
Md., 1969.

PRINDLE -- (Author unknown)
Second annual reunion of the Prindle family, held
at Sharon, Pa. ... 1887. No city, 1887.

PUMPHREY -- Bell, Raymond Martin
<u>Reason Pumphrey, 1736-1812: Maryland-Pennsylvania-West
Virginia early Methodist</u>. R. M. Bell. Washington,
Pa., 1984.

PUSEY -- Meeds, William P.
<u>The Pusey family of Chster County, Pa.</u> Washington, Pa.,
1958.

PURVES --
<u>Purves family, compiled from existing records and from
the material furnished by living descendants of Sir
William Purves</u>. Historical Publication Society.
Philadelphia, 1939.

- Q -

QUICKEL -- Quickel, David M.
    <u>Genealogical history of the three Quickel brother,</u>   (A)
    <u>Philip, George and Michael (who came from ...</u>
    <u>Germany in 1736 to Lancaster County, Pa.).</u>
    No city, 1967?

- R -

RADCLIFFE -- (Author unknown)
American Radcliffes: Carolina, Kentucky, Pennsylvania
branch. No city, 1963?

RALSTON -- Ralston, Mrs. Raymond
The search for our Ralston ancestors in Pennsylvania
(before 1800). Mrs. R. Ralston. Slippery Rock, Pa.,
1985.

RAMSEY -- Hauber, Mabel Clements
Descendants of Samuel Ramsey of Pennsylvania and
West Virgiia. Great Bend, Kans., 1946.

RANCK -- Ranck, John Allan
The ranks of the Rancks: a Ranck/Rank family history
and genealogy. Sowers Print Co. Lebanon, Pa., 1978.

RANDALL -- Randall, Leslie F.
A referenc of ancestral lines of Leslie Fairbanks   (P)
Randall, Jr. Covering a period of more than 300
years in America. Winchell Co. Philadelphia, 1963.

RANDOLPH -- Du Bin, Alexander
Randolph family and collateral lines of Parry and
Winslow. Historical Pub. Society. Philadelphia, 1946.

RANK -- McMorris, Elisabeth Runk
A brief family history. E. R. McMorris. Pennsylvania?,
1984.

RATHVON -- Sener, Samuel M.
Simon Rathvon, PH.D., Lancaster's oldest living   (A)
devotee of science. Lancaster?, Pa., 1890?

RAUB -- Raub, Michael W.
Extracts from genealogy of the Raub family in North   (P)
America, 1732-1914. Lancaster, Pa., no date.

RAUDENBUSH -- Price, Charles H.
Descendants of George Raudenbush who settled in   (P)
Upper Hanover Township, then Philadelphia County,
now Montgomery County, Pa. Telford, Pa., 1967.

RAUP -- Meiser, Joseph A.
A genealogy of selected Northumberland County, Pennsylvania
pioneer families. Guelph, Ontario, Canada, 1977.

RAY -- Froehlich, Dean
Ray families in Noble County, Indiana, Guernsey County,
Ohio, Ohio County, Virginia, and Washington County,
Pennsylvania. D. Froehlich. No city, 1982.

READ -- Reed, W. H.
History and genealogy of the Reed family; Johann Philib
Ried, Rieth, Riedt, Ritt, Rit, Rudt, etc., in Europe and
America, an early settler of Salford Township, (New
Goshenhoppen region) Philadelphia County, Pennsylvania.
Including Reeds other than our family of this locality,
an addenda, etc. The Norristown Press. Norristown,
Pa., 1929.

READ -- Seaver, J. Montgomery
... Reed family records. American Historical-Genealogical
Society. Philadelphia, 1929.

READ -- Talcott, S. V.
The Reed family. Martin & Allardyce. Frankford, Pa., 1912.

READ -- Wurts, John S.
Descent of Colonel George Reade, from medieval and modern
kings, Knights of the garter, and from thirteen sureties
and seven other barons for the Magna charta of A.D. 1215.
Brookfield Pub. Co. Philadelphia, 1941.

READING -- Leach, Josiah Granville
Genealogical and biographical memorials of the Reading,
Howell, Yerkes, Watts, Latham and Elkins families.
Philadelphia, 1898.

REAGER -- Rigor, Joseph E.
Genealogical records of; Reiger, Rieger, Reagor, Reager,
Regur, Raygor, Reger, Ragar, Rager, Rigour ... Rigor and
allied families. South Bend?. Ind., 1964.

REAM -- Thompson, A. W.
Ream family of Ursina, Pa. (formerly called Turkey   (A)
Foot) (region of Somerset County). Pittsburgh,
Pa., 1924.

REAMAN -- Finnell, E. M. G.
Rayman-Reiman family of Somerset County, Pa.   (A)
Monticello, Ind., 1973.

REBER -- Reber, Morris B.
Genealogy of the Reber family. Reading, Pa., 1901.

REDFIELD -- (Author unknown)
Recollections of John Howard Redfield (with ancestry).
Philadelphia, 1900.

REED -- Heath, Franklin W.
Child's history, Reed. Philadelphia, 1932.

REED -- Lytle, John P.
Reed family; a history of the descendants of Robert   (A)
Reed, Sr. Marion Center, Pa., 1909.

REED -- Nicholas, Ella C.
Family record: genealogies of the Reed, Eyster,   (P)
Slagel, Eckert and Shaffer families. Pittsburgh,
Pa., 1914.

REED -- Reed, Alexander P.
Alexander Reed (1776-1842) Washington, Pennsylvania   (P)
and his descendants. Reed and Whiting Co. Pittsburgh,
Pa., 1960.

REED -- Reed, Herbert R.
The Tulpehocken Reeds; a family sketch. Reed.
Philadelphia, 1974.

REED -- Reed, Willoughby Henry
History and genealogy of the Reed family; Johann Philib
Reid, Rieth, Riedt, Ritt, Rit, Rudt of Salford Township
(New Goshenhoppen region), Philadelphia County, Pa.
Norristown, Pa., 1929.

REED -- Seaver, J. Montgomery
The Reed genealogy. Philadelphia, 1929.

REES --Daskam, Faith G. S.
Rees(e)-Lee and allied families of Pennsylvania   (A)
and Maryland. Washington, D.C., 1947.

REES -- Streets, Thomas Hale
David Rees of Little Creek Hundred; and the descendants
of John Rees, his son. Philadelphia, 1904.

REEVES -- Reeves, Francis Brewster
1700-1900: ancestry and posterity of Johnson Reeves,
born October 16, 1799, died July 19, 1860, and a
memorial sermon by Samuel Beach Jones. Allen, Lane &
Scott. Philadelphia, 1900.

REICHNER -- Reichner, L. Irving
Reichner and Aiken genealogies. Philadelphia, 1918?

REIFSNYDER -- Glenn, Thomas Allen
    <u>Reifsnyder-Gillam ancestry</u>. Philadelphia, 1902.

REINEMANN -- Young, Henry James
    <u>American descendants of Eberhard Reinemann</u>. H. J.
    Young. Carlisle, Pa., 1982.

REIST -- Reist, Henry G.
    <u>Peter Reist of Lancaster County, Pennsylvania and some</u>
    <u>of his descendants</u>. Schenectady, N. Y., 1933.

REITZ -- Reitz, James J.
    <u>Family history and record book of the descendants of John</u>
    <u>Friedrich Reitz, the pioneer</u>. Walnutport, Pa., 1930.

REITZEL -- Reitzel, Albert E.
    <u>This is a record of the descendants of Michael</u>   (A)
    <u>Reitzel and Margaret Coble, his wife</u>. Philadelphia,
    1950.

RENNINGER -- Reninger, Jerilyn J.
    <u>Wendel Renninger and descendants of Pennsylvania</u>.   (P)
    Myers Print. Lansing, Mich., 1974.

RETTEW -- RETTEW, Edward W.
    <u>Genealogy of the Elijah Bull Rettew branch of the</u>   (P)
    <u>Rettew family</u>. West Chester, Pa., 1960.

REYNOLDS -- Imhof, Olive Reynolds
    <u>Reynolds of Anne-Arundel and Washington Counties,</u>
    <u>Maryland, and of Lawrence County, Pennsylvania</u>.
    Wooster, Ohio, 1973.

REYNOLDS -- Reynolds, Joseph B.
    <u>The Peter Reynolds family of Lawrence County, Pennsylvania</u>.
    Ann Arbor, Mich., 1940.

REYNOLDS -- Reynolds, Thomas A.
    <u>Ancestors and descendants of William and Elizabeth</u>
    <u>Reynolds of North Kingstown, R.I.</u> J. B. Lippincott.
    Philadelphia, 1903.

REYNOLDS -- Seaver, J. Montgomery
    <u>... Reynolds family records</u>. American Historical-
    Genealogical Society. Philadelphia, 1929.

RHOAD -- Rhoad, Robert R.
    <u>Rhoad and affiliated families, the journey to</u>   (P)
    <u>Pennsylvania</u>. No city, 1961.

RHOADS -- Gastner, S.
The Rhoads family of Pennsylvania. G. H. Buchanan. (P)
Philadelphia, 1901.

RHODES -- Mikula, Evelyn Rhodes
Henry Rhodes of Hill Valley, Pa. and descendants,
1773-1979. Sycamore Press. Elm Grove, Wisc., 1979.

RHYS -- Griffith, John T.
Rev. Morgan John Rhys, "the Welsh Baptist hero of (P)
civil and religious liberty of the 18th century."
Leader Job Print. Lansford, Pa., 1899.

RICE -- (Author unknown)
The fourth annual meeting of the Hench, Dromgold,
Hartman, Rice and Ickes reunion. Groff's park,
Perry County, Pensylvania. On Thursday, August 9,
1900. New Bloomfield?, 1900?

RICH -- Hurst, Charles W.
Early Rich families in Eastern Pennsylvania. (P)
Milford, Conn., 1958.

RICH -- Rich, Paul
The Riches of Reading. No city, 195_?

RICH -- Townroe, Frederick Rathbun
Rathbun-Rich and allied families; a manuscript covering
the ancestry of Dyer Dana and Susan Rathbun who
settled at Howard, Steuben County, New York, in the
year 1918. Harrisburg, Pa., 1947.

RICHARDS -- Richards, Louis
A sketch of some of the descendants of Owen Richards, (P)
who migrated to Pennsylvania previous to 1718. Collins
Printers. Philadelphia, 1882.

RICKETTS --Welker, Betty Ricketts
200 years in Clearfield County. Vision Press.
Coalport, Pa., 1983.

RICKRODE -- Yake, Donna Rickrode
John Rickrode and his descendants: nine generations
from 1760 to 1982. Mercury Press. Hanover, Pa., 1982.

RIDDELL -- Wood, John Maxwell
Robert Burns and the Riddell family. Norwood Editions.
Norwood, Pa., 1976.

RIDGWAY -- Hoagland, Edward C.
Notes on the Ridgway families of Bradford County,   (P)
Pa., descendants of David, Richard, Robert and
Burr Ridgway, pioneers. Sacred Art Press. Towanda,
Pa., 1958.

RIGHTER -- Goshow, Mildred
Study of the Righter family of Foxborough Township   (A)
in the 18th century. Philadlephia, 1957.

RITTENHOUSE -- Cassel, Daniel K.
A genea-biographical history of the Rittenhouse family
and all its branches in America, with sketches of their
descendants, from the earliest available records to the
present time, including the birth of Wilhelm in 1644 ...
The Rittenhouse Memorial Association. Philadelphia,
1893.

RITTENHOUSE -- Cassel, Daniel K.
The family record of David Rittenhouse; including his
sisters Esther, Anne and Eleanor. Also, Benjamin
Rittenhouse and Margaret Rittenhouse Morgan. Herald
Printing. Norristown, Pa., 1897.

RITTENHOUSE -- Cassel, Daniel K.
A record of the family of Joseph Rittenhouse.   (P)
Norristown, Pa., 1896.

RITTENHOUSE -- Gilfert, John W.
Ancestors and descendants of Charles Rittenhouse of   (P)
Sugarloaf Township, Luzerne County, Pennsylvania.
No city, 1949.

RITTENHOUSE -- Rittenhouse, Albert P.
Pedigree and history of the Rittenhouse family for   (P)
more than a thousand years in Europe and America.
No city, 1924.

RITTENHOUSE -- Rubincam, Milton
William Rittenhouse and Moses Dissinger, two eminent
Pennsylvania Germans. Pennsylvania German Society.
No city, 1959.

RITTER -- Ritter, Philip John
Family register of George Christian Ritter of Leiningen,
Rheinpfalz, Baiern, Germany, and his descendants from
the year of our Lord 1735 to the year 1905. Walther
Printing House. Philadelphia, 1905.

ROBB -- Meginness, John F.
Life and times of Robert Robb, esq. Muncy Township,
Lycoming County, Pa. Luminary Press. Muncy, Pa.,
1899.

ROBERTS -- Roberts, Clarence V.
Ancestry of Clarence V. Roberts & Frances A. (Walton)
Roberts; comprising a chart and sketches of some fifty-
six ancestral families who settled mostly in or near
Philadelphia, Pennsylvania. Wm. F. Fell Co.
Philadelphia, 1940.

ROBERTS -- Roberts, Ellwood
Old Richland families; including descendants of Edward
Roberts, Thomas Roberts, Thomas Lancaster, Peter Lester,
Casper Johnson, Hugh Foulke, Jacob Strawn, Richard Moore,
William Jamison, Robert Penrose, Joseph Ball, Morris
Morris, The Greens, Shaws, Edwardses, Heacocks, Thomsons,
Hallowells, and Spencers. Historical and genealogical
data being derived largely from the records of Friends and
other original sources. M. R. Wills, Norristown, Pa.,
1898.

ROBERTS -- Roberts, Ellwood W.
Roberts family genealogy, kith and kin for 300 years   (P)
1610 (to) 1932. 15 families ... 52 pioneer colonial
ancestors from England, Wales, Ireland, French
Flanders, and the Rhine ... Philadelphia, Pa., 1932.

ROBERTS -- Roberts, Isaac
Roberts family of Norristown, Pa., being the descen-   (A)
dants of Robert Ellis ... who emigrated from Wales
in 1690. New York, N. Y., 1912.

ROBERTS -- Seaver, J. Montgomery
... The Roberts genealogy. American Historical-
Genealogical Society. Philadelphia, 1928?

ROBESON -- Osborne, Kate Hamilton
An historical and genealogical account of Andrew Robson,
of Scotland, New Jersey and Pennsylvania, and of his
descendants from 1653 to 1916. J. B. Lippincott.
Philadelphia, 1916.

ROBINSON -- Boyer, Nathalie Robinson
A Virginia gentleman and his family. Philadelphia, 1939.

ROBINSON -- Coleman, Dorothy S.
Pioneers of Pittsburgh, the Robinsons.   (A)
Pittsburgh, Pa., no date.

ROBINSON -- Robinson, Thomas H.
     <u>Fragments of family and contemporary history</u>.
     Pittsburg, Pa., 1867.

ROBINSON -- Robinson, Thomas Hastings
     <u>Thomas Robinson and his descendants</u>. Harrisburg Pub. Co.
     Harrisburg, Pa., 1902.

ROBISON -- Thompson, Robert P.
     <u>A genealogy of the Robison family of Juniata County,</u>
     <u>Pennsylvania, 1732-1938</u>. San Diego, Calif., 1938.

ROCKWELL -- Rockwell, Charles F.
     <u>Jabez Rockwell, a biographical sketch; including a</u>   (P)
     <u>genealogy and brief history of the Rockwell family</u>.
     Philadelphia, 1901.

RODDY -- McComb, Virginia M.
     <u>The Hackett, Roddy, Moon families in Pennsylvania</u>.
     No city, 1939.

ROE -- (Author unknown)
     <u>Brief record of certain descendants of David Roe of</u>
     <u>Flushing, Long Island, New York, including John</u>
     <u>Martindale of Philadelphia, Pennsylvania and Martin</u>
     <u>Tichenor of New Haven, Connecticut and Newark, New</u>
     <u>Jersey, including Theophilus Blake of Greenbrier</u>
     <u>County, Virginia</u>. New York?, 1965?

ROGERS -- (Author unknown)
     <u>History and genealogy of the Jonathan Rogers family</u>.
     Norristown?, Pa., no date.

ROGERS -- Seaver, J. Montgomery
     <u>The Rogers genealogy</u>. Philadelphia, 1929.

ROGERS -- Van Valin, Minnie D.
     <u>Aquilla Wayne Rogers, Revolutionary patriot of Pennsylvania,</u>
     <u>Kentucky and Indiana</u>. No city, 1941.

ROGERS -- Ward, George S. L.
     <u>A sketch of some of the descendants of Samuel Rogers,</u>   (P)
     <u>of Monmouth County, New Jersey</u>. Collins Print. House.
     Philadelphia, 1888.

ROHRBACH -- Rohrbach, Jacob H.
     <u>Hans Jurg Rohrbach and descendants</u>. H. F. Temple.   (P)
     West Chester, Pa., 1941.

ROHRBACH -- Rohrbaugh, Lewis B.
Rohrbach genealogy; descendants of nine Rohrbach immigrants
to Colonial America, 1709-1754, and more than one hundred
Rohrbach immigrants to America 1825-1900. Dando-Schaff
Print. Philadelphia, 1970-77.

RONEY -- Keith, Laurence Prescott
The John Roney family of Philadelphia, including
references to the allied families Cresson, Jones,
Eckel, Morris, Cox, and Keith. Chicago, Ill., 1948.

ROOF -- Hoagland, Edward C.
Charles and James Roof, of Bradford County, Pa., and   (P)
some of their descendants. Sacred Art Press.
Towanda, Pa., 1959?

ROSE -- Allen, William J.
The Rose family in America; Isaac Rose (1747-1822)   (P)
Revolutionary War veteran, his ancestry and
descendants. No city, no date.

ROSE -- Rose, Christine
Andrew Rose family of Bucks County, Pennsylvania, and
Mercer County, Pennsylvania: the first five generations
in America. Rose. San Jose, Calif., 1977.

ROSENBERGER -- Rosenberger, Francis Coleman
Some notes on the Rosenberger family in Pennsylvania and
Virginia. Richmond, Va., 1950.

ROSENBERGER -- Fretz, Rev. A. J.
A genealogical record of the descendants of Henry
Rosenberger of Franconia, Montgomery County, Pa.
Together with historical and biographical sketches,
and illustrated with portraits and other illustrations.
Milton, N.J., 1906.

ROSENBERGER -- Kramer, Paulyne M.
A genealogical record of the descendants of Joseph   (A)
Detweiler Rosenberger. H. B. Rosenberger. Perkasie,
Pa., 1953.

ROSENBERGER -- Mathews, Edward
The Rosenberger family of Montgomery County. Historical
and genealogical sketches. I. R. Haldeman. Harleysville,
Pa., 1892.

ROSENBERGER -- Rosenberger Family Association
   The Rosenberger family; a collection of books,   (P)
   pamphlets, and updated genealogical material on
   the Rosenberger family in America. · Rosenberger
   Family Association. Hatfield, Pa., 1973.

ROSENBERGER -- Rosenberger, Francis Coleman
   A partial list of the descendants of Erasmus Rosenberger
   who lived in Hanover Township, Lancaster County,
   Pennsylvania, in the 1750's and settled in Berkeley
   County, Virginia, now West Virginia, in 1776. Washington,
   1951.

ROSENBERGER -- Rosenberger, Jesse Leonard
   The Pennsylvania Germans; a sketch of their history
   and life, of the Mennonites, and of side lights from
   the Rosenberger family. The University of Chicago
   Press. Chicago, Ill., 1923.

ROSENGARTEN -- Du Bin, Alexander
   Rosengarten family. Historical Pub. Society.
   Philadelphia, 1939.

ROSS -- (Author unknown)
   Ross memorial. William Sterling Ross and Ruth Tripp Ross
   (with genealogy). Reports of committees of Wyoming
   Historical and Genealogical Society. Wilkes-Barre,
   Pa., 1884.

ROSS -- Seaver, J. Montgomery
   ... Ross family records. American Historical-Genealogical
   Society. Philadelphia, 1929.

ROSSETTI -- Waller, Ross Douglas
   The Rossetti family, 1824-1854. Norwood Editions.
   Norwood, Pa., 1976.

ROSSETTI -- Waller, Ross Douglas
   The Rossetti family, 1824-1854. R. West. Philadelphia,
   1977.

ROWLAND -- (Author unknown)
   Rowland genealogy, Joseph Rowland of Lancaster Co.,   (A)
   Pa. and Ashland and Wyandotte Cos., Ohio, 1760-1927.
   Michigan State Lib. Lansing, Mich., 1952.

ROWLAND -- Roland, Charles Thomas
   The Roland and Spicer families of Maryland and Dorset,
   England. C. T. Roland. Bethel Park, Pa., 1983.

ROWLAND -- Rowland, Henry J.
A genealogical sketch of the posterity of John Rowland of
Rhosybayvil, parish of Bayvil, Pembroke, Wales, and after-
wards of East Whiteland, Chester Co., Pa. J. B. Lippincott.
Philadelphia, 1893.

ROYER -- Francis, J. G.
Genealogical record of the Royer family in America.
Lebanon, Pa., 1928.

ROYER -- Metz, W. Ray
The Royer family, ironmaster of Blair County,   (P)
Pennsylvania ... Hollidaysburg?, Pa., 1951.

ROYER -- Royer, John
First four generations of the family of Sebastian   (A)
Royer in America. Harrisburg, Pa., 1945.

RUBINCAM -- Rubincam, Milton
The German background of the Rubincam-Revercomb family of
Pennsylvania and Virginia. Washington, D.C., 1938.

RUBENKAM -- Rubincam, Milton
The Rubenkam family of Hessen, parent stock of the
Rubincam-Revercomb family of Pennsylvania and
Virginia. From Pennsylvania Genealogical Magazine.
No city, 1961.

RUBENKAM -- Rubincam, Milton
The Rubenkam family of Hessen, parent stock of the   (A)
Rubincam-Revercomb family of Pennsylvania and
Virginia. Philadelphia?, 1961.

RUFFNER -- Sweinberger, Jane S.
Ruffners of Pennsylvania and collateral lines, 1743-
1978. Sweinberger. San Diego?, Calif., 1979.

RUPP -- Rupp, I. Daniel
A brief biographic memorial of Joh. Jonas Rupp, and
complete genealogical family register of his lineal
descendants, from 1756 to 1875.. With an appendix.
L. W. Robinson. Philadelphia, 1875.

RUSH -- (Author unknown)
Descendants of John Rush. Philadelphia, 1893.

RUSH -- Biddle, Louis Alexander
A memorial containing travels through life or sundry
incidents in the life of Dr. Benjamin Rush, born
Dec. 24, 1745 (old style) died April 19, 1813;
written by himself; also extracts from his common-
place book as well as a short history of the Rush
family in Pennsylvania. Made at the Sign of the Ivy
Leaf. Philadelphia, 1905.

RUSH -- Rush, John L.
The Rush family of the Appalachians. Uniontown, Pa.,
1965.

RUSH -- Wiley, Sara L.
The Rush family of the Appalachians; descendants of   (P)
Captain John Rush. W. H. Farwell. Uniontown, Pa.,
1965.

RUSLING -- Rusling, James F.
The Rusling family. Philadelphia, 1907.

RUSSELL -- Russell, Alexander
Biographical sketch of the Russell family and   (A)
connections. H. F. Ward. Washington, Pa., 1887.

RUSTERHOLTZ -- Rusterholtz, Wallace P.
The Swiss family Rusterholtz in America; a history
and genealogy of Jacob and Catherine Kaufman Rusterholtz
of Erie County, Pennsylvania, and their descendants.
Erie, Pa., 1972.

RUTH -- Kriebel, Warren R.
"Ruth genealogy" (sic) a partial record of the decendants
of pioneer Henry Ruth, and other Ruth families mainly
Bucks and Montgomry Counties in southeastern Pennsylvania.
Fountain Press. Freeport, Pa., 1972.

RUTH -- Kriebel, Warren R.
The Ruth families. Fountain Press. Freeport, Pa., 1981.

RUTHERFORD -- Rutherford, W. F.
Dedication of the Rutherford monument and reunion of   (A)
the family, Jan.27, 1898. Harrisburg, Pa., 1898.

RUTTER -- Beaumont, Andre A.
Rutter wills. Wilkes-Barre, Pa., 1940.

RYDER -- Du Vernet, Margaret Binkley
Adam Ryder of Fort Loudon,Pennsylvania. Hagerstown,
Maryland, 1980.

- S -

SALKELD -- By a descendant
    The Salkeld family, from John who emigrated in 1705,
    to the fourth generation so far as known.   Jacob
    Painter.   No city, 1867.

SAMUEL -- Samuel, J. Bunford
    Records of the Samuel family, collected from essays, mss.,
    and other sources.   J. B. Lippincott.   Philadelphia, 1912.

SANDERS -- Helmer, Richard Bryan
    James and Alvin Sanders, Livestock Journalists of the
    Midwest.   Bryn Mawr, Pa., 1985.

SANTEE -- Santee, Ellis M.
    Genealogy of the Santee family in America.   Wilkes-Barre,
    Pa., 1927.

SARGENT -- Sargent, M. P.
    Pioneer sketches.   Erie, Pa., 1891.

SATTERTHWAITE -- Satterthwaite, Amos
    Genealogy of the Satterthwaite family descended from   (P)
    William Satterthwaite, who settled in Bucks County,
    Pa., in 1734, with some account of his ancestors in
    England.   Press of Franklin Print.   Philadelphia, 1910.

SAUDER -- Sauder, George G.
    History of the Bishop John M. Sauder family and   (A)
    related groups.   Goodville, Pa., 1956.

SAUDER -- Sauder, George G.
    History of the John M. Sauder family and related groups,
    1729-1966.   Ensinger Print Service.   Adamstown, Pa.,
    1966.

SAUDER -- Weaver, Laura G. M.
    Christian M. Sauder and Barbara G. Good Sauder,   (A)
    Magdalena C. Martin Sauder, etc   Ensinger Print.
    Adamstown, Pa., 1967.

SAUNDERS -- Helmer, Richard Bryan
    James & Alvin Sanders, livestock journalists of the
    Midwest.   Dorrance.   Bryn Mawr, Pa., 1985.

SAVAGES -- Burghard, August
    America's first family, the Savages of Virginia.
    Philadelphia, 1974.

SAVERY -- Savery, Addison H.
A genealogy and brief biography of the Savery family   (P)
of Philadelphia. Philadelphia, 1911.

SAYLOR -- Flickinger, Robert E.
In memory of Polly Weimer and the Saylor family of   (N)
which she was the last surviving member. Port
Royal, Pa., 1896.

SCAIFE -- Schoyer, William T.
Scaife Company and the Scaife family, 1802-1952; a   (A)
history of the oldest manufacturing company west of
the Alleghenies under five generations. Davis & Warde.
Pittsburgh, Pa., 1952.

SCARBOROUGH --
Photostat facsimiles of manuscripts relating to the
ancestry of Henry W. Scarborough of Philadelphia
(July 24, 1870 - October 10, 1935) and of his wife
Clara Hagerty Scarborough (1870-1932). Bequeathed by
him to the Library of Congress. Washington, D.C., 1936.

SCHAEFER -- Schaefer, John W.
Green grapes; a series of letters, personal and
genealogical. Hobson Book Press. New York, N.Y.,
1947.

SCHAEFFER -- Schaeffer, David I.
History and genealogy of the Georg Schaeffer family.   (P)
H. Ray Haas. Allentown, Pa., 1949?

SCHEFFER -- Crawford, Hazel Sheffer
The John Adam Scheffer family history and lineage,
1751-1958. Emlenton, Pa., 1958.

SCHEIRER -- Scheirer Family Reunion Association
Scheirer family directory and historical forward.
Slatington, Pa., 1950.

SCHEIRER -- Scheirer, David
Brief historic statement and directory of the present   (N)
Scheirer family. The Cement News Print. Northampton,
Pa., 1911.

SCHERMERHORN -- Schermerhorn, Louis Y.
Genealogy of a part of the third branch of the
Schermerhorn family in the United States.
J. B. Lippincott. Philadelphia, 1903.

SCHILLAT -- Iliff, Kathryn Hepburn
   The Schillat family in America. K. H. Iliff. West
   Chester, Pa., 1983.

SCHIMPF -- Shimp, Charles James
   Schimpf families of Philadelphia, Pennsylvania.
   Springfield?, Ill., 1971.

SCHLABACH -- Schlabach, Jacob C.
   Memorial history of Daniel and John Schlabach and   (A)
   their lineal descendants ... 1834-1967. Print Shop.
   Gordonville, Pa., 1967.

SCHLABACH -- Slayback, George Pendleton
   The Schlabach family of Northampton County, Pennsylvania.
   Schlechter's. Allentown, Pa., 1969.

SCHMOYER -- Dickson, Elmer
   The Schmoyer family (Schmeyer, Schmeier, Schmyer, Smoyer)
   descendants of Philip Schmeyer of Lehigh County, Pa.
   Chico, Calif., 1986.

SCHNECK -- Williams, Laurine Schneck
   Im Schneckengang = "At a snail's pace!": a genealogy and
   early history of several Schneck families in America,
   1741-1985. H. R. Schneck. Allentown, Pa., 1985.

SCHNEIDER -- Brossman, Schuyler C.
   Notes on the ancestors and descendants of Robert   (P)
   Isaac Schneider, born ... 1903, Bethel, Berks Co.,
   Pa. and his wife Jane Seidel Kuhlman ...
   R. I. Schneider. Reading, Pa., 1974.

SCHOCH -- Mousley, Franklin
   Michael Schoch (1733-1819) of the Northern Liberties.   (P)
   "Some of his descendants." Philadelphia, 1949.

SCHOFER -- Shofer, H. M.
   History of the descendants of John George and Regina
   Dorothea Shofer. East Greenville, Pa., 1897.

SCHOLL -- Scholl, A. G.
   Descendants of John Peter Scholl and his wife Anna.
   Susanna Dorothea Scholl, and genealogical family
   history, with short sketch of Philip Scholl and
   descendants. The Juniata Herald Pub. Co.
   Mifflintown, Pa., 1903.

SCHOONOVER -- Hoagland, Edward Coolbaugh
   The Schoonover and allied families. Wysox, Pa., 1954.

SCHOONOVER -- Hoagland, Edward Coolbaugh
The Schoonover & allied families; or, Jacob Schoonover
of Standing Stone, Pa., and his descendants, from records
gathered largely by Neva Schoonover Robinson. Wysox,
Pa., 1954.

SCHOTT -- Curry, Kate S.
Frederick Schott of Derry Township, Lancaster County,
Pennsylvania, and descendants. Washington, D.C., 1933.

SCHOTT -- Curry, Kate Singer
Frederick Schott, Derry Township, Lancaster County,
Pennsylvania. No city, 1934.

SCHOTT -- Shott, Joseph W.
Schott/Shott: John Jacobs Schott of Tulpehocken Township,
Berks County, Pa., and Ludwig Schott of Lebanon Township,
Lebanon County, Pa., and related families. Shott.
Lacey, Wash., 1978?

SCHROCK -- Miller, Elsie J.
Descendants of Samuel J. Schrock. Print Shop.   (A)
Gordonville, Pa., 1968.

SCHUCKER -- Schucker, Morris Gunther
Commemorative biographical and genealogical record of
the descendants of Johann Heinrich Schucker. Pittsburgh,
Pa., 1952.

SCHULTZ -- Berky, Andrew S.
An account of Dr. Benjamin Schultz of Pennsylvania.
Pennsburg, Pa., 1952.

SCHWARIE -- Swarey, Ezra B.
Family history of Christian Schwarie and Annie   (A)
(Hauder) Schwarie and their descendants. Berlin
Pub. Berlin, Pa., 1973.

SCHWEINITZ -- Rubincam, Milton
The de Schweinitz family of Pennsylvania. Penn. Historical
Junto. No city, 1955.

SCHWENK -- Strassburger, Ralph Beaver
Genealogy of the Schwenk family. Norristown, Pa.,
1929.

SCOTT -- Chance, Maria Scott Beale & Mary Ellen Evans Smith
Scott letters; the letters of John Morin Scott and his ife,
Mary Emlen Scott; with notes relating to them, their
ancestors and descendants. Biddle Press. Philadelphia,
1930.

SCOTT -- Hayward, Elizabeth
    <u>To thee this temple; the life, diary, and friends</u>   (A)
    <u>of Jacob Richardson Scott, 1815-1861</u>. Am. Baptist
    Historical Society. Chester, Pa., 1955.

SCOTT -- Scott, George Wilson
    <u>Quotations and excerpts from"McGinness and Scott</u>
    <u>families..." with additional supplementary historical</u>
    <u>and genealogical data of the John P. Scott branch of</u>
    <u>the Scott family and their relations with the White,</u>
    <u>May, Welch, Reed, Farrar, Cook and Gladden families of</u>
    <u>Yohogania County, Virginia ...</u> Imperial Press.
    Imperial, Pa., 1953.

SCOTT -- Scott, George Wilson
    <u>The Scott-White and related families of Western,</u>
    <u>Pennsylvania</u>. No city, 1953.

SCOTT -- Scott, Thomas Jefferson, D. D.
    <u>Our clan; a biological and genealogical account of the</u>
    <u>family of Rev. Andrew Scott, its ancestry and posterity</u>.
    Lancaster, Pa., 1920.

SCOTT -- Seaver, J. Montgomery
    <u>... Scott family records</u>. American Historical-Genealogical
    Society. Philadelphia, 1929.

SCULL -- (Author unknown)
    <u>The family of Scull ...</u> John C. Winston Company.
    Philadelphia, 1930.

SEAMAN -- Seaman, George S.
    <u>History of the Seaman family in Pennsylvania, with</u>   (P)
    <u>genealogical tables</u>. Reading, Pa., 1911.

SEAMAN -- Seaman, William Millard
    <u>The Seaman family of the Middle West; an account of</u>
    <u>the descendants of William Seaman, who died in</u>
    <u>Washington County, Pennsylvania, in 1814</u>. East
    Lansing, Mich., 1952.

SEAMAN -- Vogt, Helen Elizabeth
    <u>Descendants of William Seaman of Washington County,</u>
    <u>Pennsylvania, and allied families: Hurt, Brasher,</u>
    <u>McCammant, Wright</u>. H. E. Vogt. Brownsville, Pa.,
    1981.

SEARIGHT -- Searight, James Allison
A record of the Searight family (also written Seawright).
Established in America by William Seawright, who came from
near Londonderry ... to Lancaster County, Pennsylvania,
about 1740; with an account of his descendants as far as
can be ascertained. M. Cullaton & Co. Uniontown, Pa.,
1893.

SEATON -- Crosby, Jane Snowden
The Seatons of western Pennsylvania. The Hobson Book Press.
New York, N.Y., 1945.

SEAVER -- Seaver, Jesse
The Seaver genealogy. Philadelphia, 1924.

SEELY -- Hanners, Irving C.
General Samuel C. Seely, 1759-1819. Springtown,   (P)
Pa., 1961.

SEELYE -- Owlett, Mrs. E. H.
A pioneer family. A history of the family of
Ebenezer Seelye ... Press of the Agitator.
Wellsboro, Pa., 1910.

SEIBERT -- Bell, Raymond Martin
The Seibert family. Washington, Pa., 1959.

SEIBERT -- Bell, Raymond Martin
The families of George Nicholas Seibert (d. 1858) and
Leonard Miller (d. 1864) of Lebanon County, Pennsylvania,
Conrad Smith (d. 1879) and John Care (d. 1864) of Dauphin
County, Pennsylvania. R. M. Bell. Washington, Pa., 1981.

SEIBERT -- Sherman,Charles P.
First report on the Seibert estate. Times Printing House.
Philadelphia, 1883?

SELDEN -- Rogers, Sophie Selden
Selden ancestry; a family history, giving the ancestors
and descendants of George Shattuck Selden and his wife,
Elizabeth Wright Clark. E. van D. Selden. Oil City,
Pa., 1931.

SELL -- Sell, Jas. A.
History of the Sell family. Keystone Press. Altoona,
Pa., 1931.

SELL -- Sell, William D.
Descendants of Andoni Sell, Pennsylvania. Charleston   (A)
Electric Blue Print Co. Charleston, W. Va., 1913.

SELLERS -- Sellers, Edwin Jaquett
Partial genealogy of the Sellers and Wampole families
of Pennsylvania. J. B. Lippincott. Philadelphia,
1903.

SELLERS -- Sellers, Edwin J.
Supplement to genealogies. Allen. Philadelphia, 1922.

SELLERS -- Sellers, Edwin Jaquett
Sellers family of Pennsylvania, and allied families.
Allen, Lane & Scott. Philadelphia, 1925.

SELLERS -- Sellers, Sarah Pennock
David Sellers, Mary Pennock Sellers (written in 1916).
Innes & Sons. Philadelphia, 1928.

SELTZER -- West Virginia D.A.R., G.R.C.
The Seltzer family of Pennsylvania. No city, 1949.

SENSEMAN -- Senseman, Abraham H.
Historical incidents in the lives of Joachim and   (P)
Anna Catharine Senseman, and his son, Gottlob Senseman,
and his wife ... Senseman & Son. Philadelphia, 1881.

SENSEMAN -- Senseman, Charles M.
One hundred and seventieth anniversary of the landing   (N)
in America of Heinrich Joachim and Ann Catherine
Senseman. Carlisle, Pa., 1912.

SEYMOUR -- Du Bin, Alexander
Seymour, Taylor, Varian, Burt, Pierce, Baker.   (N)
Historical Publication Society. Philadelphia, 1954.

SHADE -- Hoffman, Walter R.
Pioneers of Pennsylvania, Ohio and Alabama; empire
builders extraordinary ... Piedmont, Calif., 1966.

SHAFER -- Schaeffer, Austin M.
History and genealogy of the George Schaeffer family.   (A)
H. R. Haas. Allentown, Pa., 1949.

SHAFER -- Shaffer, Mr. & Mrs. A. Nello and Frederick S. Weiser
Genealogical data concerning the ancestors and descendants
of John Jacob Shaffer, 1763-1816, of Mercerburg, Franklin
County, Pennsylvania. With supplementary data on the
Lesch, Kopp, Reiss, and Krafft families of Heidelberg and
Tulpehocken Townships, Berks County, Pennsylvania.
Gettysburg, Pa., 1958.

SHAFFER -- Shaffer, A. Nello
Genealogical data concerning the ancestors and descendants
of John Shaffer (1763-1816) of Mercersburg, Franklin
County, Pennsylvania. Gettysburg, Pa., 1958.

SHAMBACH -- Shambach, LeRoy Franklin
My ancestors and genealogical history of the Shambach
family. Middleburg, Pa., 1968.

SHANEFELT -- (Author unknown)
The Shanefelt family of Maryland and Pennsylvania.
No city, 1968.

SHANER -- Gustafson, Elaine Laura Shaner
Shaner family lineage in eastern Pennsylvania and
southern New Jersey. No city, 1975.

SHARP -- Eastwood, Elizabeth Cobb Stewart
Henry Sharp (c. 1737-1800) of Sussex County, New Jersey
and Fayette County, Pennsylvania, and his wife Lydia
Morgan, and some of their descendants, including Chalfant,
Depuy, Silverthorn, and Wheatley families. Eastwood.
Cleveland, Ohio, 1975.

SHARP -- Eastwood, E. C. S.
First supplement of additions and corrections to the   (A)
Henry Sharp (of Sussex Co., N.J. and Fayette Co.,
Pa.) genealogy. Cleveland, Ohio, 1978.

SHARP -- (Author unknwon)
Sharp family; from the estate of Hon. Geo. M. Sharp.   (A)
No city, 1911.

SHARP -- Sharp, Peter E.
Peter Sharp family history: emphasizing the descendants
of Christian and Mattie (Zook) Sharp. Sharp. Elkhart,
Ind., 1980.

SHARPLES -- Anderson, Bart
The Sharples-Sharpless family. West Chester, Pa.,
1966-1971.

SHARPLES -- Cope, Gilbert
Genealogy of the sharples family descended from John and
Jane Sharples, settlers near Chester, Pennsylvania, 1682.
Philadelphia, 1887.

SHARPLES -- Sharpless, Joseph
Family record containing the settlement, and genealogy to
the present time of the Sharples family in North America.
Philadelphia, 1816.

SHARPLESS -- Du Bin, Alexander
Sharples family, with collateral lines of Hunn and Jackson.
Historical Pub. Society. Philadelphia, 1948.

SHARPLESS -- Sharpless, Joseph
Family record; containing the settlement, and genealogy to
the present time, of the Sharples family, in North America.
With an appendix, containing memorials of the dying,
sayings, &c., of several deceased members of the family;
not before published. Philadelphia, 1816.

SHARP -- Sharpe, William Carvosso
The Sharps of Chester County, Pennsylvania, and abstracts
of records in Great Britain. W. C. Sharpe. Seymour,
Conn., 1903.

SHEARER -- Starkey, William Lowell
A genealogy of the Jacob Shearer family: descendants of
Jacob Shearer, 1744-1823, and Elizabeth Deal, 1750-1825,
who came from Cordorus Township, York County, Pennsylvania
to Washington County, Pennsylvania and then to Mapleton,
Stark County, Ohio in 1813. W. L. Starkey. Fremont,
Calif., 1978.

SHEELY -- Weiser, Frederick S.
Notes on the Sheelys of Adams and Cumberland Counties,   (A)
Pennsylvania. Lancaster, Pa., 1964.

SHELBY -- Shelby, Cass H.
A report on the first three generations of the Shelby
family. Holidaysburg, Pa., 1927.

SHELLEY -- Rolleston, Maud
Talks with Lady Shelley. Folcroft Library. Folcroft,
Pa., 1977.

SHELLEY - Rolleston, Maud
Talks with Lady Shelley. Norwood Editions. Norwood, Pa.,
1978.

SHELLEY -- Shelley, E. Herman
Descendants of Christian Shelly of Lancaster County,   (A)
Pa. Camp Hill, Pa., 1955.

SHEPARD --
Isaac A. Sheppard: a brief account of his ancestors and
some collateral relatives, together with an autobio-
graphical sketch. Philadelphia, 1897.

SHEPPARD -- Sheppard, Walter L.
    Ancestry and descendants of Isaac Applin Sheppard   (N)
    and Caroline Mary Holmes, his wife. Havertown?, Pa.,
    1973.

SHERMAN -- Sherman, Roger
    (The) Shermans; a sketch of family history and   (A)
    genealogical record, 1570-1890 ... Butler, Pa.,
    1946?

SHERRARD -- Sherrard, Robert Andrew
    The Sherrard family of Steubenville. Together with
    letters, records and genealogies of related families.
    J. B. Rodgers. Philadelphia, 1890.

SHERRARD -- Sherrard, Thomas Johnson
    The Sherrard family of Steubenville. Philadelphia, 1890.

SHERRICK -- Sherrick, James Wiley, II
    Beginning with the nation: a Sherrick family history.
    Sherrick. Edinboro, Pa., 1976.

SHIELDS -- Shields, John Edgar
    A history of the Shields family. Harrisburg, Pa., 1968.

SHILLITO -- Smith, Samuel M.
    Shillito family in Scotland, Ireland and America;   (A)
    520 descendants of George and Agnes Miller Shillito ...
    Beaver, Pa., 1931.

SHIMER -- Shimer, Allen R.
    History and genealogy of the Shimer family in America.
    Berkemeyer, Keck & Co. Allentown, Pa., 1908-1931.

SHIPPEN -- Armes, Ethel
    Nancy Shippen, her journal book; the international
    romance of a young lady of fashion of colonial
    Philadelphia, with letters to her and about her.
    J. B. Lippincott. Philadelphia, 1935.

SHIPPEN -- Balch, Thomas Willing
    The English ancestors of the Shippen family and Edward
    Shippen of Philadelphia. Philadephia, 1904.

SHIPPEN -- Klein, Randolph Shipley
    Portrait of an early American family: the Shippens of
    Pennsylvania across five generations. University of
    Pennsylvania Press. Philadelphia, 1975.

SHIREY -- Hanlon, LaVonne R.
   The marriage of Catherine & David: a history of
   southwestern Pennsylvania families. Fay-West
   Heritage Publications. Laurel, Md., 1982.

SHIREY -- Shirey, Clarence R.
   Parentage and descendants of John Shiry, Sr. and   (A)
   Mary "Polly" (Shaffer) Shiry. Shippenville,
   Pa., 1974.

SHIRK -- Shirk, Noah M.
   Family record of Joseph Shirk and his wife, Esther   (A)
   Horning. Kinsinger. Gordonville, Pa., 1966.

SHIRK -- Wenger, Eli D.
   History of Henry G. Shirk (fifth generation) ancestors (A)
   and descendants. Manheim, Pa., 1966.

SHIVELY -- Black, Arthur Geiger
   Descendants of Christian Shively of Warwick Twp.,
   Lancaster County, and later York Twp., York County,
   Pennsylvania. Kansas City, Mo., 1941.

SHRIVER -- Shriver, Robert Campbell
   History of the Shriver family and their connections.
   Hershey, Pa., 1976.

SHRIVER -- Shriver, Robert Campbell
   1981 supplement to the Shriver family history 1684-1976,
   (bicentennial ed.). R. C. Shriver. Mechnicsburg,
   Pa., 1981.

SHRIVER -- Shriver, Samuel S.
   History of the Shriver family and their connections,
   1684-1888 -- abridged and rev. Bicentennial ed. by
   Robert Campbell Shriver. R. C. Shriver. Hershey,
   Pa., 1976.

SHOEMAKER -- Blair, William T.
   The Michael Shoemaker book (Schumacher). International
   Text Book Press. Wyoming, Pa., 1924.

SHOEMAKER -- (Author unknown)
   The Shoemaker family. Reading, Pa., 1909.

SHOEMAKER -- (Author unknown)
   The Shoemaker family of Shoemakersville, Pennsylvania,
   1682-1909. L. S. Mohr. Reading, Pa., 1909.

SHOEMAKER -- Shoemaker, Benjamin H.
Shoemaker Pioneers. A guide to the Shoemaker families   (P)
of colonial America. Germantown, Pa., 1955.

SHOEMAKER -- Shoemaker, Benjamin H.
Shoemaker pioneers: the early genealogy and history of   (P)
the colonial Shoemaker families who came to America
before the Revolution. Shoemaker. Germantown,
Pa., 1975.

SHOEMAKER -- Shoemaker, Benjamin H.
Genealogy of the Shoemaker family of Cheltenham,
Pennsylvania. J. B. Lippincott. Philadelphia, 1903.

SHOEMAKER -- Shoemaker, Hubert Bastian
A genealogical and biographical record of the Shoemaker
family of Gloucester and Salem Counties, N.J., 1765-
1935. Temple Type-Crafters. Philadelphia, 1935.

SHOEMAKER -- Shoemaker, Thomas H.
The Shoemaker family. J. B. Lippincott. Philadelphia,
1893.

SHOEMAKER -- Shoemaker, William M.
Shoemakers and their descendants in the Wyoming   (P)
Valley, Pennsylvania. Rosemont, Pa., 1954.

SHOMO -- Joyner, Peggy S.
Ancestors and descendants of Joseph Shomo (Shammo),
immigrant to Pennsylvania, 1750. Gateway Press.
Baltimore, Md., 1983.

SHOWALTER -- Howes, Floyd
"Pennsylvani Ditesch" family of Showalter. Cheyenne,   (A)
Wyo., 1971.

SHRYOCK -- (Author unknown)
... Genealogical fan chart showing many "Shryock"
collateral lines ... Washington, D.C., 1930.

SHRYOCK -- Johnson, Rhea Duryea
The Shryock line. Cornwall, Pa., 1945.

SHUEY -- Shuey, D. B., A.M.
History of the Shuey family in America, from 1732 to
1876. Lancaster, Pa., 1876.

SHULTZ -- Shultz, Charles Ross
A genealogy of the Shultz, Cupp, Weyand and Pisel families
which have descended from Michael Shultz, a pioneer settler
in Somerset County, Pennsylvania, many of whose descendants
have also been pioneers throughout the United States and
Canada. Pittsburgh?, Pa., 1945.

SHUMWAY -- Shumway, Asahel Adams
Genealogy of the Shumway family in the United States of
America. G. Shumway. York, Pa., 1972-.

SIDMAN -- Wachter, Evelyn S.
Col. Isaac Sidman of Easton, Pa. Westfield, N.J.,   (A)
1972.

SIDWELL -- (Author unknown)
Sidwell family of Pennsylvania. No city, 1927.

SIDWELL -- A member of the family
A genealogy of the Pennsylvania, Maryland and Ohio
branches of the Sidwell family, compiled from various
published and unpublished sources. Washington, D.C.,
1930.

SIEGFRIED -- Stoudt, John B.
The life and times of Col. John Siegfried (with
ancestry. Northampton, Pa., 1914.

SIEGRIST -- Brechbill, L. T.
Pedigree of the Siegrists. Lancaster, Pa., 1972.   (A)

SIGGINS -- White, Emma Siggins
Genealogical gleanings of Siggins and other Pennsylvania
families. Kansas City, Mo., 1918.

SIGLER -- Bell, Raymond Martin
Our Sigler ancestors: early settlers in Mifflin County,
Pennsylvania. Carlisle, Pa., 1934.

SIGLER -- Bell, Raymond Martin
The Sigler family of Mifflin County, Pennsylvania.
Washington, Pa., 1958.

SILL -- Duermyer, L. A.
Sells chronology; a chronological index to early   (A)
records of the Sells, Sills, Zell and vonZellen
family of Pennsylvania. Staten Island, N.Y., 1962.

SILL -- Rudder, Edith Attkison
   My mother's family, Shannon-Sill, Pennsylvania and
   Ohio, Hamilton-Robinson, Virginia and Indiana.
   Salem?, Ind., 1942?

SILLIMAN -- Silliman, Robert B.
   The Silliman family; Pennsylvania and South Carolina
   lines. Silliman University Press. Dumaguette City,
   Philippines, 1966.

SILVER -- Keefer, Norman D.
   James Silver and his community. Paper read at Cumberland
   County, Pa., Historical Society and Hamilton Library
   Association, March 20, 1969.

SIMCOCK -- Liddle, Edna E.
   Simcock (Simcox), Liddle (Liddell) and related   (N)
   families, 1966. D. A. R. Lycoming Chapter.
   Williamsport, Pa?, 1966.

SIMPSON -- (Author unknown)
   The Simson and Gillespie genealogy. Philadelphia, 1902?

SIMPSON -- Bladen, Elizabeth Simpson
   The Simpsons of Rye Top, Cumberland Valley, Pennsylvania.
   Allen, Lane & Scott. Philadelphia, 1905.

SIMPSON -- Massey, George Valentine
   The Simpsons of Paxtang and Sunbury, Pennsylvania. No
   City, 1949.

SIMPSON -- Simpson, Helen A.
   Early records of Simpson families in Scotland, North
   Ireland, and eastern United States, with a history of
   the family of the compiler, and including genealogies
   of allied families Hout, Stringer, Potts and Dawson.
   J. B. Lippincott. Philadelphia, 1927.

SIMPSON -- Simpson, Helen A.
   Additions and correction to early records of Simpson
   families and allied families of Hout, Stringer, Potts,
   and Dawson. J. B. Lippincott. Philadelphia, 1929.

SIMPSON -- Simpson, Helen J.
   Genealogy of James Simpson, Westmoreland County,   (A)
   Pa., 1787-1957. Cordova, Ill., 1957.

SIMS -- Morris, Jane
   Adam Symes and his descendants. Dorrance and Company.
   Philadelphia, 1938.

SIMS -- Platt, Charles
     John Sims. Glenside, Pa., 1968.

SINCLAIR -- Baker, Wilma S.
     Father and his town: a story of life at the turn of
     the century in a small Ohio River town. Three
     Rivers Press. Pittsburgh, Pa., 1961.

SINCLAIR -- Daub, St. Claire (L.)
     Sinclair - Mulholland families of Ireland and   (P)
     America, 1679-1954. Springfield, Pa., 1954?

SINCLAIR -- Daub, St. Claire (Lappe)
     The Sinclaire family of Belfast, N. Ireland and their
     descendants, 1660-1960. Springfield, Pa., 1960.

SINCLAIR -- Daub, St. Claire (Lappe)
     The Sinclaire family of Belfast, N. Ireland and their
     descendants (sic) 1660-1964. Springfield, Pa., 1964?

SINCLAIR -- Kelsey, Jeannette G. W.
     A diverted inheritance. Philadelphia, 1904.   (A)

SINNOTT -- Sinnott, Mary Elizabeth
     Annals of the Sinnott, Rogers, Coffin, Corlies, Reeves,
     Bodine, and allied families. Philadelphia, 1905.

SITLER -- Sitler, Jacob
     Record of the Solomon and Samuel Sitler families.   (A)
     Zelienple, Pa., 1927.

SITMAN -- Wachter, Evelyn S.
     Rev. John R. Sitman, pioneer (United Brethren)   (P)
     preacher of Cambria County, Pa., and his descendants.
     Wachter. Westfield, N.J., 1973.

SKILLMAN -- Atkinson, Margaret A. S.
     To the water's edge; Skillman, Galley, Atkinson and
     allied families. Philadelphia, 1967.

SKILLMAN -- Skillman, William J.
     Skillmans and their kin. Philadelphia, 1903.   (P)

SKINNER -- Wahl, Doris S.
     The Skinner kinsmen; the descendants of Joseph and   (A)
     Martha (Kinne) Skinner of Connecticut, New York and
     Pennsylvania. Niagara Falls, N.Y., 1958.

SLAYMAKER -- Slaymaker, Henry Cochran
<u>History of the descendants of Mathias Slaymaker, who</u>
<u>emigrated from Germany and settled in the eastern</u>
<u>part of Lancaster County, Pennsylvania, about 1710</u>.
Lancaster, Pa., 1909.

SLAYMAKER -- Slaymaker, Henry C.
<u>History of the Slaymaker family</u>.   Lancaster Print.   (A)
Lancaster, Pa., 1969.

SLEAR -- Miller, Augustus D.
<u>A history of the Slear family</u>.   J. W. Shamp.   (P)
Lewisburg, Pa., 1902.

SLEAR -- Miller, A. D.
<u>... Slear genealogy, a history of the Slear family ...</u>
<u>with data furnished by Miss Mary C. Slear ... (Rev. ed.)</u>.
Eureka Printing Co.   Norristown, Pa., 1929.

SMEDLEY -- Cope, Gilbert
<u>Genealogy of the Smedley family, descended from George</u>
<u>and Sarah Smedley, settler in Chester County, Pa.;</u>
<u>with brief notices of other families of the name, and</u>
<u>abstracts of early English wills.   Published pusuant</u>
<u>to the will of Samuel Lightfoot Smedley, of Philadelphia,</u>
<u>Pa.</u>   Wickersham Print.   Lancaster, Pa., 1901.

SMEDLEY -- Hilles, Raymond W.
<u>Smedley (William Webster Smedley), Hilles (Albert</u>   (P)
<u>Letchwort Hilles), Whitaker (James Whitaker) ....</u>
Historical Publication Society.   Philadelphia, 1944.

SMITH --(Author unknown)
<u>Genealogy of the descendants of Robert Smith, who settled</u>
<u>near Castle Shannon, Washington Co.   Now Allegheny Co.,</u>
<u>Pennsylvania.   1772</u>.   Williamsport Print & Binding.
Williamsport, Pa., 1923.

SMITH -- (Author unknown)
<u>Record of the Smith family descended from John Smith, born</u>
<u>1655 in County Monaghan, Ireland</u>.   G. F. Lasher.
Philadelphia, 1906.

SMITH -- Andrews, Roberta G.
<u>Thirteen generations: ancestors and descendants of</u>   (N)
<u>Lemuel Hawley Smith and Mary Elizabeth Colby, 1580-</u>
<u>1974</u>.   Media, Pa., 1974?

SMITH -- Barnes, Mrs. Harriet Southworth (Lewis)
Smith, with collateral lines: Chipman, Divine, Huckins,
Jones, Lewis (Barnstable Branch) and Mayflower connection;
ancestral record of Frances Amelia (Smith) Lewis.
Philadelphia, 1910.

SMITH -- Harris, Joseph S.
Record of the Smith family. Philadelphia, 1906.

SMITH -- Hartman, Blanche T.
The Smiths of Virginia; a history and genealogy of the
Smiths of "Big Spring plantation", Frederick County,
Virginia, together with a chronicle of the Drugan and
the Carnahan families of Pennsylvania and Ohio.
Pittsburgh, Pa., 1929.

SMITH -- Heyward, Mary J. M.
The Smith family of Pennsylvania; a genealogy of the
descendants of the Smith family ... together with an
account of the origin of the name. Pasadena,
Calif., 1937.

SMITH -- Highland, Scotland G.
Fourth annual Christmas plea ... Dedicated by the author
to his maternal ancestor John Smith, born 1655, great
grandfather of Robert Fulton, born at Fulton house,
Fulton (then Little Britain) Township, Lancaster County,
Pennsylvania, November 14, 1765, died in New York,
February 24, 1815. An historical and genealogical
narrative ... Clarksburg, W. Va., 1926.

SMITH -- Michigan D.A.R., G.R.C.
Record of the Smith family of Washington Township,
York County, Pennsylvania. No city, 1934.

SMITH -- Nolan, J. Bennett
The Smith family of Pennsylvania, Johann Friederich
Schmidt, 1756-1812. Reading, Pa., 1932.

SMITH -- Oxenreider, Clayton D.
The Smith family record, made in 1912, with some
additions in 1953. Reading?, Pa., 1955

SMITH -- Seman, David
Pedigree of John Smith, Esq. of England, and a list of
unreclaimed estates. Philadelphia, 1859.

SMITH -- Smith, Charles W.
The history and genealogy of an American family: (N)
The Smiths of Herricks, who settled on Long Island
about 1639 ... 1635-1945. Glenside?, Pa., 1965?

SMITH -- Smith, Edward U.
Genealogy of the descendants of Robert Smith who settled near Castle Shannon, Washington County, now in Allegheny County, Pennsylvania, 1772. Polyanthus. Cottonport, La., 1971.

SMITH -- Smith, Elbert
The descendants of Joel Jones; a revolutionary soldier, born in Charlton, Mass., in 1764, and died in Crawford County, Pa., in 1845. Together with an account of his ancestors, back to Lewis and Ann Jones, of Watertown, Mass., who came to America about 1635, also the descendants of Lemuel Smith, born in Ware, Mass., in 1770, came to Crawford County, Pa., in 1817, and died in 1855. With an account of such of his ancestors as can now be located. The Tuttle Company. Rutland, Vt., 1925.

SMITH -- Smith, Josiah B.
Genealogy of William Smith, of Wrightstown, Bucks County, Pa., 1684. Collins Print. Newton, Pa., 1883.

SMITH -- Smith, Josiah B.
Genealogy of Robert Smith, of Buckingham, Bucks County, Pa., 1719. Newton, Pa., 1885.

SMITH -- Smith, Josiah B.
Genealogy of William Smith of Wrightstown, Bucks County, Pennsylvania, 1684. No city, 1937.

SMITH -- Smith, Marshall M.
A history of the descendants of Peter Smith. Marion Center, Pa., 1927.

SMITH -- Smith, Sarah W.
Brief history and a complete record of the American   (A)
descendants of John and Mary Smith, who lived and died in County Derry, Ireland. Allegheny, Pa., 1892.

SMITH -- Waters, Margaret R. & Donald D. Murphy
Smith family, descendants of George and Barbara (Bash) Smith of Westmoreland County, Pennsylvania, and Coshocton County, Ohio, whose children migrated westward through Hancock County, Indiana, and Madison County, Iowa, with allied lines of Bash, Waters, Ruby, Hogle, and Murphy. Indianapolis, Ind., 1946.

SMOUSE -- Smouse, J. Warren
The history of the Smouse family of America, 1738-1969, with revisions and additions by Mary Smouse Yohe. Havertown?, Pa., 1969?

SMOUSE -- Smouse, J. Warren
   The history of the Smouse family of America. Herald Print.
   Martinsburg, Pa., 1908.

SMUCKER -- Davidson, Jane L. S.
   Descendants of David Renno Smoker and Lydia Stoltzfus
   Smoker, Lancaster County, Pennsylvania. Chester County
   Trade Talk. Downington, Pa., 1978.

SMUCKER -- Davidson, Jane L. S.
   Christian Schmucker, a colonial Pennsylvania farmer.
   Davidson. Glen Moore, Pa., 1976.

SMUCKER -- Smucker, John R.
   Jonas Smucker, ancestors and descendants.   (A)
   Harleysville, Pa., 1975.

SMULL -- Egle, William H.
   Memorial of John Augustus Smull. L. S. Hart Print.
   Harrisburg, Pa., 1881.

SMYSER -- (Author unknown)
   Bicentennial meeting of the Smyser family in America,
   York fair grounds, June twenty-second, nineteen hundred
   and forty-six, York, Pennsylvania. Maple Press Company.
   York, Pa., 1947.

SMYSER -- (Author unknown)
   Minutes of the centennial celebration, held by the   (P)
   descendants of the elder Matthias Smyser, May 3,
   1845, on the farm of Samuel Smyser, in West
   Manchester Township, York Co., Pa. Stroman & Wagner.
   York, Pa., 1846.

SMYSER -- Laucks-Xanders, Amanda Lydia
   History of the Smyser family in America, September 1731 -
   September 1931. York Printing. York, Pa., 1931.

SNAVELY -- Compton, Lake F.
   Notes on Casper Snavely covering period 1723 to 1894   (P)
   (approx.) Berks, Dauphin, Lebanon and Lancaster
   Counties, Pa. D.A.R. Washington, D.C., 1975?

SNAVELY -- Weiser, Frederick S.
   Some notes on the ancestors of Esther Snavely (1803-   (A)
   1832), widow of Michael Bergtold and wife of Jacob
   Tanger. Gerttysburg, Pa., 1957.

SNOWBERGER -- Chance, Hilda Snowberger
   Family records of Snowberger and Kegarise. Chester?,
   Pa., 1964.

SNOWBERGER -- Chance, Hilda
Snowberger and Kegarise supplement, 1970, with index.
Liberty?, Pa., 1970.

SNOWDEN -- Snowden, Virginia Whitman
The descendants of Joseph Snowden (1725-1799): Amboy,
N.J., Washington County, Pa., Brooke Co., (W.) Va.
Gateway Press. Baltimore, Md., 1981.

SNYDER -- (Author unknown)
History of the Hough family and Snyder family. Uniontown,
Pa., 1940.

SNYDER -- Grove, Anna Barbara Snyder
History of John Peter Snyder, his wife Mary Cath.
Elizabeth Stantz Snyder, and their descendants.
Marion, Pa., 1892.

SNYDER -- Horlacher, Vaneta Thomas and Levi Jackson Horlacher
Family of John and Anna Margaret Lowald Snyder of
Northampton and Centre Counties, Pennsylvania.
Lexington, Ky., 1972.

SNYDER -- Suloff, Jean Aurand
History of the Snyder farm in Ferguson Valley, Mifflin
County, Pennsylvania. No city, 1976.

SOMERS -- Somers, Constantine
A short history of the Somers family, who first   (P)
settled on Somers Point. Collins. Philadelphia,
18__.

SOUTHWORTH -- Barnes, Harriet Southworth (Lewis)
Southworth, with collateral lines: Buckingham, Collier,
Kirtland, Pratt, Shipman; ancestral record of Henry
Martyn Lewis. Philadelphia, 1903.

SOUTHWORTH -- Southworth, G. C.
Genealogy of the Southworth family. Grove City,   (A)
Pa., 1925.

SOUTHWORTH -- Southworth, G. C.
Hiram Southworth, his ancestors and descendants. A
history of the Southworths of northwestern Pennsylvania.
Edwards Brothers. Ann Arbor, Mich., 1943.

SOWER -- Auge, M.
David Sower. The Sower Family. Philadelphia?, 1879?   (N)

SOWER -- Sower, Charles G.
Genealogical chart of the descendants of Christopher
Sower, printer of Germantown, Philadelphia, Pa.
C. G. Sower. Philadelphia, 1887.

SPANGLER -- Farley, Belmont
Eight centuries of Spanglers; twenty-two generations from
1150 A.D. to 1939 A.D., descendants of George Spangler
(1150-1190) ... with special reference to those sons of
Rudolph Spangler of Adams County, Pennsylvania, who
emigrated to Ohio between 1800 and 1825. Washington,
D.C., 1939.

SPARE -- Summers, William
The Speare family: Leonard and his descendants. Norristown,
Pa., 1931.

SPEAKMAN -- Webster, Emma Speakman
The Speakman family in America, including descendants of
Thomas and Ann (Harry) Speakman of Chester County,
Pennsylvania, married in 1714, and of William and Mary
(Townsend) Speakman of Berkshire in England, married in
1738. H. Ferris. Philadelphia, 1930.

SPEARS -- Delahunt, Mary Lou
Thomas and Nancy Lemmon Speer of Allegheny County,
Pennsylvania and Fulton County, Illinois. M. L. Delahunt.
Avon, Ill., 1981.

SPENCER -- Clark, Flora S.
Spencer genealogy. Elkins Park, Pa,m 1963-65.   (N)

SPENCER -- Jenkins, Howard M.
Genealogical sketch of the descendants of Samuel Spencer
of Pennsylvania. Ferris & Leach. Philadelphia, 1904.

SPENCER -- Spencer, Rachel and Herbert Reynolds Spencer
Spencer descendants of Gerard Spencer the emigrant.
Erie, Pa., 1941.

SPENCER -- Walter, Judith A.
1876 diary of Abraham Spencer of Clearfield County,   (A)
Pa. Bothell, Wash., 1973.

SPENGLER -- Spangler, Edward W.
The annals of the families of Caspar, Henry, Baltzer,
and George Spengler who settled in York County
respectively in 1729, 1732, 1732, and 1751. York, Pa.,
1896.

SPIELMANN -- Spielmann, Percy Edwin
The early history of the Spielmann family and of Marion
Harry Alexander Spielmann (1858-1948) to the year of his
marriage (1880), together with some associated excursions
and diversions. Reading, Pa., 1951.

SPITTLER -- Honeyman, Gale Edwin Spitler
The house of Spittler-Spitler, 1736-1976: de[s]cendents
of Johannes and Catharina (Schaffner) Spittler, emigrants
from Bennwil, Canton Basel Switzerland, to Bethel Township, Lancaster County, Pennsylvania. Honeyman.
Laura, Ohio, 1977.

SPRENCKEL -- Young, Henry J.
Report on the Sprenckel family of York County, Pa.,   (N)
prior to the year 1850. Historical Society of York
County. York, Pa., 1972.

SPRINGER -- Springer, M. C.
A genealogical table and history of the Springer family,
in Europe and North America, for eight centuries, from
the earliest German princes; origin of the name, etc.
Dickson & Gilling. Philadelphia, 1881.

SPRINGER -- Springer, Moses C.
Chart No. 1. Showing the derivation of Louis II (the
Springer). Printed especially for the Newberry library,
and given with the compliments of Mrs. Warren Springer,
1897. Philadelphia?, 1897.

SPOON -- Finfgeld, Lois Ryno
Descendants of Ulrich Spoon/Spohn (1717-1781) of Lancaster
County, Pennsylvania. Henry, Ill., 1977.

SPOON -- Finfgeld, Lois Ryno
Descendants of Ulrich Spoon/Spohn (1717-1781) of Lancaster
County, Pennsylvania: a record of descendants through
seventh and eighth generations with various related
documents, letters, and pictures. Finfgeld. Canton,
Ill., 1977.

STABLER -- Frey, Frank H.
Stabler family of Pennsylvania, Maryland, Illinois.   (A)
Chicago, Ill., 1938.

STAGER -- Fisher, Clerice Joy Zehrbach
The posterity of John Adam Stager: who arrived in
Philadelphia in 1732, and settled in Avon,
Pennsylvania. Gateway Press. Richland, Wash., 1983.

STAM -- Hornsby, Lillie S.
   The descendants of Jacob Stam (Stamm), Pennsylvania,   (A)
   Maryland. No city, no date.

STANDISH -- Cass, Earle Millard
   Ada Ball Cass, a descendant of Captain Myles Standish.
   New Catle, Pa., 1949.

STANTON -- Stanton, William Henry
   A book called our ancestors the Stantons. Philadlephia,
   1922.

STAPLES -- Ralston, Mrs. Raymond
   The ancestry of Job Staples of Canterbury, Connecticut,
   and Butler County, Pennsylvania. Mrs. R. H. Ralston,
   Slippery Rock, Pa., 1983.

STAUDT -- Staudt, Richard W.
   The Staudt-Stoudt-Stout family of Pennsylvania and their
   ancestors in the Palatinate. Allentown, Pa., 1925.

STAUFFER -- (Author unknown)
   A Stouffer line of descent that originated in Lancaster
   County, Pennsylvania. No city, 1951.

STAUFFER -- (Author unknown)
   Records of the proceedings of the John Stauffer memorial
   association ... Ringtown, Pa., 1911 -.

STAUFFER -- Bower, Henry S.
   A genealogical record of the descendants of Daniel Stauffer
   and Hans Bauer and other pioneers, together with historical
   and biographical sketches, and a short history of the
   Mennonites ... With a history of the house of Hohenstaufen,
   by Fred. Raumer, of Germany. News Printing House.
   Harleysville, Pa., 1897.

STAUFFER -- Fretz, Abraham James
   The descendants of Henry Stauffer and other Stauffer
   pioneers. Harleysville, Pa., 1899.

STAUFFER -- Stauffer, Ezra N.
   Stauffer genealogy of America and history of the descendants
   of Jacob Stauffer, from the earliest available records to
   the present time. With a few illustrations. Mennonite
   Pub. House. Scottdale, Pa., 1917.

STAUFFER -- Stauffer, Richard E.
   Stauffer, Stouffer, Stover, and related families.
   Stauffer. Old Zionsville, Pa., 1977.

STAYROOK -- Stayrook, Sarah R.
Family record of Nicholas Stayrook and Mary (Plank)   (A)
Stayrook and their descendants. Berlin Pub.
Berlin, Pa., 1970.

STEELE -- (Author unknown)
The Holy Bible ... Philadelphia. M. Carey & Son.
Philadephia, no date.

STEELE -- McKinstry, Loraine S.
Laurel; a leaf from Chester County's past; with   (P)
biography of Hugh E. Steel and genealogy of his
descendants. West Chester?, Pa., 1928.

STEELE -- Stone, Frederick D., Jr.
The descendants of George Steele of Barthomley, Cheshire,
England, and Chester County, Pennsylvania. Philadelphia,
1896.

STEELE -- Welfley, William H.
Steele family genealogy. Somerset, Pa., 1909.   (A)

STEELE -- Welfley, William Henry
A genealogy of the descendants of George Steele and
his wife Margaret, late of Hopewell Township,
Bedford County, Pa. No city, 1976.

STEER -- (Author unknown)
... The Steer family. Philadelphia, 1943.

STEER -- Johnson, Rhea Duryea
Abstracts of wills and administration papers: the Steer
family ... Philadelphia, 1946?

STEIGERWALT -- Steigerwalt, Mabel
The Steigerwalt family, 1767-1967. Stutzman Print.
Mifflintown, Pa., 1967.

STEINMAN -- Brubaker, John H.
The Steinmans of Lancaster: a family and its enterprises.
Steinman Enterprises. Lancaster, Pa., 1984.

STEPHENS -- Bell, Raymond M.
Alexander Stephens, 1727-1814, Scotland, Pennsylvania,   (A)
Georgia; grandfather of Alexander Hamilton Stephens.
Washington and Jefferson College. Washington, Pa.,
1962.

STEVENS -- Bell, Raymond Martin
The Alexander Stephens family, Pennsylvania-Georgia.
R. M. Bell. Washington, Pa., 1981.

STEVENSON -- Stevenson, George Urie
James Stevenson, Senior, of Strabane Township, York
County, Pennsylvania. No city, 1964.

STEWART --Stewart, Archibald G.
History of the Robert Stewart family; which came from   (A)
Ireland in 1774 ... and settled in Westmoreland Co.,
Pa. Grove City Pub. Grove City, Pa., 1908.

STICHTER -- Stichter, Joseph L.
Genealogy of the Stichter family. Pottsville, Pa., 1902.

STICHTER -- Stichter, Joseph L.
Genealogy of the Stichter family, 1189-1902. Daily
Republican Books Room. Pottsville, Pa., no date.

STIEFEL -- Stiefel, Ira B.
Genealogy Stiefel and Jones families. Wilkinsburg,   (A)
Pa., 1959.

STIEGEL -- Heiges, George L.
Henry William Stiegel and his associates. Manheim,
Pa., 1948.

STILES -- Nichols, Jeannette Paddock
James Styles of Kingston, New York, and George Stuart
of Schoolcraft, Michigan; their descendants and allied
families with an historical narrative. Swarthmore,
Pa., 1936.

STOCKER -- Stewart, Jennie E.
Records from six families of Northampton and Berks
County, Pennsylvania. No city, 1938.

STOCKTON -- Cregar, William Francis
The Stockton family in England and the United States.
Patterson and White. Philadelphia, 1888.

STOCKTON -- Glenn, Thomas A.
Morven and the Stocktons. H. T. Coates.   (P)
Philadelphia, 1899.

STOCKTON -- Stockton,J. W.
A history of the Stockton family. Press of Patterson &
White. Philadelphia, 1881.

STOCKTON -- Stockton, T. H.
Poems: with autobiographic and other notes. W. S. & A.
Martin. Philadelphia, 1862.

STOEVER -- Staver, Addie Johnston
    <u>A genealogical and biographical sketch of a branch of a</u>
    <u>family tree</u>. Lock Haven, Pa., 1931.

STOLTZFUS -- Stoltzfus, John
    <u>Family history; memories of the past with a glance</u>   (A)
    <u>into the future, and the legacy of a minister</u>.
    S. Ernst. Millwood, Pa., 1873.

STONE -- Seaver, J. Montgomery
    <u>Stone family records</u>. Philadelphia, 1927.

STONER -- Stoner, Robert T.
    <u>A genealogical study of the antecedents of Calvin C.</u>   (P)
    <u>Stoner, b. 1875, d. 1959, and Lucy C. Stoner, of</u>
    <u>Shiremanstown, Cumberland County, Pa., and their</u>
    <u>descendants...</u> Fry Publications, Inc. Mechanicsburg,
    Pa., 1973?

STORK -- Morris, John G.
    <u>The Stork family in the Lutheran church: or, Biographical</u>
    <u>sketches of Rev. Charles Augustus Gottlieb Stork, Rev.</u>
    <u>Theophilus Stork, D.D., and Rev. Charles A. Stork, D.D.</u>
    Lutheran Publication Society. Philadelphia, 1886.

STOUT -- Stout, Edmund B.
    <u>Stout marriages in Berks County, Pennsylvania</u>.   (A)
    No city, 1976.

STOUT --
    <u>The history of the Stout family, first settling in</u>
    <u>Middletown, Monmouth County, New Jersey, in 1666 ...</u>
    <u>Originally compiled and published in 1823 by Capt.</u>
    <u>Nathan Stout. Reprinted in 1878 with additions by</u>
    <u>Mrs. Sarah Weart and other descendants, and by</u>
    <u>Joab B. Stout ... in May 1906</u>. G. A. Chandler.
    Bethlehem, Pa., 1929.

STOUT -- Streets, Thomas H.
    <u>The story of Penelope Stout as verified by the events</u>   (P)
    <u>of history and official records (with genealogical</u>
    <u>data)</u>. Philadelphia, 1897.

STOVER -- Fretz, Rev. A. J.
    <u>A genealogical record of the descendants of Henry Stauffer</u>
    <u>Stauffer pioneers, together with historical and biographical</u>
    <u>sketches</u>.   Press of the Harleysville News. Harleysville,
    Pa., 1899.

STRASSBURGER -- Strassburger, Ralph Beaver
<u>The Strassburger family and allied families of Pennsylvania;</u>
<u>being the ancestry of Jacob Andrew Strassburger, esquire, of</u>
<u>Montgomery County, Pennsylvania.</u> Gwynedd Valley, Pa., 1922.

STRAUSBAUGH -- Strausbaugh, Stella F.
<u>Strausbaugh, Bringman, Carr, and Nisly families,</u>
<u>Pennsylvania.</u> No city, 1957-1958.

STRAW -- Straw, Albert Y.
<u>Some genealogies and family records.</u> Clearfield,   (A)
Pa., 1931.

STRAYER -- Strayer Historical Committee
<u>Record of John Peter Strayer.</u> York County Strayer Reunion.
Dover, Pa., 1968.

STRICKLER -- Strickler, Abigail M.
<u>Stricklers of Pennsylvania ...</u> Mennonite Pub. House.   (P)
York, Pa., 1966?

STRITE -- Robinson, Carl E. and Amos W. Strite
<u>The history and genealogical records of the Strite and</u>
<u>allied familis of Lancaster, Dauphin, and Franklin</u>
<u>Counties, Pa. and Washington County, Md.</u> A. Strite.
Hagerstown, Md., 1963.

STRITTMATTER -- Strittmatter, Rev. Blase
<u>A Strittmatter family tree.</u> Latrobe, Pa., 1936.

STRONG -- Barr, Lockwood
<u>Biography of Dr. Joseph Strong, 1770-1812,</u>   (N)
<u>Philadelphia physician ...</u> Pellham Manor, N.Y., 1940.

STROTHER -- Owen, Thomas McAdory
<u>William Strother, of Virginia, and his descendants.</u>
Harrisburg, Pub. Harrisurg, Pa., 1898.

STROUD -- Stroud, Lester M.
<u>History of the name of Stroud and the descendants of</u>   (A)
<u>John Thomas Stroud and Ida Ann Smith Stroud.</u> Trout
Run, Pa?, 1962.

STUART -- Stewart, Archibald G.
<u>History of the Robert Stewart family.</u> Grove City Pub. (A)
Grove City, Pa., 1908.

STUKEY -- Denniston, Elmer Leonidas
<u>Genealogy of the Stukey, Ream, Grove, Clem, and</u>
<u>Denniston families.</u> Harrisburg, Pa., 1939.

STURGIS -- Sturgis, Charles Inches
  The descendants of Robert Shaw Sturgis & Susan Brimmer Inches. Wm. F. Fell Co. Philadelphia, 1943.

STURTEVANT --Sturtevant, Percy G.
  Lineage and descendants of Charles Henry Sturtevant and Rolinda Sherman Sturtevant, Minnesota pioneers, with other family information. Erie, Pa., 1956.

SUMMERS -- (Author unknown)
  A history of George Summers of Douglass and Lower Dublin Townships, Montgomery County, Pennsylvania. No city, 1918?

SUMMERS -- (Author unknown)
  Seventh annual reunion of the Summers family ...   (P)
  Hunting Park, Philadelphia. Philadelphia?, 1922.

SUMMERS -- Summers, G. Byron
  A history of George Summers of Douglass and Lower   (N)
  Dublin Townships, Montgomery County, Pa. No city, 1926?

SUMY -- Summy, John A.
  Family record of John and Elizabeth Sumy and their   (A)
  descendants. Comm. Print. Meyersdale, Pa., no date.

SUNDAY -- (Author unknown)
  Sunday family history; first member settles at   (P)
  Cocalico, in Conestoga Valley. Reading, Pa., 1921?

SUNDAY -- (Author unknown)
  Sunday-Sontag family of Berks and Lehigh Counties,   (A)
  Pennsylvania; correspondence on family between Lammas Klopp and Mrs. Elton Herring and a few others, 1963-1969. No city, 1963-1969.

SUNDAY -- Sunday, John H.
  History of the Sunday-Sonntag-Sondagh family, or   (A)
  Hendk, Sondagh and his descendants of Berks and Lehigh Counties, Pa. Washington, D.C., 1890-1925.

SUNDAY -- Sunday, John L.
  Descendants of my great-great-grandparents Henry   (P)
  Sunday (1757-1831) and Mary Ann Sunday (1757-1846). Philadelphia, 1950.

SUPPLEE -- Conard, Mrs. Irene D. S.
  History of the Supplee-De Haven family. Norristown, Pa., 1935?

SWAIN -- Swayne, Norman Walton
<u>The descendants of Francis Swayne and others</u>. J. B.
Lippincott. Philadelphia, 1921.

SWAN -- Swan, S. D.
<u>Family record of John Swan of Greene County, Pa.</u> New
Nonpareil Co. Council Bluffs, Iowa, 19__?

SWARTLEY -- Swartley, Samuel R.
<u>Genealogy record of descendants of Elizabeth Gehman</u>   (A)
<u>and Abraham R. Swartley of Franconia, Montgomery</u>
<u>County, Pa.</u> Lansdale, Pa?, no date.

SWAYNE -- Swayne, Norman W.
<u>Swaynes descended from Francis Swayne of East</u>   (P)
<u>Marlborough Township, Chester County, Pa.</u>
Stephenson Bros. Philadelphia, 1955.

SWIFT -- Balch, Thomas Willing
<u>The Swift family of Philadelphia</u>. Philadelphia, 1906.

SWING -- Swing, Albert Holmes
<u>The Swing family in America</u>. Bryn Mawr, Pa., 1961.

SWOPE -- Swope, Gilbert Ernest
<u>History of the Swope family</u>. Lancaster, Pa., 1896.

SWOPE -- Swope, Gilbert Ernest
<u>History of the Swope family and their connections.</u>
<u>1678-1896</u>. T.B. & H.B. Cochran. Lancaster, Pa., 1896.

SWOPE -- Swope, Harper E.
<u>The Swope family in central Pennsylvania</u>. Pittsburgh,
Pa., 1946.

SWOPE -- Swope, Harper E.
<u>Some interesting facts relative to members of the</u>   (A)
<u>Swope family in central Pennsylvania</u>. Pittsburgh,
Pa., 1946.

SYNG -- (Author unknown)
<u>Syng of Philadelphia</u>. Sherman & Co. Philadelphia, 1891.

- T -

TALBOT -- (Author unknown)
Talbot (family). Printed at the Herald. Honey Brook,
Pa., 19__.

TALLEY -- Talley, George A.
A history of the Talley family on the Delaware, and
their descendants; including a genealogical register,
modern biography and miscellany. Early history and
genealogy from 1686. Moyer & Lesher. Philadelphia,
1899.

TALMAGE -- Talmage, T. Dewitt
The almond tree in blossom; or, The beauty of age. A
sermon commemorative of the life and death of Hon.
David T. Talmage. Philadelphia, 1866.

TANGER -- Weiser, Frederick Sheely
The Tanger-Metzger genealogy. Gettysburg, Pa., 1955.

TANGER --
The Tanger-Metzger genealogy, with a record of the
descendants of John and Catharine (Metzger) Tanger,
1773-1950, and data on the Lottman, Rudisil, Snavely,
Hess, Harnish, Zercher, and Gall families of Lancaster
County, Pennsylvania. Gettysburg, Pa., 1955.

- Some notes on the ancestors of Esther Snavely, 1803-
1832, widow of Michael Bergtold and wife of Jacob Tanger.
Gettysburg, Pa., 1957.

TANNENBERG -- Armstrong, William H.
The life and work of David Tannenberg. Philadelphia,
1967.

TATTERSON -- Tatterson, Benjamin F.
The Tatterson family of America and allied families.
B. F. Tatterson. Pittsburgh, Pa., 1983.

TATUM -- Tatum, Richard P.
Tatum narrative, 1626-1925. Philadelphia, 1925.

TAYLOR -- Bye, Arthur Edwin
A friendly heritage along the Delaware. The Taylors   (P)
of Washington Crossing and some allied families in
Bucks County ... Vantage Press. New York, N.Y.,
1959

TAYLOR -- Cope, Gilbert
Descendants of Joseph Taylor, of Kennet, Chester Co.,
Pa. West Chester, Pa., 1891.

TAYLOR -- Cope, Gilbert
Taylor family, Chester County, Pa. West Chester, Pa.
1869.

TAYLOR -- Du Bin, Alexander
The Taylor family of Philadelphia, and collateral   (N)
lines of Alkins-Hayes-Holder-Goddard... Historical
Publication Society. Philadelphia, 1948.

TAYLOR -- Jacobs, G. W.
Family record of the descendants of Dr. Edward Taylor.
G. W. Jacobs. Philadelphia, 1903-54.

TAYLOR -- Justice, Alfred Rudolph
Descendants of Robert Taylor. Philadelphia, 1925.

TAYLOR -- Justice, Alfred Rudolph
Descendants of Robert Taylor, one of the colonizers and
early settlers of Pennsylvania under William Penn, with
special reference to the descendants of his son Isaac,
and his daughters, Rachel Livesey and Mary Lewis.
Philadelphia, 1925.

TAYLOR -- Seaver, J. Montgomery
Taylor family history. Philadelphia, 1929.

TAYLOR -- Stewart, Thomas M.
History of the Taylor family, the descendants of William
and Ann (Wilson)̇ Taylor of Lawrence County, Pensylvania.
Taylor Family Association. Filley, Nebr., 1925.

TAYLOR -- Taylor, Mary Snyder
Annals of a Bucks County family of Old Taylorsville,
Pennsylvania. No city, 1940.

TEDFORD -- Detty, Victor Charles
A Tedford family history. Carlisle, Pa., 1956.

TEETER -- Teeter, Banjamin F.
Ancestors and descendants of Benjamin Franklin   (A)
Teeter (1860-1941); including genealogy of some
other relatives. Berlin Pub. Berlin, Pa., 1961.

TELLER -- Teller, Chester Jacob
Teller family in America, record of a hundred years.
Cousins' Pub. Committee. Philadelphia, 1944.

TELLER -- Teller, Chester Jacob
New Teller generations; sequel to Teller family in
America. Cousins' Pub. Committee. Philadelphia,
1953.

TENER -- Tener, Francis J.
The Teners of Tyrone, Ireland and of the United States   (N)
of America. Pittsburgh, Pa., 1932.

THEAL -- Theal, Charles T.
My family genealogy, Theal, 1800-1984: project of the
Theal Heritage Resource Center. C. T. Theal. Camp
Hill, Pa., 1984.

THOM -- Thom, Jay Webb
The Thom family, the descendants of Joseph Thom and
Elizabeth Craig Thom of Westmoreland County, Pennsylvania.
Franklin, Ind., 1931.

THOMAS -- Bacon, Henry
Christian old age: a discourse preached in the Church   (P)
of the Messiah ... on the death of Jacob Thomas.
Crissy & Markley. Philadelphia, 1854.

THOMAS -- Levick, James J.
The early history of Merion. And An old Welsh pedigree.
Collins Printing House. Philadelphia, 1880.

THOMAS -- Lyle, William Thomas
The Thomas family, as descended from David and Anna Noble
Thomas. J. B. Hoff. Philadelphia, 1907.

THOMAS -- Mathews, Edward
The Thomas family of Hilltown, Bucks County, Pennsylvania.
A. K. Thomas. Landsdale, Pa., 1884.

THOMAS -- Meginnis, John F.
Address at the annual reunion of the descendants of   (P)
"Iron" John Thomas, held at Williamsport, Pa. ...
Gazette and Bulletin Print House. Williamsport,
Pa., 1896.

THOMAS -- Seaver, J. Montgomery
Thomas family history. Philadelphia, 1927.

THOMEN -- Thomen, Harold O.
Martin Thomen, who came from Switzerland to America
in 1803, his descendants and some of their ancestors.
Tavern Press. Boalsburg, Pa., 1970.

THOMPSON -- (Author unknown)
The Thompson family ... Pottsville, Pa., 1887.

THOMPSON -- Morrell, John Dorrance
1800 census of Pennsylvania for the surname Thompson.
Copied for the Thompson family magazine by Beverly Margaret
Stercula. With appendix of 1820 census records of Tioga
Co., Pa.; Union Co., Pa.; Warren Co., Pa.; Washington Co.,
Pa.; Venango Co., Pa. (and) York Co., Pa. Thompson Family
Association. Fullerton, Calif., 1963.

THOMPSON -- Thompson, David G.
Gordon and Jane Clemens Thompson ... Science Press Print.
Lancaster, Pa., 1940.

THOMPSON -- Thompson, John Bodine
John Thomson and family. Gazette and Bulletin Print House.
Williamsport, Pa., 1889.

THOMPSON -- Thompson, William Baker
Thompson lineage, with mention of allied families.
Telegraph Printing Co. Harrisburg, Pa., 1911.

THOMSON -- Bassett, Josephine R.
Ancestry and some of the descendants of Thomas Thomson   (A)
(d. 1770) of County Down, Ireland and Donegal Township,
Lancaster Co., Pa. Minneapolis, Minn., 1948.

THOMSON -- Herndon, John Goodwin
John Thomson. Lancaster, Pa., 1943.

THOMSON -- McAllister, Addams S.
The descendants of John Thomson. Easton, Pa., 1917.

THORNE -- Thorne, John M.
The Thorne family, its branches from the parent tree.
Lancaster Press. Lancaster, Pa., 1935?

THORPE -- King, Edward Thorp
Genealogy of some early families in Grant and Pleasant
districts, Preston County, West Virginia, also the
Thorpe family of Fayette County, Pennsylvania, and
the Cunningham family of Somerset County, Pennsylvania.
Marshalltown?, Iowa, 1933.

THRESHER -- Kaup, Paul Edwin
The de(s)cendants of Edmund Henry and Louisa Sabin Thresher.
This is an account of the origin, migration, and generations
of the de(s)cendants of Edmund Henry and Louisa Sabin
Thresher. Pittsburgh, Pa., 1965.

TIERS -- Tiers, Clarence Van Dyke
Some branches from the Tier's tree ... Oakmont, Pa.,
1941.

TIESENHAUSEN -- Lawrence, Schuyler
Genealogical notices of the von Tiesenhausen family.   (N)
Towanda, Pa., 1936.

TILTON -- Lochner, Edwin F.
The ancestry of Earle Barrett Tilton, 1899. E. F. Lochner.
Philadelphia, 1983.

TITUS -- Titus, Clarence Edwin
A Titus genealogy: the direct line of descendant of
Titus Syrachs de Vries. C. E. Titus. Philadelphia,
1979.

TODD -- Chamberlain, Gretchen French
Descendants of Hugh Todd of Pennsylvania. No city, 1948.

TOMKINSON -- Tomkinson, Newton Powers
Genealogical memoirs of various families of Tomkinson,
1620-1904. Philadelphia, 1904.

TORRENCE -- Dieckmann, Paul
Ancestry of the Torrence families of Cincinnati, Ohio.
New Kensington, Pa., 1965.

TORRENCE -- Handy, William Torrence
Chart of the Torrence, Findlay, Brownson, Paull, Irwin,
McDowell and Smith families of Pennsylvania. Published
as a memorial to Hon. John Findlay Torrence of Cincinnati
by his sister Harriet Rebecca Torrence Stewart. Commenced
in 1859 by John Findlay Torrence. The Henderson-Achert-
Krebs Lith. Co. Cincinnati, Ohio, 1894.

TORRENCE -- Torrence, Robert M.
Torrence and allied families ... under the auspices of
the Genealogical Society of Pennsylvania. Wickersham
Press. Philadelphia, 1938.

TORREY -- Torrey, Rev. David, D.D.
Memoir of Major Jason Torrey, of Bethany, Wayne County,
Pensylvania. J. S. Horton. Scranton, Pa., 1885.

TORREY -- Torrey, John
Genealogical notes, showing the paternal line of descent
from William Torrey, of Combe St. Nicholas, Somerset County,
England, A.D. 1557, to Jason Torrey, of Bethany, Penn., with
the descendants of Jason Torrey, and of his brothers and
sister, to A.D. 1884. J. S. Horton. Scranton, Pa., 1885.

TOWNSEND -- Townsend, Ida C.
Ancestry and descendants of Joseph Townsend and Martha (P)
Wooderson of Chester County, Pa. Philadelphia, 1958.

TRABUE -- Harper, Lilli Du Puy Van Culin
Colonial men and times; containing the journal of Col.
Daniel Trabue, some account of his ancestry, life and
travels in Virginia and the present state of Kentucky
during the revolutionary period; the Huguenots, genealogy,
with brief sketches of the allied families. Innes & Sons.
Philadelphia, 1916.

TRACY -- Dickson, Tracy Campbell
Some of the descendants of Lieutenant Thomas Tracy of
Norwich, Connecticut. John C. Winston Co. Philadelphia,
1936.

TRANSUE -- Transue, Wendell F.
Genealogy of Transue (Dransu-Transu-Transou-Transeau) (A)
family. Bethlehem, Pa., 1937.

TRAUTMANN -- Trautman, Mrs. DeForest (1966),
              Brossman, Schuyler C. (1967)
Trautman-Troutman family of Tulpehocken Township, Berks
County, Pennsylvania, reunion leaflets of 1966 and 1967.
Trautman-Troutman Family Association. Rehrersburg, Pa.,
1967?

TREE -- Leach, Josiah Granville
Some account of the Tree family and its connections in
England and America. J. B. Lippincott. Philadelphia,
1908.

TRESSLER -- Scott, George Tressler
The family of John Tressler and Elizabeth Loy Tressler;
a sketch. Loysville, Pa., 1949.

TREVASKIS -- Trevaskis, Allan Edward and Robert James Trevaskis
Trevaskis; directory of a surname. Allentown, Pa., 1973.

TREXLER -- (Author unknown)
Minutes and proceedings of the reunion of the Trexler (N)
family. Allentown, Pa?, 1970.

TREXLER -- Warren, John Trexler
History and genealogy of the Trexler family. Trexlertown,
Pa., 1972.

TRIMMER -- Bell, Raymond Martin
The family of Paul Trimmer (1750-1834) of Washington
County, Pennsylvania. Washington, Pa., 1971.

TRIPP -- Dean, Arthur D.
Genealogy of the Tripp family descended from Isaac Tripp,
of Warwick, R.I. and Wilkes-Barre, Pa. F. H. Gerlock & Co.
Scranton, Pa., 1903.

TROTH -- Troth, Samuel
Henry Troth. Philadelphia, 1903.

TROTTER -- Trotter, Newbold H.
Chart of the Trotter family. Philadelphia, 1868.   (P)

TROUT -- Trout, Mary D.
Trout family and related families from Blair and   (A)
Bedford Counties, Pa., including the Ake, Harrison
and Smith forebears. Harrisburg, Pa., 1975.

TROUTMAN -- Brossman, Schuyler C.
Notes on Johann Philip Trautman (also known as Philip
Troutman and Phil. Troutman) 9 August 1758-23 Feb. 1830,
of Tulpehocken Township, Berks County, Pennsylvania.
Rehrersburg, Pa., 1968.

TROYER -- Coblentz, Mrs. Mose E.
Descendants of David C. Troyer and Lydia Speicher,   (A)
1870-1971. Print Shop. Gordonville, Pa., 1971.

TROYER -- Troyer, Dan G.
Descendants of David Troyer and Katherine Holly.   (A)
Print Shop. Gordonville, Pa., 1968.

TRUAX -- Hires, Thura Truax
Bedford County, Pennsylvania Revolutionary soldiers
of the Truax-Truex family. No city, 1948.

TRUAX -- Hires, Thura Colby Truax
Thura Truax Hires manuscripts: a genealogical study of
the names du Trieux, Truax, Trueax, Truax in the states
of Pennsylvania and Ohio. Association of Phillippe
Du Trieux Descendants. Ann Arbor, Mich?, 1983.

TRUBY -- Graff, Mary Truby
Early history of Truby-Graff and affiliated families.
Kittanning, Pa., 1941.

TRUESDALE -- Truesdell, Karl
Descendants of John Truesdale of Cumberland County,
Pennsylvaia. No city, 1952.

TRUMBAUER -- Price, Charles H.
History and genealogy of the Trumbauer family. Telford,
Pa., 1968.

TRUXAL -- Truxal, Isaiah P.
   <u>Biographical sketch of the life of Abraham Drachsel</u>   (P)
   <u>(Troxal-Truxal) and list of descendants</u>.   Tribune Press.
   Greensburg, Pa., 1914.

TURNER -- Rawle, William B.
   <u>Some genealogical notes regarding Robert Turner and</u>   (P)
   <u>his descendants</u>.   Philadelphia, 1900.

TUTHILL -- Tuthill, William H.
   <u>Genealogy of the Tuthill and Kent families ...</u>   (P)
   Philadelphia, 1880.

TYLER -- Tyler, Frederick Stansbury
   <u>Fifty years of yesterdays (1882-1932)</u>.   Harrisburg, Pa.,
   1932.

TYSON -- Du Bin, Alexander
   <u>Tyson family and collateral lines</u>.   Historical Publ.
   Society.   Philadelphia, 1948.

- U -

UHLER -- Uhler, George H.
Genealogy of the Uhler family from the year 1735 to the younger generation. The Report Pub. Co. Lebanon, Pa., 1901.

ULREY -- (Author unknown)
Ulrey family in Ohio and Pennsylvania. No city, no date.

UNDERWOOD -- Underwood, Lucien Marcus
The Underwood families of America. The New Era Printing Co. Lancaster, Pa., 1913.

URNER -- Urner, Isaac N.
Genealogy of the Urner family and sketch of the Coventry Brethren Church in Chester County, Pennsylvania. J. B. Lippincott. Philadelphia, 1893.

- V -

VAN BUSKIRK -- Van Buskirk, George W.
The records of the genealogies of the Van Buskirk   (N)
and Lesher families. The records of the genealogy
of the Ellmaker family, as compiled by Watson
Ellmaker, Lancaster, Pa. Dr. G. Van Buehler.
Bost, 1937.

VANCE -- Dixon, Elizabeth Williamson
The Vance family of Virginia, Pennsylvania, North
Carolina, Tennessee; the Brank family of North
Carolina and Kentucky. No city, 1958.

VAN CULEMBORG -- Sellers, Edwin J.
Allied ancestry of the van Culemborg family of   (N)
Culenborg, Holland; being the ancestry of Sophia
van Culemborg, wife of Johan de Carpentier ...
Allen, Lane & Scott. Philadelphia, 1915.

VANDERPOOL -- Hoagland, Edward C.
Isaac Vanderpool of Swartwood, N.Y., and his descen-   (P)
dants. Sacred Art Press. Wysox, Pa., 1957.

VAN DERSLOOT -- Vandersloot, Lewis
History and genealogy of the von der Sloot family.
Harrisburg, Pa., 1901.

VAN DEUSEN -- Du Bin, Alexander
Van Deusen family and collateral lins of Pawling, Wallace,
Kitts, Roach (and) Sproul. Historical Publ. Society.
Philadelphia, 1947.

VAN HORN -- (Author uknown)
... annual report of the Van Horn and Vansant   (P)
Association. Philadelphia, 1879-.

VAN HORN -- Marvin, Francis M.
The Van Horn family history. East Stroudsburg, Pa.,
1930.

VAN HORNE -- Baber, Jean
A New Jersey Dutch lineage to Christian Barentsen   (P)
Van Horne. Replica. Philadelphia, 1976.

VAN LEUVENIGH -- Leach, Josiah Granville
... Hendrick van Leuvenigh of Newcastle County, Delaware,
and some of his descendants. Genealogical Society of
Pennsylvania. Philadelphia, 1920.

VAN RENSSELAER -- Glenn, Thomas A.
     The Patroonship of Van Rensselaers. H. T. Coates.   (P)
     Philadelphia, 1899.

VEAZEY -- Ardinger, Dennis B.
     The Veazey family of Beaver County, Pennsylvania,
     1750-1900: with related information on the Rutter,
     McClelland, Reed, and White families of Hopewell
     Township. Ardinger. Bridgeville, Pa., 1979.

VERRILL -- Round, Harold F.
     The history & genealogy of the Varrell-Verrill and
     associated families. Bryn Mawr, Pa., 1968.

VUNK -- Sanwick, Charles M.
     The Vunk family; a record of some descendants of   (N)
     Hendrick Vunke, soldier of the American Revolution.
     Easton?, Pa., 1957.

- W -

WAGAMAN -- Wagaman Family Reunion Association
     Miscellaneous papers on the Wagaman family.
     Greensburg, Pa., 1940.

WAGENSELLER -- Wagenseller, George Washington
     The history of the Wagenseller family in America,
     with kindred branches. Wagenseller Publishing Co.
     Middleburgh, Pa., 1898.

WAGER -- Glenn, Thomas A.
     Notes on the families of Wager, Witz, Houser, Baker,   (P)
     Schriener and Potter, of Philadelphia, Penn.
     Herald Print. Norristown. Pa., 1900.

WALBRIDGE -- Wallbridge, William Gedney
     Descendants of Henry Wallbridge, who married Anna Amos,
     December 25, 1688, at Preston, Conn., with some notes
     on the allied families of Brush, Fassett, Dewey, Fobes,
     Gager, Lehman, Meech, Stafford, Scott. Franklin Print.
     Philadelphia, 1898.

WALKER -- Coddington, John Insley
     The family of George Walker of Philadelphia. New Haven,
     1943.

WALKER -- Elston, James S.
     George Walker (of Northumberland County, Pa. and   (A)
     Tioga County, N.Y.) and his descendants. Winter
     Park, Fla., 197_.

WALKER -- Streets, Priscilla Walker
     Lewis Walker of Chester Valley and his descendants:
     with some of the families with whom they are connected
     by marriage. 1686-1896. A. J. Ferris. Philadelphia,
     1896.

WALKER -- Walker, George G.
     Francis William Walker of the Beaver Valley in Beaver
     County, Pennsylvania, 1855-1933. G. G. Walker.
     Manchester, Conn., 1984.

WALL -- Reed, Ardelle McMillen
     Wahl ancestors, descendants and related families of
     Alsace and Butler County, Pennsylvania, 1632-1982.
     A. M. Reed. Cedar Bluffs, Va., 1982.

WALLACE -- Reader, F. S.
  <u>Some pioneers of Washington County, Pa.</u> New Brighton,   (N)
  Pa., 1902.

WALLACE -- Seaver, J. Montgomery
  <u>Wallace genealogical data; suggestions for a Wallace</u>
  <u>family association, a national Wallace family reunion,</u>
  <u>and a complete Wallace genealogy.</u> American Historical-
  Genealogical Society. Washington, D.C., 1927.

WALSH -- (Author unknown)
  <u>Walsh, the name and the arms.</u> Martin and Allardyce.
  Frankford, Pa., 1910.

WALTER -- Ratcliff, Ruth Walters
  <u>The descendants of Aaron Walters: Fayette County,</u>
  <u>Pennsylvania, 1788 to present.</u> Exponent Publishers.
  Hagerstown, Ind., 1981.

WALTON --
  <u>Walton family; one of the series of sketches to be</u>   (N)
  <u>embraced in the "old Philadelphia famillies."</u>
  The Historical Pub. Society. Philadelphia, 1936.

WALTON -- Du Bin, Alexander
  <u>Walton family and collateral liners of Bonnell, Donnell,</u>
  <u>Dyre, Earle, England, Knight, Lamb, Nicholson, Potts,</u>
  <u>Root, Spittall, Trask, Wiedersheim.</u> Historical Pub.
  Society. Philadelphia, 1947.

WALTON -- Martindale, Joseph C., M.D.
  <u>The Walton family.</u> Martin & Allardyce. Frankford,
  Pa., 1911.

WALTON -- Swayne, Norman Walton
  <u>Byberry Waltons; an account of four English brothers,</u>   (P)
  <u>Nathaniel & Thomas & Daniel & William Walton who</u>
  <u>settled about 1683 in Byberry Township, Philadelphia</u>
  <u>County, Pa.</u> Stephenson Bros. Philadelphia, 1958.

WALTON -- Townsend, Annette (Mrs. Townsend Phillips)
  <u>The Walton family of New York, 1630-1940.</u> The Historical
  Publication Society. Philadelphia, 1945.

WALTON -- Windle, Harry Smith
  <u>Genealogy of the Walton, Smith and Windle families.</u>
  Philadelphia, 1971.

WANGER -- (Author unknown)
  <u>Genealogical chart of the descendants of Henry Wanger ...</u>
  Pottstown, Pa., 1910.

WANGER -- (Author unknown)
Genealogical chart of Helen Grubb Wanger ... Pottstown,
Pa., 1910.

WARDEN -- Worden, O. N.
Some records of persons by the name of Worden,
particularly of over one thousand of the ancestors,
kin, and descendants of John and Elizabeth Worden of
Washington County, Rhode Island. Covering three
hundred years, and comprising twelve generations in
America ... J. R. Cornelius. Lewisburg, Pa., 1868.

WARE -- Ware, Franklin
Genealogy of the descendants of Joseph Ware of Fenwick   (P)
colony, 1675. Ware Bros. Philadelphia, 1891?

WARING -- Waring, R. N.
A short history of the Warings. The Herald. Tyrone,
Pa., 1898.

WARNER -- Hiday, Nellie E. C.
The William Warner family of Pennsylvania. No city,
no date.

WARNER -- Justice, Theodore
The Warner family. Germantown, Pa., 1914.   (N)

WARREN -- Boyer, Carol Constance (Younker)
Warren family descendants in Pennsylvania/Indiana.
Denver, Colo., 1981.

WARREN -- Cassd, Earle Millard
Ada Ball Cass, a descendant of Warren of the Mayflower.
New Castle, Pa., 1946.

WARREN -- Davis, Betsey Warren
The Warren, Jackson, and allied families; being the
ancestry of Jesse Warren and Betsey Jackson.
J. B. Lippincott. Philadelphia, 1903.

WARREN -- Davis, Betsey W.
The ancestry of Mary Bolton Warren (Mrs. Frederick   (N)
Wooley). W. A. Cooper. Conshohocken, Pa., 1892.

WATSON -- Brey, Jane W. T.
A Quaker saga; the Watsons of Strawberry-Howe, the
Wildmans, and allied families from England's north
counties and Lower Bucks County in Pennsylvania.
Dorrance. Philadelphia, 1967.

WATT -- Herr, Fred R.
   <u>George Watt of York Co., Pennsylvania</u>. Havertown,   (A)
   Pa., 1959.

WATT -- Herr, Frederick R.
   <u>Descendants of George Watt, Adams County, Pa.</u>
   Havertown, Pa., 1959.

WAY -- Way, Charles G.
   <u>Pennsylvania Way family</u>. No city, no date.   (A)

WAYNE -- Glenn, Thomas A.
   <u>Waynesborough</u>. H. T. Coates. Philadelphia,   (P)
   Pa., 1900.

WAYNE -- Sellers, Edwin Jacquett
   <u>English ancestry of the Wayne family of Pennsylvania</u>.
   Allen, Lane & Scott. Philadelphia, 1927.

WEAVER -- (Author unknown)
   <u>Family history of Samuel B. Weaver and Mary N.</u>   (A)
   <u>Martin Weaver, 1855</u>. Juniata Globe. Thompsontown,
   Pa., 1967.

WEAVER -- Hoover, Anna W.
   <u>History and descendants of the John B. Weaver family,</u> (A)
   <u>1711-1974</u>. Ephrata, Pa., 1974.

WEAVER -- Hurst, Frances W. M.
   <u>Reuben M. and Lydia Shirk Weaver family, 1851-1966,</u>   (A)
   <u>genealogy</u>. Ensinger Print. Adamstown, Pa., 1966.

WEAVER -- Imhof, Olive R.
   <u>Weaver family history, Maryland, Pennsylvania, Ohio,</u> (A)
   <u>Illinois</u>. Pittsburgh, Pa., 1962.

WEAVER -- Leid, Noah W.
   <u>Family history of the descendants of Levi and Esther</u> (A)
   <u>(Sauder) Weaver; including some of their ancestry,</u>
   <u>1690-1969</u>. Print Shop. Gordonville, Pa., 1969.

WEAVER -- Rutt, Anna M. W.
   <u>Isaac M. Weaver and Elizabeth W. Burkholder family</u>   (A)
   <u>history, 1854-1971</u>. Ensinger Print. Adamstown,
   Pa., 1971.

WEAVER -- Weaver, Aaron D.
   <u>Weavers of New California, Pa.</u> Macungie, Pa., 1953.   (A)

WEAVER -- Weaver, Esther S.
   <u>Descendants of Henry B. Weaver</u>. Ephrata, Pa., 1953.   (A)

WEAVER -- Weaver, Robert Kean
Indices & supplement to Who was Henry Weaver (1732-1807), buried Pine Bank Cemetery, Mount Joy Township, Adams County, Pennsylvania. Anundsen Pub . Co. Decorah, Iowa, 1985.

WEBSTER -- Cozert, James A.
Philo Webster: his ancestors snd descendants. Canonsburg, Pa., 1966.

WECKESSER -- Whaley, Miriam
Four American settlers: the children of Johann Georg Weckesser and their descendants. Gateway Press. Baltimore, Md., 1979.

WEEKS -- Hoagland, Edward C.
Some brief notes on the Weeks and Wicks families of Bradford, Pa. Sacred Art Press. Wysox, Pa., 1957.   (P)

WEEKS -- Weeks, Ralph R.
Descendants of David Weeks, a pioneer settler of Bath, New Hampshire, 1774. Upper Darby, Pa., 1965.   (P)

WEGMAN -- Wegman, Charles S.
History of the Wegman families; or, The genealogy of the Wegmans ... The generations of Jacob Wegman, the first Wegman in America, 1715 to 1946, chronology of the Wegman reunions in Berks County, Pennsylvania. Wm. O. Flatt Co. Reading, Pa., 1946.

WEIKERT -- (Author unknown)
History of the Weikert family from 1735-1930 ... The Telegraph Press. Harrisburg, Pa., 1930.

WEISER -- Croll, P. C.
Conrad Weiser and his memorial park. Reading Eagle Press. Reading, Pa., 1926.

WEISER -- Graeff, Arthur D.
Conrad Weiser, man of affairs. John Conrad Weiser   (A)
Family Association. Manheim, Pa., 1964.

WEISER -- Mattice, Paul B.
Conrad Weiser wife was Ann Eve Feeck; old will found   (P)
in Philadelphia settled long quest for a lost identity ... Saint Johnsville, N.Y., no date.

WEISER -- Richards, Henry Melchoir Muhlenberg
The Weiser family. Lancaster, Pa., 1924.

WEISER -- Weiser, Frederick Sheely
"A good Christian man"; the story of Jacob Weiser and
his family. Compiled for his descendants on the occasion
of their reunion, June 29, 1952, at Pine Grove Furnace,
Pennsylvania. No city, 1952.

WEISER -- Weiser, Frederick S.
The Weiser family. Mechanicsburg, Pa., 1960.

WEISER -- Weiser, Frederick S.
The Weiser family; a genealogy of the family of John
Conrad Weiser, the elder (d. 1746). Prepared on the
two hundred fiftieth anniversary of his arrival in
America, 1710-1960. Manheim, Pa., 1960.

WEISER -- Weiser, Frederick S.
The German origins of the Weisers. Manheim, Pa., 1965.

WEISER -- Weiser, Frederick S.
The German origins of the Weisers. Research into the   (P)
ancestry of John C. Weiser (1696-1760) and of his wife,
Ann Eve Feg (1706-1781). John C. Weiser Family Assoc.
Manheim, Pa., 1965.

WEISER -- Weiser, Frederick S.
Letters from the Mahantongo Valley; correspondence from
Jacob Weiser in Mahantongo Valley, Northumberland County,
Pennsylvania, to Frederick Weiser, his brother, in
Delaware County, Ohio. Weiser Family Association.
Manheim, Pa., 1967.

WEISER -- Weiser, Frederick S.
Weiser family album; designed by L. Z. Stahl.   (A)
John C. Weiser Family Assoc. Manheim, Pa., 1971.

WEISER -- Weiser, J. F.
Johan Friederich Weiser's buch (comp. ca. 1696-1760)   (A)
containing: The autobiography of John Conrad Weiser
(1696-1760). J. C. Weiser Family Assoc. Hanover,
Pa., 1976.

WEITZEL -- Hayden, Rev. Horace Edwin
The Weitzel memorial. Historical and genealogical
record of the descendants of Paul Weitzel, of Lancaster,
Pa. 1740. Including brief sketches of the families of
Allen, Byers, Bailey, Crawford, Davis, Hayden, M'Cormick,
Stone, White, and others. E. B. Yordy Printer. Wilkes-
Barre, Pa., 1883.

WELDIN -- Weldin, Lewis Cass
History and genealogy of the Weldin family in America.
Pittsburgh, Pa., 1939.

WELLS -- Wells, George H.
History of the Wells and allied families of the   (P)
Eastern Shore of Maryland and Delaware.   Allen,
Lane & Scott. Philadelphia, 1958.

WELSH -- Welch, Edwin Charles
The family of John Welsh, 1704-1754, of Middletown,
Dauphin County, Pennsylvania: being one of a series
of genealogies on the Welch-Welsh-Walsh family in
America. Santa Barbara, Calif., 1953.

WENDELL -- Du Bin, Alexander
Wendell family. Historical Publication Society.
Philadelphia, 1939.

WENDELL -- Wendell, Henry A.
Ancestry and descendants of the late Isaac Wendell of
Portsmouth, N.H. Philadelphia, 1911.

WENGER -- Wenger, Aaron M.
Wenger family history record 1727 to 1959; containing   (A)
1050 families ... Ensinger Print. Adamstown, Pa.,
1959.

WENGER -- Wenger, Ezra
Genealogy of Edward Meyer Wenger and his wife, Emma   (A)
Meyer Wenger; v.1, A record of seven generations.
Fredericksburg, Pa., 1972.

WENGER -- Wenger: Jonas G., Martin D., Joseph H.
History of the descendants of Christian Wenger who
emigrated from Europe to Lancaster County, Pa., in
1727, and a complete genealogical family register ...
With a few illustrations. Mennonite Pub. Co.
Elkhart, Ind., 1903.

WENTZ -- Wentz, Helen
Wentz. Kennett Square, Pa., 1939.

WESLAGER -- Weslager, C. A.
August Weslager and his family of Pittsburgh, Pa.
Wilimgton, Del., 1964.

WESLEY -- Whitehead, John
    The life of Rev. John Wesley ... Collected from his
    private papers and printed works; and written at the
    request of his executors. To which is prefixed some
    account of his ancestors and relations; with the life
    of the Rev. Charles Wesley ... Collected from his
    private journal, and never before published.
    W. S. Stockton. Philadelphia, 1845.

WESTBROOK -- Coulter, W. J.
    Vital records of the Westbrook family and allied families
    as found in Orange County, New York, Sessex County, New
    Jersey, Pennsylvania, Ohio, Michigan, Illinois of the
    1850 and 1860 period as noted. Zephyrhills, Fla., 1953.

WETHERILL -- Wetherill, Charles and W. Bleddyn Powell
    Records, English and colonial, of the Wetherill family.
    The English records collected by George W. Marshall, 1897.
    Philadelphia, 1898?

WETHERILL -- (Author unknown)
    Genealogical sketch, tracing the descent of the children
    of Robert and Phoebe Ann (Delany) Wetherill through the
    Sharp, Keen, Sandelands, Taylor, Thomas, Henvis, Kite,
    Delany, West, Price and Wetherill families ...
    J. Spencer. Chester, Pa., 1902.

WEYERMAN -- Kennedy, Maude (Wierman)
    History of the Wierman family. York Springs?, Pa., 1952.

WEYTZEL -- Hayden, Horace E.
    A genealogical sketch of the descendants of Johan Paul   (P)
    Weytzel of Lancaster, Pa., 1742. No city, no date.

WHALEY --Foelsch, Donald H.
    An index to Rev. Samuel Whaley's "English record of
    the Whaley family and its branches in America."
    D. H. Foelsch. Williamsport, Pa., 1985.

WHARTON -- (Author unknown)
    The Wharton family of Philadelphia, Pa., Newspaper
    account with portraits, etc. Philadelphia, Pa.,
    1896.

WHARTON -- Lippincott, Joanna Wharton
    Biographical memoranda concerning Joseph Wharton,
    1826-1901. J. B. Lippincott. Philadelphia, 1909.

WHARTON -- Moorhouse, Robert Wharton
    Notes on the Wharton family. Bryn Mawr, Pa., 1958-60.

WHARTON -- Wharton, Anne H.
Genealogy of the Wharton family of Philadelphia, 1664-1880. Collins Printers. Philadelphia, 1880.

WHARTON -- Wharton, Mrs. Helen Elizabeth (Ashhurst)
Francis Wharton. Philadelphia, 1891.

WHARTON -- Wharton, Nathan Earl
The Wharton sleeve. Bryn Mawr, Pa., 1963.

WHITAKER -- Pennypacker, Samuel Whitaker
Joseph Rusling Whitaker, 1824-1895, and his progenitors. Philadelphia, Pa., 1896.

WHITAKER -- Smeltzer, Wallace Guy
Homestead Methodism (1830-1933) the history of Methodism in Mifflin Township, Allegheny County, Pa., being the story of the first Methodist Episcopal church in that township, variously named the Whitaker church, the Franklin church, etc. ... D. K. Murdock Co. Pittsburgh, Pa., 1933.

WHITAKER -- Whitaker, William Alexander
The Whittaker and allied families. Altoona?, Pa., 1962.

WHITALL -- Smith, H, W. S. (Hannah Whitall)
John M. Whitall. The story of his life. Written for his grandchildren by his daughter. Philadelphia, 1879.

WHITCRAFT -- Whitcraft, Frances Kotras
The Whitcrafts of Pennsylvania. Gateway Press. Baltimore, Md., 1980.

WHITE -- Briggs, Aubrey Roy
A genealogy of the de(s)cendants of Giles White and Sarah Dodd, as compiled for their de(s)cendants. Briggs. Youngsville, Pa., 1958.

WHITE -- Cregar, William Francis
Ancestry of Samuel Stockton White ... With accounts of the families of White, Newby, Rose, Cranmer, Stout, Smith, Stockton, Leeds, Fisher, Gardiner, Mathews, Elton, Revell, Stacye, Tonkin, Carey, and Johnson. Patterson and White. Philadelphia, 1888.

WHITE -- Cregar, William Francis
Ancestry of the children of James William White, M.D.,
with accounts of the families of White, Newby, Rose,
Cranmer, Stout, Smith, Stockton, Leeds, Fisher, Gardiner,
Mathews, Elton, Revell, Stacye, Tonkin, McLorinan, Dowse,
Jewett, Hunt, Reddinge, Isbell, and Griswold. Patterson
and White. Philadelphia, 1888.

WHITE -- White, William
White family papers, volume III. Haverford, Pa., 1950.

WHITMER -- Nolt, Paul M.
Roots to Joseph S. Whitmer, 1842-1905. P. M. Nolt.
New Holland, Pa., 1981.

WHITMORE -- Purdy, Jessie Whitmore Patten
The Whitmore genealogy. Reading, Pa., 1907.

WICKERSHAM -- (Author unknown)
First reunion of the Wickersham family; held at the   (A)
old homestead ... near Kennett Square, Pa. ...
Wickersham Print. Lancaster, Pa., 1921.

WICKERSHAM -- (Author unknown)
Second reunion of the Wickersham Family. Held at the
Old Kennett Meeting House. No city, 1925.

WIELAND -- Bartol, William C.
The old home farm. Lewisburg, Pa., 1935.

WIGTON -- Reeve, Mary Wigton
Wigton family. Clearfield, Pa., 1962.

WILCOX -- Wilcox, William Alonzo
A Wilcox-Brown-Medbery genealogy. Scranton, Pa., 1902.

WILCOX -- Willcox, Joseph
Ivy Mills, 1729-1866, Willcox and allied families.
Supplement - Memoir of Mrs. Mary Brackett Willcox.
G. H. Buchanan Co. Philadelphia, 1917.

WILEY -- Kober, David M.
Life and work of Samuel Thomas Wiley, historian and   (A)
educator, 1850-1905. W. H. Farwell Co. Uniontown,
Pa., 1968.

WILEY -- Wylie, Jennie Dwight
The Wylie family from Pennsylvania and Ohio. New York,
N.Y., 1959.

WILHELM --
A history of the Wilhelms and the Wilhelm charge,
by the Historical Committee of St. Paul's church,
Meyersdale, Pa.). The Wilhelm Press. Meyersdale,
Pa., 1919.

WILHELM -- Cox, Clara V.
Genealogy of the David and Margaret Wilhelm family   (A)
of Maryland; including members of the family in
Pennsylvania, Illinois, Indiana, Michigan, California,
and other states. The Reunion Committee. Reistertown,
Md?, 1959.

WILLCOX -- McIver, Helen H.
Willcox family of Pennsylvania, North Carolina, South
Carolina, Georgia. No city, 1930.

WILLETT --Bartlett, Ted Lawrence
The Willits family: descendants of Richard Willets of
Long Island, through the Willits brothers, Isaiah
(and wife Susanna (Boone)) and Isaac (and wife
Elizabeth), of Pennsylvania. T. L. Bartlett.
Chicago, Ill., 1982.

WILLIAMS -- Douglas, Bessie P.
The families of Joshua Williams of Chester County, Pa.,
and John McKeehan of Cumberland County, Pa., with some
allied families. Augsburg Press. Minneapolis, Minn.,
1928.

WILLIAMS -- Ehrig, Frances Hansen
A Williams chronicle; descendants of Thomas Williams of
Sullivan County, New York, and Jefferson County,
Pennsylvania, including some families of Horton, Morris
Hickox, Foster, Elwood, Rice, Zum Brunnen, Nolph,
Crissman, Hastings, Edelblute, McKnight, and others.
J. W. Ehrig. Richland, Wash., 1969.

WILLIAMS -- Myers, Albert E.
Asa Williams (1828-1894) and Direxa Dunn of Great   (A)
Pond, Maine: their ancestors and descendants. Myers.
Harrisburg, Pa., 1976.

WILLIAMS -- Williams, John Francis
The ancestor; the world of William Williams.   (N)
Dorrance. Philadelphia, 1971.

WILLIAMS -- Williams, Olin E.
A Williams genealogy: ancestors and descendants of
Luke Stanton Williams and his wife, Olive Miller
Williams. Williams. Pittsburgh, Pa., 1976.

WILLIAMS -- Williams, Richard J., Jr.
Genealogy of the Williams family, descendants of George
Williams. Germantown, Pa., 1908.

WILLIAMS -- Williams, W. A., D.D.
Early American families, the Williams, Moore, McKitrick,
Fonda, Van Alen, Lanning, King, Justice, Cunningham,
Longacre, Swanson and Cox families, with numerous related
families, embracing the ancestors of perhaps 100,00 or
more covering over 330 years, from 1588 to 1916 ...
Philadelphia, 1916.

WILLIAMS -- Williams, William
Major William Williams' family, an uncompleted   (A)
record ... Hollidaysburgh, Pa., no date.

WILLIAMSON -- New Jersey D.A.R.
A record of the Williamson family and Crozer family of
Bucks County, Pennsylvania. No city, 1939.

WILLIAMSON -- Williamson, Edward H.
A brief lineage of the descendants of William   (P)
Williamson of Thornbury Township, Chester County,
Pa. Philadelphia, 1884.

WILLING -- Du Bin, Alexander
Willing family and collateral lines of Carroll, Chew,
Dundas, Gyles, Jackson, McCall, Moore, Parsons,
Shippen. The Historical Publication Society.
Philadelphia, 1941.

WILMOTH -- Wilmeth, James Lillard
Wilmot-Wilmoth-Wilmeth. Philadelphia, 1940.

WILSON -- (Author unkown)
Register of David Shields Wilson's family.   (A)
Descendants of Marcus Wilson (1721-1812).
Waynesburg, Pa?, 1907.

WILSON -- Ely, Warren S.
Genealogy of the Wilson-Thompson families; being an
account of the descendants of John Wilson, of County
Antrim, Ireland, whose two sons, John and William,
founded homes in Bucks County, and of Elizabeth MvGraudy
Thompson, who with her four sons came from Ireland and
settled in Bucks County about 1740. Intelligencer.
Doylestown, Pa., 1916.

WILSON -- Haley, James B.
The Wilson family ancestry of Matthew James Wilson   (A)
(1830-1924) of Oxford, Chester Co., Pennsylvania.
Berkeley, Calif., 1964.

WILSON -- Justice, Alfred Rudolph
Wilson and allied families; Billew, Britton, Du Bois,
Longshore, Polhemus, Stillwell, Suebering.
Philadelphia, 1929.

WILSON -- Seaver, J. Montgomery
Wilson genealogical data and suggestions for a Wilson
family association, a national Wilson family reunion,
and a complete Wilson genealogy. American Historical-
Genealogical Society. Philadelphia, 1927.

WINNER -- Siegel, Ernestine
The ancestry and descendants of James Winner, 1759-   (N)
1829, of Sussex County, N.J. and Lycoming County,
Pa. E. Siegel. Tampa, Fla., 1969-70.

WINNETT -- Brown, Edna W. R.
Genealogy of William and Sarah (Strange) Winnett,
Fallowfield Township, Washington County, Pennsylvania.
Verona, Pa., 1965.

WINSLOW --
Autobiography of George W. Porter, reminiscences,
observations and writings ... The Spirit Pub. Co.
Punxsutawney, Pa., 1929.

WIRSING -- Wiley, Sara L.
History and genealogy of the Wirsing family of   (A)
Pennsylvania. Uniontown, Pa., 1967.

WIRZ --
Wurts family; one of a series of sketches written
for the Philadelphia North American, 1907-1913.
Based on the manuscript of John S. Wurts, comp.
1903 and by him brought down to date. Historical
Pub. Society. Philadelphia, 1931.

WISE -- Champlin, Grascer M. B.
   Family Wise: a story of the Kausler-Wise family of
   Maryland, Pennsylvania, Ohio, Indiana, 1753-1975.
   Champlin. Minneapolis, Minn., 1975.

WISTAR -- (Author unknown)
   Caspar Wistar, born at Hilspach in the electorate   (P)
   of Heidelberg in Germany ... 1696. Arrived in
   Philadelphia ... 1717. No city, no date.

WISTAR -- (Author unknown)
   Observations in the European derivation of the American
   family of Wistars and Wisters. Philadelphia, 19__?

WISTAR -- Davis, Richard Wistar
   The Wistar family. A genealogy of the descendants
   of Caspar Wistar, emigrant in 1717. Philadelphia,
   1896.

WISTAR -- Haines, Caspar W.
   Some notes concerning Caspar Wistar (immigrant) and   (P)
   on the origin of the Wistar and Wister families.
   Wistar Institute Press. Philadelphia, 1926.

WISTAR -- Ruschenberger, W. S. W.
   A sketch of the life of Caspar Wister ... W. J. Dornan.
   Philadelphia, 1891.

WISTAR -- Wister, Fanny Kemble
   That I may tell you: journals and letters of the Owen
   Wister family. Haverford House. Wayne, Pa., 1979.

WITCRAFT -- Witcraft, John R.
   Origin of the Witcraft family. B. Hepworth & Co.
   Philadelphia, 1912?

WITHEROW -- Wantz, Mary Witherow
   A history of David and Nancy Walker Witherow, Fairfield,
   Pennsylvania, and their descendants. No city, 1955.

WITMER -- Witmer, Mary M.
   Brief history of ancestors and descendants of Amos S.   (A)
   Witmer and wife Mary (Brubaker) Witmer ... Ensinger
   Print. Adamstown, Pa., 1970.

WITTER -- Buchanan, Merwyn R.
   Descendants of James D. and Margaret (Humes) Witter.   (P)
   Ambler, Pa?, 1962.

WITTMAN -- Kohl, Helen Wittman
    Wittman family and allied lines of Pennsylvania.
    Allentown, Pa., 1972.

WOLF -- Beck, Clara A.
    Kith and kin of George Wolf, Governor of Pennsylvania,
    1829-1835. Easton, Pa., 1930.

WOLFE -- Bell, Raymond Martin
    The Wolf family of Washington County, Pennsylvania
    (also Wolff, Wolfe). R. M. Bell. Washington, Pa.,
    1984.

WOLFERSBERGER -- Bell, Raymond Martin
    John Wolfersberger, Alsace to Pennsylvania, 1730.
    R. M. Bell. Washington, Pa., 1983.

WOLFF -- Wolff, Raymond Alvin
    The Wolf, Wolfe, Wolff families of Pennsylvania.
    Baltimore, Md, 1971.

WOLGEMUTH -- Wolgemuth, Daniel M.
    Genealogy of Daniel N. and Anna Engle Wolgemuth,
    1844 to 1979. D. M. Wolgemuth. Mount Joy, Pa.,
    1979?

WOMMER -- Bell, Raymond Martin
    The Wommers of Saarland and Pennsylvania: also spelled
    Woomer, Womer, Wummer, Wumer. R.M. Bell. Washington,
    Pa., 1980.

WOOD -- (Author unknown)
    Family records; Wood, Dewees, Farmer, Gilpin, Porter,   (P)
    Craige, Harper, Horsefall, Heberton, Craig, Robinson,
    Brooke, Porter. J. B. Lippincott. Philadelphia, 1911.

WOOD -- Koedel, Mrs. R. Craig
    From John Wood of Rhode Island to Hubert Wood of
    Pennsylvania. No city, 1975.

WOOD -- Kussart, Mrs. S.
    The early history of the Fifteenth ward of the city of
    Pittsburgh. Suburban Printing. Bellevue, Pa., 1925.

WOOD -- McLean, Crosby C.
    The Wood family of Montgomery County, Pennsylvania.   (P)
    Altadena, Calif., 1963.

WOOD -- Wood, Arnold
    The John Wood family of Bucks County, Pa. Washington,
    D.C., 1974.

WOOD -- Wood, C. E.
A genealogical history. Wood. Read at the reunion of the
Woods at East Smithfield, Pa., September 4, 1882. Alvord
& Son. Towanda, Pa., 1882.

WOOD -- Wood, Day
A record of the descendants of Joseph and Catherine   (P)
Day Wood, who settled in West Nottingham, Chester
Co., Pa., in 1758, with some historical account of
him and his ancestors. Goshen?, Pa., 1903.

WOODCOCK -- Woodcock, William Lee
History of the Woodcock family from 1692 to Sept. 1, 1912.
Altoona Tribune. Altoona, Pa., 1912.

WOODLING -- Fisher, Charles A.
A biographical history and genealogy of the Woodling
family. Selinsgrove, Pa., 1936.

WOODRING -- Bell, Raymond M. and Mabel G. Granquist
The Vautrin-Wotring-Woodring family, Lorraine-Alsace-
Pennsylvania, 1640-1790. Washington, Pa., 1953.

WOODRING -- Bell, Raymond Martin
The Wotring-Woodring family of Pennsylvania. R. M. Bell.
Washington, Pa., 1981.

WOODRING -- Granquist, Mabel Armstrong (Ghering)
Descendants of Nicholas and Margaret (Frantz) Wotring.
Warren, Pa., 1948.

WOODS -- Delafield, Joseph L.
Notes on the Woods family, of Bedford, Pennsylvania.   (N)
J. B. Lippincot. Philadelphia, 1908.

WOODS -- Whedon, Nellie E. W.
James Woods family of Pennsylvania and Ohio; an   (A)
account of the descendants of Allen Sr., Samuel Sr.,
and Nathaniel Sr., the three sons of James Woods,
1736-1942. Edwards Bros. Ann Arbor, Mich., 1942.

WOODSIDE -- Southworth, George
The Woodsides of northwestern Pennsylvania; the story   (P)
of John and Mary Woodside and their twelve children.
Southworth. No city, 1971.

WOODWARD -- Ostrom, Laurence E.
The descendants of John Jackson Woodward and Hannah
Mattson Woodward. L. E. Ostrom. Media, Pa., 1981.

WOODWARD -- Woodward, Lewis
Genealogy of the Woodward family of Chester County,
Pennsylvania, with an appendix giving a brief account
of the Woodwards of some other portions of the United
States. Ferris Bros. Wilmington, Del., 1879.

WOOLLEY -- Parkinson, Preston Woolley
The Utah Woolley family, descendants of Thomas Woolley
and Sarah Coppock of Pennsylvania. With brief notices
of other families of the name. Salt Lake City, Utah,
1967.

WOOLSEY -- Austin, Anne L.
The Woolsey sisters of New York; a family's involvement
in the Civil War and a new profession. Philadelphia,
Pa., 1971.

WORDEN -- Eastwood, Eric K.
The Worden family; an account of some of the   (A)
descendants of Peter Worden of Yarmouth, Mass ...
Pittsburgh, Pa.,   1951.

WORDEN -- Worden, O, N.
First supplement to: Some records of persons by the name
of Worden. Lewisburg, Pa., 1869.

WORK -- Steele, M. T.
Work family. Marion Center, Pa., 1894.

WORK -- Work, Edith
Work family, a history of the descendants of William   (A)
and John Work. Independent Office. Marion Center,
Pa., 1894.

WORRALL -- Cope, Gilbert
Worrall chart ... W. Chester, Pa., 1917.   (A)

WORRALL -- Foster, Mary K.
The Worrall-Worrell family of Pennsylvania.   (P)
Philadelphia, 1950.

WORTH -- Lewis, William
The Worth genealogy; descendants of Samuel and Hannah   (A)
Prentice Worth of Greenfield, Lackawanna County,
Pennsylvania. Waverly?, Pa., 1956.

WOTRING -- Bell, Raymond Martin
The Vautrin-Wotring-Woodring family, Lorraine-Alsace-
Pennsylvania, 1640-1790. Washington, Pa., 1953.

WOTRING -- Bell, Raymond Martin
The Vautrin-Wotring-Woodring family, Lorraine-Alsace-
Pennsylvania, 1640-1790. Washington, Pa., 1958.

WOTRING -- Bell, Raymond M.
The Wotring-Woodring family of Pennsylvania.   (P)
Washington, Pa., 1968.

WRIGHT -- By some of his descendants
History of the Joseph Wright family of Pennsylvania.
No city, 1914.

WRIGHT -- Talcott, S. V.
The Wright family. Martin & Allardyce. Frankford, Pa.,
1912.

WUNDERLICH -- Cornman, Charles Albert
Genealogical record of the Wunderlich family in America.
Carlisle, Pa., 1911.

WURTS -- Leach, Frank Willing
Wurts family; one of the series of sketches written for the
Philadelphia North America, 1907-1913. Based on the manuscript of John S. Wurts, comp. 1902 and by him brought down
to date. Historical Pub. Society. Philadelphia, 1931.

WYANT -- Wion, John H.
John Wiant of Mifflin County, Pennsylvania: a history of
the Wian-Wion-Wyan family in America and Australia
through eight generations, with notes on the possible
origins of the family in Germany and colonial Pennsylvania
and including brief histories of the allied Pennsylvania
families of Gerberic, Graf, Jager, Moser, Schwab, and
Wagner. Wion. Wion, New York, 1976.

WYCKOFF -- (Author unknown)
Annual meeting and social gathering of the Wyckoff house
and Association Inc. in Stroudsburg, Pa. ... No City,
no date.

WYCKOFF -- (Author unknown)
The Old World progenitors of the Wyckoff family. Upper
Darby, Pa?, 1930.

WYCKOFF -- Wyckoff, William L.
The old world progenitors of the Wyckoff family: (P)
a genealogy prepared from the genealogical collections
of the late Wm. Forman Wyckoff of Jamaica, N.Y.
The Claesen Press. Upper Darby, Pa., 1936?

WYLIE -- Wylie, Jennie D.
 <u>The Wylie family from Pennsylvania and Ohio.</u>
 New York, N.Y., 1959.

WYNN -- Cook, Richard Y.
 <u>Ancestry of Dr. Thomas Wynne, speaker of the first</u>
 <u>Assembly of Pennsylvania, etc. Who was born in the</u>
 <u>parish of Yskeiviog, near Caerwys, in Flintshire,</u>
 <u>North Wales, in the year 1627, and who removed to the</u>
 <u>province of Pennsylvania with William Penn, in the good</u>
 <u>ship "Welcome," in the year 1682. (From the authorities</u>
 <u>cited in proof)</u>. Philadelphia, 1904.

WYNN -- Deem, T. B.
 <u>The Wynnes; a genealogical summary of the ancestry of the</u>
 <u>Welsh Wynnes, who emigrated to Pennsylvania with William</u>
 <u>Penn</u>. Aetna Printing. Indianapolis, Ind., 1907.

WYSONG -- Marquiss, John and Beulah Wysong Whistler
 <u>Some descendants (sic) of Ludwig and Mary Wysong; whose</u>
 <u>first written record was found in York, Pennsylvania,</u>
 <u>as of the year 1740</u>. Eustis, Fla., 1972.

- Y -

YAPLE -- Crowe, Grace Vandervort
<u>History and genealogy of the Yaple family</u>. Erie, Pa., 1977.

YARDLEY -- Yardley, Thomas W.
<u>Genealogy of the Yardley family, 1402-1881</u>. W. S. Schofield. Philadelphia, 1881.

YARNALL -- Du Bin, Alexander
<u>Yarnall family and collateral lines</u>. Historical Publication Society. Philadelphia, 1948.

YATES -- Yates, William A.
<u>Genealogy of James Yates, the immigrant to Pennsylvania, 1684</u>. W. A. Yates. Ozark, Mo., 1984.

YEAGER -- Yeager, Hon. James Martin
<u>A brief history of the Yeager, Buffington, Creighton, Jacobs, Lemon, Hoffman and Woodside families, and their collateral kindred of Pennsylvania</u>. Lewistown, Pa., 1912.

YENZER -- Coppersmith, Donald Yentzer
<u>The farmers' children</u>. Enterprise Pub. Assoc. Coudersport, Pa., 1981.

YERKES -- Leach, Josiah Granville
<u>Chronicle of the Yerkes family, with notes on the Leech and Rutter families</u>. J. B. Lippincott. Philadelphia, 1904.

YODER -- Hershberger, Emanuel J.
<u>Descendants of Christian and Barbara Yoder</u>. U. G. Kinsinger. Gordonville, Pa., 1965.

YODER -- Swartzentruber, Esther C. Y.
<u>Family record of Elias A. Yoder and his descendants</u>.   (A)
Berlin Pub. Berlin, Pa., 1951.

YODER -- Yoder, Bennie C.
<u>Family history of Elias A. Yoder and descendants, 1834 to 1981</u>. B. C. Yoder. Springs, Pa., 1981.

YODER -- Yoder, Christian Z.
<u>Genealogical records of descent from John Yoder,</u>   (A)
<u>Jacob Zook, Daniel Conrad and Nathan Smiley</u>.
Mennonite Pub. Scottdale, Pa., 1932.

YODER -- Yoder, Mattie S.
    <u>Family record of Simeon H. Yoder and his descendants</u>.   (A)
    A. S. Kinsinger. Gordonville, Pa., 1964.

YODER -- Yothers, Richard J.
    <u>Descendants of Jacob Yothers, Bucks County, Pennsylvania</u>.
    Gateway Press. Baltimore, Md., 1984.

YOHE -- (Author unknown)
    <u>Descendants of Northampton County families</u>.   (P)
    Germantown, Pa., 1907.

YOUNG -- Herchenroether, Nell Young
    <u>Genealogy of Charles Herman Young and Una May Brown,</u>
    <u>including families of Young, Russell, Taylor, Brown,</u>
    <u>Miller, Aughenbaugh & Harter, Houlette & Bryant</u>.
    Herchenroether. Pittsburgh, Pa., 1974.

YOUNG -- Seaver, J. Montgomery
    <u>Young family record</u>. Philadelphia, 1929.

- Z -

ZAHNISER -- Zahniser, Kate M.
The Zahnisers. Mercer, Pa., 1906.

ZANE -- Hoagland, Robert Elwood
Robert Zane of Newton, Gloucester County, West New
Jersey, 1642-1694/5 and some of his descendants.
Philadelphia, 1984.

ZEHNER -- Carpenter, Mrs. Ellen Priscilla (Zehner)
The first Zehner-Hoppes family history; Adam Zehner,
John Michael (Habbas) Hoppes of Schuylkill County,
Pennsylvania, and descendants, pioneer farmers and
millers, by the Zehner Indiana branch of the
Pennsylvania, Ohio, Indiana, Illinois, Wisconsin
relative societies, 1939 A.D. Mirror Press.
South Bend, Ind., 1939.

ZERBE -- Elliott, Mrs. Ella Zerbey
Blue book of Schuylkill County; who was who and why in
interior eastern Pennsylvania, in colonial days. The
Huguenots and Palatines; their service in Queen Anne's
French and Indian, and revolutionary wars. History of
the Zerbey, Schwalm, Miller, Merkle, Minnich, Staudt,
and many other representative families. "Republican."
Pottsville, Pa., 1916.

ZIEGLER -- Warren, Walter E.
Descendants of Christopher Ziegler. Beaver Falls, Pa.,
1965.

ZIEGLER -- Ziegler, Gertrude Mohlin
The Ziegler family and related families in Pennsylvania.
C. Campbell Print. Co. Zelienople, Pa., 1970.

ZIEGLER -- Ziegler, Jesse
The Ziegler family record. Royersford, Pa., 1906.

ZIMMERMAN -- Zimmerman, Milo H.
John and Catherine and Drusilla Mishler Zimmermann family
register, 1843-1974. Akron, Pa., 1975.

ZOOK -- Zook, Harry D.
Zug/Zuck/Zouck/Zook genealogy. H. D. Zook. Gateway
Press. Baltimore, Md., 1983.

ZOOK -- McCone, Percy V.
John Zuck, Sr. of Erie, Pennsylvania, descendants &
ancestors. P. V. McCone. Tucson, Ariz., 1982.

ZUG -- Zook, Lois Ann
     <u>Only a twig; a branch of the Zugs/Zooks from</u>
     <u>Pennsylvania</u>. Strasburg, Pa., 1979.

ZWEMER -- Zwemer. Adrien
     <u>Genealogy and history of the Zwemer-Boon family,</u>   (A)
     <u>recorded for his children. (Trans. from the</u>
     <u>original Dutch ms. with suppplement, notes,</u>
     <u>bibliography and illustrations)</u>. Nungesser Print.
     Harrisburg, Pa., 1935.

This cross-reference table lists secondary surnames and variations of primary names given in the titles.

STYLES, 219
SUEBERING, 247
SUMNER, 22
SUPPES, 96
SUTTON, 5
SWANSON, 246
SWISHER, 143
SYMES, 62 208
SZTYNBERG, 17
TAGGART, 164
TANGER, 213
TAYLOR, 7 25 46 52 82 172 201
   242 255
TEDROW, 25
TENEYCK, 100
TENHEUVEN, 57
TERRELL, 86
TERRY, 36
THOMAS, 138 242
THOMPSON, 247
THOMSON, 189
THORN, 83
TICHENOR, 190
TILL, 138
TISON, 22
TONKIN, 243 244
TOWNSEND, 215
TRACEY, 154
TRACY, 31 154
TRANSEAU, 229
TRANSOU, 229
TRANSU, 229
TRASK, 236
TRAUTMAN, 230
TRIEUX, 230
TRIMBLE, 170
TRIPP, 192
TROUTMAN, 146 229
TROXAL, 231
TRUEAX, 230
TRUEX, 230
TUMLIN, 18
TWAIN, 45
TYRRELL, 36
UNDERHILL, 39
UPDIKE, 177
UPHOUSE, 111
VALLEUAX, 71
VANALEN, 246
VANCE, 117

VANCORTLANDT, 48
VANDERHEGGEN, 79
VANDERSAAL, 98
VANDERVEER, 100
VANGEZEL, 46
VANMETRE, 63
VANNIEUKIRK, 164
VANPELT, 100
VANSANT, 233
VANSCIVER, 80
VANVOORHEES, 91
VARIAN, 201
VARRELL, 234
VAUGHAN, 138
VAUTRIN, 250-252
VOGELEN, 71
VOLLMAR, 75
VOLPELL, 72
VONDERSLOOT, 233
VONTIESENHAUSEN, 228
VONZELLEN, 207
WADDELL, 148
WAGNER, 252
WAKEFIELD, 138
WALBECK, 28
WALKER, 5 14 93
WALLACE, 233
WALLBRIDGE, 235
WALSH, 241
WALTON, 189
WAMPOLE, 201
WAPLES, 95
WARD, 138
WARDER, 28
WARREN, 48
WATERS, 212
WATSON, 107
WATTS, 184
WEART, 220
WEAVER, 10 155
WEBB, 4 46
WEIMER, 196
WELCH, 51 199 241
WELLS, 113
WEST, 242
WESTALL, 91
WEYAND, 207
WHEATLEY, 202
WHITAKER, 113 176 210
WHITE, 63 159 199 234 240

WHITING, 22
WHITTING, 69
WIAN, 252
WIANT, 252
WICKS, 239
WIEDERSHEIM, 236
WIERMAN, 242
WILCOX, 31
WILDMAN, 237
WILKIN, 113
WILLCOX, 244
WILLETS, 245
WILLIAM THE CONQUEROR,
   63 106
WILLIAMS, 43 63 123 138 149
WILLING, 11
WILLIT, 245
WILLITS, 245
WILMETH, 246
WILMOT, 246
WILSON, 22 39 82 113 225
WINDLE, 236
WINSLOW, 74 183
WINTER, 173
WINTERS, 2
WION, 252
WISTER, 248
WITMER, 119
WITZ, 235
WOLF, 66
WOLFERSBERGER, 156
WOMER, 249
WOOD, 25 138
WOODERSON, 229
WOODRING, 251 252
WOODSIDE, 254
WOOLEY, 237
WOOMER, 249
WORDEN, 237
WORDSWORTH, 138
WORRELL, 251
WORTH, 91
WOTRING, 250
WRIGHT, 57 136 199 200
WUMER, 249
WUMMER, 249
WURTS, 247
WYAN, 252
WYNNE, 253
YEAKLEY, 58